More praise for
Mipham's Sword of Wisdom

"The great scholar and advanced spiritual master Jamgon Mipham's *Sword of Wisdom* is a classic work that explicates valid cognition. I am happy to see it now available in English with commentary and scholarly appendices that will be very helpful for serious students in understanding this profound and important text."

—His Holiness the Sakya Trichen

"I am very pleased that this seminal text by the first Mipham has been translated and made available in English. This book presents direct perception and reasoning as the most valid way to know reality, starting with the truth of cause and effect and extending to the realization of nondual wisdom."

—Sakyong Mipham Rinpoché

"*Mipham's Sword of Wisdom* is the essence of the Dharma itself! Khenchen Palden Sherab was a true lineage holder and scholar, a compassionate and humble man whose work can be trusted to be in perfect accord with the teachings of all the lineage masters, so we can rely on his teachings with absolute confidence. This text contains the power, blessing, and kindness of the incomparable Mipham Rinpoché, so it is like the very soul and heart of Manjuśrī himself! It is my heartfelt prayer that everyone read this text and take these teachings purely and honestly into their hearts."

—Ven. Gyatrul Rinpoché

"Although we think we have understood emptiness as the ultimate teaching of the sutras and tantras, we haven't really delved into the depths of its meaning and still continue to see things with ordinary perception and are unable to rest freely in the ultimate true nature. Mipham provides the tools for us to actualize the supreme timeless awareness and become naturally liberated and boundlessly compassionate, which is the final result of our practice."

—His Holiness Shenpen Dawa Norbu Rinpoché

"I have found it to be extremely well written and with great blessings. I am reminded constantly of Khenchen Rinpoché's teachings and his kindness, and I found boundless joy in this sublime work."

—Khenpo Tsewang Gyatso

Mipham's Sword of Wisdom

The Nyingma Approach to Valid Cognition

KHENCHEN PALDEN SHERAB

Translated by ANN HELM with KHENPO GAWANG

Wisdom Publications
199 Elm Street
Somerville, MA 02144 USA
wisdompubs.org

Library of Congress Cataloging-in-Publication Data is available.
LCCN 2017026912

ISBN 978-1-61429-428-3   ebook ISBN 978-1-61429-440-5

22 21 20 19 18
5 4 3 2 1

Cover and interior design by Tim Holtz. Set in DGP 11.5/15.
Cover image © Padmasambhava Buddhist Center. Reprinted by permission.

Wisdom Publications' books are printed on acid-free paper and meet the guidelines for permanence and durability of the Production Guidelines for Book Longevity of the Council on Library Resources.

♲ This book was produced with environmental mindfulness. For more information, please visit wisdompubs.org/wisdom-environment.

Printed in the United States of America.

MIX
Paper from
responsible sources
FSC® C011935

Please visit fscus.org.

Contents

Translator's Introduction

ON THE CONTENTS OF THIS BOOK

This book contains the root text of 104 verses by Jamgön Mipham Rinpoché titled *The Sword of Wisdom That Ascertains Reality*, followed by a commentary by Khenchen Palden Sherab Rinpoché titled *The Radiant Light of the Sun and Moon*. Also included in this volume is Mipham's autocommentary on *The Sword of Wisdom*. These annotations to the verses make Mipham's intended meaning clear and form the basis for Khenchen Palden's commentary.

Perhaps the greatest value of this very rich, classical text is in being a clear and concise primer on Buddhist philosophy and valid cognition. Its core subject matter is the Buddhist view of the two truths—the relative truth of conventional appearances and the absolute truth of emptiness and buddha nature—and how the two truths are inseparable. The main questions this text poses are: How can we actually know the two truths? And how can we be certain that our knowledge is accurate? Mipham's answer is that to know the two truths we need *pramāṇa* or valid cognition, as demonstrated through reasoning, and to gain certainty we need the four reliances. This is summed up in verse 92:

92.   The supreme, stainless cause
      is the possession of the four reliances,
      which come from contemplating how the Dharma of the two truths
      is established by the four types of reasoning.

This book excels in giving an easily understandable overview of valid cognition. What is valid cognition? It is accurate knowing, which we experience through direct perception and correct inference. Valid cognition is a topic of Buddhism rarely taught to Westerners, as it can seem either too simplistic or too complex, and it requires sustained study to get a good foundation in it. This text provides that foundation by explaining direct perception and inference according to the traditional Indian treatises of Dharmakīrti and Dignāga, and then by laying out the four reasonings: the efficacy of causes, the dependency of effects, the relative and ultimate natures of things, and the construction of valid proofs.

Along with valid cognition, the commentary discusses several of the topics traditionally studied in the *shedras*, the monastic colleges of Tibetan Buddhism. For instance, there are topics from Abhidharma such as the six causes, five effects, and four conditions, a discussion of general and specific phenomena, and the ten fields of knowledge. The section on *pramāṇa*, or valid cognition, includes material used for formal debate, such as various types of correct and false reasons, and these are illustrated with sample syllogisms. The section on direct perception includes a discussion of yogic direct perception and self-aware direct perception, so it also touches on meditation. As well, there is some discussion of the schools of Madhyamaka philosophy when Khenchen Palden points out the distinctions between Prāsaṅgika Madhyamaka and Svātantrika Madhyamaka in their approach to the absolute truth.

This root text and commentary exemplify the view of the Nyingma lineage of Tibetan Buddhism as set forth by Jamgön Mipham. It is one of the first books in English to present the Nyingma lineage understanding of valid cognition and its usage in Buddhist philosophy in general and in the Vajrayāna teachings in particular. The Vajrayāna section of the book follows the *Guhyagarbha Tantra* in discussing the two truths from the perspective of purity and equality: the relative truth is the purity of all phenomena and the absolute truth is the equality of all phenomena. Echoing the *Guhyagarbha*, Jamgön Mipham and Khenchen Palden introduce the Vajrayāna reasoning of the four realizations, the six parameters and four styles of interpretation, the Buddha's eight intentions, and the primacy of self-knowing awareness. Mipham's text makes it clear that higher realization depends on valid cognition, so we need to know what valid cognition consists of, how to train in it, and how to apply it in practice. As he says in the section on fruition, these methods are undoubtedly a genuine path because they result in genuine realization.

It might be useful to add that Khenchen Palden's commentary is written in the classical Tibetan scholarly style. Each section begins with a root verse, commentary that usually includes every word of the root verse, and then scriptural citations to support the statements made in the root verse. From one point of view this style of adding quotation after quotation can seem redundant, but from another point of view this is a chance to read in English portions of the greatest Indian philosophical works by Nāgārjuna, Candrakīrti, Candragomin, Dharmakīrti, Dignāga, and others. There are also quotations from the early Buddhist masters of Tibet, such as King Trisong Detsen, Kawa Paltsek, and Chokro Lui Gyaltsen. Most of us will never read their books on valid cognition, particularly since so few have been translated into Western languages. By including numerous quotations, we come to know what some of the most famous Buddhist masters said on the topics in this text.

Another feature of the classical Tibetan teaching style is its many categories or perspectives on a topic. For example, the two truths are discussed according to their essences, definitions, characteristics, functions, and purposes. As we go through these categories, looking at the two truths from all these different angles, it becomes more and more apparent what they entail. Understanding comes about from having several ways of approaching and contemplating the same topic.

For example, one way of looking at the two truths is to divide them into the pure and impure relative and the expressible and inexpressible absolute. This way of discussing the two truths is a special feature of Mipham Rinpoché's view, which follows Śāntarakṣita's view in the *Adornment of the Middle Way*. This very insightful presentation is particularly upheld by the Nyingma lineage. Another aspect of the two truths discussed in this text is how the relative nature is comprised of functional things and designations, and the ultimate nature is comprised of the three doors of liberation.

This rich text provides a thorough grounding in the core teachings of Buddhist philosophy as well as the views of the Nyingma lineage and Jamgön Mipham. As Mipham says, if we follow the four reliances by relying on the definitive meaning of the Buddha's teachings and nondual wisdom in particular, we can gain certainty about the nature of reality.

ON THE CREATION OF THIS BOOK

Khenchen Palden Sherab began teaching Jamgön Mipham's *Sword of Wisdom That Ascertains Reality* in 1967, the opening year of the Central University of Tibetan Studies in Sarnath, India. The university had been formed after a meeting called by the Tibetan government in exile to determine how to preserve and further the Tibetan Buddhist heritage. Representatives of all four schools of Tibetan Buddhism attended this meeting, and His Holiness Dudjom Rinpoché, then head of the Nyingma lineage, asked Khenchen Palden

Sherab to represent the Nyingma lineage. Khenchen Palden began teaching at the Central University in 1967, and for the first few years he was the only faculty member and administrator in the Nyingma department, where he taught up to twelve classes daily. He continued teaching at the Central University for seventeen years.

During that time, Mipham's *Sword of Wisdom* was the first text studied in the sequence of courses in the Nyingma department. Since there was no textbook, Khenchen Palden would write notes on the blackboard and students would copy them before the notes were erased at the end of each class. Eventually some of the students compiled their notes and Khenchen used them as the basis for this commentary, *The Radiant Light of the Sun and Moon*, which he wrote in full in 1984 and the Central University published in 1986.

In the 1990s Khenchen Palden made some corrections and additions for a digital edition of his commentary, which was prepared by Anna Orlova and Alex Chernoguzov and published through Sky Dancer Press. Over the years until his death in 2010, Khenchen annotated this text with many additional scriptural quotations, and the entire text was retyped by Peter De Niro for publication by the Central University in 2013. This final version of the commentary is translated here into English. On behalf of readers of the Tibetan editions, many thanks are extended to Anna, Alex, Peter, and the publication staff of the Central University for their work.

An initial English translation of this book was undertaken by Ives Waldo in the early 1990s and published on his website and the Sky Dancer Press website.

For this particular translation, I would like to extend special thanks first to Khenchen Palden Sherab, who taught me the first four chapters of his commentary in 2006 and 2007 while we were in residence at Padma Samye Ling. Most of the notes accompanying the translation of these chapters came directly from Khenchen's explanations of the poetic allusions, scriptural citations, and meaning of the words. In the endnotes, his particular comments are noted with the abbreviation (KPS). Next I want to express special gratitude to Khenpo Gawang, who went over the entire translation with me from 2011 to 2013. We conferred via Skype ninety-seven times, which shows extraordinary patience and kindness on his part. I could never have finalized this translation without his expertise. In the endnotes, his particular comments are noted with the abbreviation (KG).

Further special thanks go to Dzigar Kongtrul Jigmé Namgyel, who taught Mipham's *Sword of Wisdom* in our Tibetan language class in 1995 at Naropa University in Boulder, Colorado. I appreciate his encouragement to translate this commentary, and also the encouragement I received from Khenpo Tsewang Dongyal and Derek Kolleeny to complete this book. I want to thank Derek Kolleeny for his outline of Mipham's verses in Appendix B, and his topical outline of Khenchen Palden's commentary in Appendix C. Special thanks also to Peter De Niro and Philippe Turenne for inserting Sanskrit diacritics in the text.

Many excellent suggestions for improving the translation came from our triweekly study group at Padma Samye Ling monastery in the fall and winter of 2013–2014. We met over fifty times to study the text together. I particularly thank the members of the study group who attended consistently: Lama Laia, Lama Dragpa, Ani Joanie Andras, Andrew Cook, Ross Hathaway, Amanda Lewis, Jeychalie Maldonado, Kate Mueller, and Carl Stuendel.

In closing, I would like to echo the aspiration of Khenpo Thubten Tsöndrü in his guru yoga sādhāna addressed to Jamgön Mipham Rinpoché:

> Through all my lives may I remain at your lotus feet,
> and study, reflect, and meditate on your texts again and again.
> Grant your blessings that I will hold, protect, and spread your teachings
> to the limits of space for as long as saṃsāra lasts.

ANN HELM
PADMA SAMYE LING, NEW YORK

The Sword of Wisdom That Ascertains Reality

by Jamgön Mipham

———

1   This philosophy is unmistaken;
    all errors have been eliminated.
    The mind is free from doubt about three points.
    I pay homage to Mañjuśrī, the treasure of wisdom.

2   The teachings of the Sugata
    are profound, vast, and difficult to realize.
    For those who wish to taste this deathless nectar,
    I will bestow the light of intelligence.

3   The Dharma taught by the buddhas
    is completely based on the two truths:
    the worldly, relative truth
    and the supreme, absolute truth.

4   If one wants to know the nature of the two truths
    with a mind that ascertains them unerringly,
    one should thoroughly establish the good, clear eyes
    of the two types of flawless valid cognition.

5   No matter how things appear,
    they arise interdependently.
    Nothing independent appears;
    that would be like a lotus appearing in the sky.

6   When the collection of causes is complete,
    it functions to produce an effect.
    Each and every effect
    depends on its own specific causes.

7   Therefore by understanding correctly or incorrectly
    how causes and effects function,
    one engages in or refrains from activities.
    All the philosophical systems and fields of knowledge, like artistry,

8   are also rooted in this.
    This is why cause and effect encompass all worldly training
    and the training that transcends the world.
    Every interdependent thing

9   has its unique defining characteristics,
    like solidity, wetness, or heat,
    because that is its own individual nature.
    This nature cannot be denied.

10 In a single thing there are a variety of attributes,
    and there are numerous facts and classifications
    of terminology that establish or exclude those attributes.
    Each thing has its own specific nature.

11 An object is thoroughly apprehended by direct perception.
    Then the conceptual mind—that which distinguishes and combines—
    uses terminology
    to label it as a separate thing.

12 Objects of knowledge will be thoroughly understood
    by categorizing them into two groups:
    substantial things and designations based on terminology.
    There are many further classifications that elaborate on this.

13 If one examines the true reality
    of causes, effects, and the nature of things,
    one cannot find any production
    and nothing that arises through dependency.

14 By its own very nature,
   appearance is essentially emptiness.
   The basic space of phenomena, having the three aspects of liberation,
   is the nature of the ultimate.

15 Although there is causal efficacy and dependency,
   the reasoning of the nature is the final reasoning.
   Once the nature of a thing has been reached,
   there are no further reasons to be sought.

16 As was just explained, valid comprehension of a thing
   accords with the nature of the two truths
   and is established through the power of fact.
   This is the reasoning of a valid proof.

17 Similarly, the way things appear and the way they are
   are comprehended according to their natures,
   either by direct perception or by inference of something else,
   which is unmistaken because it relies on what directly appears.

18 There are four kinds of direct perception:
   unmistaken sensory perception, mental perception, self-aware
       perception, and yogic perception.
   Since their objects are appearing, specific phenomena,
   direct perception is not conceptual.

19 Without direct perception,
   there would be no evidence, so there could be no inference.
   All appearances would be impossible,
   such as the way things arise from causes and then cease.

20 Therefore it is by relying on evidence
   that one understands emptiness and so forth.
   Without relying on the conventional,
   one cannot realize the absolute.

21   The sense consciousnesses, which arise from the five sense faculties,
     clearly experience their own objects.
     Without direct sense perceptions,
     one would not perceive objects, like someone who is blind.

22   Having arisen based on the mental sense faculty,
     mental direct perception clearly discerns outer and inner objects.
     Without mental direct perception,
     there would be no consciousness of all the phenomena that are
         commonly known.

23   By meditating well according to the scriptures,
     yogic direct perception clearly experiences its own object, the ultimate.
     Without yogic direct perception,
     one would not see the ultimate, which transcends ordinary objects.

24   The experience of direct perception clears away misunderstandings
     about forms being the way they are.
     If it were the same in relation to one's own mind,
     this would entail another knower, and that would be endless.

25   Therefore the mind, which is clear and knowing by nature,
     knows itself in the same way that it knows objects.
     It illuminates itself without depending on anything else.
     This is called "self-awareness."

26   Whatever the other direct perceptions experience
     is ascertained as being direct perception
     through self-awareness. Without self-awareness,
     there would be no way to establish this.

27   Inference is rooted in direct perception,
     and direct perceptions are ascertained by self-awareness.
     When the experience of an unmistaken mind is reached,
     nothing further is needed to establish that.

28   Therefore on the basis of direct perceptions
     that are nonconceptual and unmistaken,
     misunderstandings are eliminated
     about manifest phenomena.

29   Understanding happens through apprehending objects as mental
          images
     and mixing those images with names.
     This is the activity of the mental consciousness and its concepts,
     which then develop all sorts of conventional terminology.

30   Mental images appear in the mind
     even for beings who do not understand language.
     By using concepts they have the ability to mix images with names
     to either engage or not engage with objects.

31   Without the conceptual mind,
     there would be no terminology, such as negation and affirmation.
     There could be no inference, no subjects to be learned,
     and nothing whatsoever could be taught.

32   Through concepts one can comprehend and affirm
     things that are not apparent, like goals for the future.
     Without inference and its concepts,
     everyone would be like newborn babies.

33   By relying on a sign, one can understand things.
     A sign is unmistaken if it fulfills the three criteria for valid evidence:
     The sign is present in the subject,
     there is a positive pervasion and a counter pervasion.

34   An inference about a hidden phenomenon
     is proven through its relationship
     with a sign
     that is established by valid direct perception.

35   To establish a proof there is the sign of being an effect, the sign of
          having the same nature,
      and the sign of not being perceived, which refutes an object to be
          negated
      because the object is not perceived or something contradictory is
          perceived.
      These are the three types of signs.

36   When seen authentically
      all appearances are primordially equal.
      When one's mindstream is pure, one's perceptions are pure.
      Everything is pure by nature.

37   Functional things are based on their having arisen.
      Nonfunctional things are based on having been designated.
      Therefore both functional things and nonfunctional things
      are empty of essence.

38   Ultimately in the true nature, the empty basis
      and its emptiness are not two different things.
      Appearance and emptiness are inseparable and ineffable.
      This is experienced by individual, self-knowing awareness.

39   All the aspects that are established
      are encompassed by affirmation of their existence or what they are.
      All the aspects that are refuted
      are encompassed by negation, by showing their nonexistence or what
          they are not.

40   Having gained certainty about this way of using
      affirmations and negations based on valid cognition,
      one can then show others
      proofs and refutations according to reasoning.

41   In formulating refutations, one uses reasons with the three criteria for
          valid evidence
      to establish autonomous arguments,
      and one refutes others by showing the consequences,
      depending on what they assert.

42 On the conventional level, since there are appearances that do not
     accord with reality,
   there are the way things appear and the way things are.
   In dependence on impure, ordinary perception
   or pure vision,

43 there are two types of conventional valid cognition,
   which resemble human eyes and divine eyes.
   These two have their own features
   and are categorized by their natures, causes, effects, and functions.

44 A mind that is unmistaken about ordinary facts
   arises from having correctly apprehended its objects.
   Valid ordinary perception eliminates misunderstandings about objects
   and fully apprehends the facts of a situation.

45 Limitless, timeless awareness
   arises from seeing suchness just as it is.
   It eliminates misunderstandings about its objects, which are
     inconceivable,
   and results in knowing the entire extent of phenomena.

46 There are also two approaches to the absolute truth:
   the expressible and the inexpressible.
   These are comprehended by the two types of valid cognition
   that investigate ultimate reality.

47 By relying on the former, one engages in the latter.
   It is like clearing one's eye of a flaw.
   Once the eye of valid cognition is thoroughly cleansed,
   one will see the reality of purity and equality.

48 Both the nonconceptual mind and the conceptual mind
   have undeluded aspects as well as deluded aspects,
   like perceiving two moons, dreams, and a rope as a snake.
   Therefore the two categories of valid cognition and nonvalid cognition
     are established.

49   Without both valid cognition and nonvalid cognition
     it would be impossible to distinguish what is false due to delusion
     from what is true and undeluded,
     and there could be no philosophy.

50   When one investigates the authentic, absolute truth,
     one uses direct perception and inference, and valid cognition and
        nonvalid cognition.
     In the same way that these are classifications,
     they are conceptual constructs.

51   However, their nature is established as empty,
     and therefore beyond all constructs.
     Emptiness is in all conventional constructs,
     just like heat is in fire.

52   Therefore appearance and emptiness
     abide inseparably in all phenomena
     as the means and what arises from the means,
     so one cannot affirm one of them and negate the other.

53   If one asks whether someone can engage in the absolute truth
     merely by seeing the world,
     without investigating it according to valid cognition or nonvalid
        cognition,
     indeed there is nothing to prevent that from happening.

54   In seeing how "this" arose from "that,"
     worldly people use inference, which deduces the meaning
     by relying on direct perception.
     Even though they do not designate things with those words, the
        meaning is not forsaken.

55   Without both types of conventional valid cognition,
     pure vision would be false,
     and for the impure level of seeing something like a conch,
     one could not tell which is true and which is false—the white conch or
        the yellow one.

56 Without both ways of investigating the absolute truth,
one would not know the unity of the two truths,
and the absolute would be reduced to a fabricated extreme.
In this way, ultimate valid cognition would destroy itself.

57 Upon investigation, relative truth—the object being comprehended—
    is not established,
and neither are the mind and self-awareness, which do the
    comprehending.
They are like the moon in water.
Ultimately, the two truths are inseparable;

58 they are a single truth, the final reality of nirvāṇa,
because the ultimate is in all phenomena.
Consciousness and objects of knowledge are inseparable
from the appearance of the kāyas and wisdoms, which are beyond
    notions of a "center" or "limit."

59 After opening wide the excellent eye of wisdom
that is profound and vast, as explained above,
one needs to see the excellent path taken by
the highly intelligent ones,

60 the descendents of the Sugata.
So do not let your actions be fruitless
by playing around when you could train systematically
in the vehicles of the sūtras and tantras, so difficult to find.

61 Therefore those who exhibit intelligence
possess the four reasonings as described above,
and perform their investigations without depending on others.
This is how they become certain about the four reliances.

62 Without a mind like this,
it is like the blind leading the blind.
Relying on consensus, literal words, or what is easy to understand
goes against the understanding of the four reliances.

63 Therefore one should not rely on individuals;
  one should rely on the Dharma.
  One will be liberated by what is said about the path established
      through authentic reasoning,
  not by those who say it.

64 If what an individual says is correct,
  then it is suitable, no matter what the person is like.
  Even the sugatas have emanated in forms such as butchers
  in order to tame sentient beings.

65 However, if what the person teaches
  contradicts the meaning of the Mahāyāna,
  there will be no benefit, no matter how good the person looks,
  like the form of a buddha emanated by a demon.

66 When intelligent ones hear and contemplate the Dharma,
  they should rely on the meaning and not on the words.
  If the meaning is understood, there is no contradiction
  no matter how it is expressed in words.

67 Things are named because of wanting to express an understandable
      meaning.
  Once the meaning has been understood,
  if the speaker keeps trying to formulate it in words,
  it is like continuing to search for tracks after an elephant has been
      found.

68 If one elaborates further because of attachment to words,
  concepts proliferate endlessly.
  Wandering further and further from the meaning,
  immature beings just make themselves tired.

69 For any single phrase, like "Bring me the wood,"
  if wood is differentiated according to its locale, etc., the possibilities are
      endless.
  Once one has understood the meaning of the phrase,
  then the words have fulfilled their purpose.

70 When a man points to the moon with his finger,
    a childish person looks at the finger instead.
    Foolish ones who adhere to the words
    have difficulty understanding, even though they think they
        understand.

71 When one engages in the meaning,
    one should know the provisional meaning and the definitive meaning,
    and rely on the definitive
    rather than the provisional.

72 Since the Omniscient One was all-knowing,
    he taught the yānas in a sequence,
    like steps ascending a staircase,
    according to students' styles, capacities, and interests.

73 There are eight categories of intentions and indirect intentions
    based on the Buddha's purpose regarding the basis for the intention.
    He spoke this way because it suited his purpose,
    whereas taking the words literally would impair valid cognition.

74 Because of his intentions, there are various levels of teachings,
    from the four Buddhist tenets up to the sublime Vajrayāna.
    The aspects that are not understood by the lower levels
    are clarified by the higher ones.

75 Having seen which teachings are closer to reasoning that accords with
        scripture,
    one holds to the definitive meaning.
    Like swans who can extract milk from water,
    those of the highest intelligence play in the ocean of the Buddha's
        speech.

76 The profound Vajrayāna teachings
    are concealed through the six parameters and the four styles of
        interpretation.
    They are established through flawless reasoning
    along with the key instructions of the lineage.

77 All phenomena are a unity
    of primordial purity and great equality.
    The two types of accurate valid cognition
    establish exactly what this means.

78 Without contradiction, one penetrates the essence
    of the *Prajñāpāramitā*, the creation stage,
    the completion stage, and the great completion,
    by means of the four styles of interpretation through the literal,
        general, hidden, and ultimate meanings.

79 Through that, highly intelligent ones
    become confident through certainty about the meaning.
    These heirs of the Buddha hold the inexhaustible treasure of the
        Dharma
    and the victory banner of the teachings of scripture and realization.

80 When practicing the definitive meaning,
    do not rely on consciousness—
    the perceiving mind and what it perceives, which depend on words and
        concepts.
    Rely instead on nondual wisdom.

81 That which has reference points
    is the mind with a nature of apprehending the apprehended.
    Conceiving of things in this way is false.
    In reality, there is no actual contact.

82 Whether something is conceived of as an entity or a nonentity,
    or as both or neither,
    no matter how it is focused on, there are still reference points.
    The sūtras say that whatever is grasped through conceptualization

83 is the domain of demons.
    Conceptualization cannot be destroyed
    by negating or affirming.
    But if one sees without removing or adding anything, there is
        liberation.

84 Completely free from perceiver and perceived,
    naturally occurring, timeless awareness is natural luminosity.
    Since all fabrications of the four extremes are brought to an end,
    timeless awareness is said to be supreme.

85 Just like someone blind from birth looking at the form of the sun,
    immature beings have not previously seen this.
    No matter how they imagine it, they don't actually know it,
    so immature beings feel anxious.

86 However, by means of authentic scriptures,
    reasoning that refutes all extreme views,
    and the guru's key instructions,
    just like a blind man gaining sight, one will see it for oneself.

87 At this time, those with devotion taste the nectar
    of the Dharma of the Tathāgata,
    and their eye of increasing joy
    turns toward the wisdom body of the sugatas.

88 At this time, all phenomena without exception
    are resolved in the state of equality.
    One gains the inexpressible confidence of certainty
    and skill in explaining the inexhaustible treasure of the Dharma.

89 By gaining expertise in the way the two truths are,
    one sees the reality of the two truths in union.
    When this happens, it is like removing the husk to reveal the essence.
    One knows how to endeavor in all the skillful means.

90 Since the sugatas know about skillful means,
    all their methods are said to be a genuine path.
    This is why one gives rise to irreversible confidence
    in one's teachers and their teachings.

91   By actualizing supreme, nondwelling, timeless awareness,
     one is naturally liberated from the extremes of cyclic existence and
          peace.
     Continuous, effortless, great compassion
     boundlessly pervades all directions and times.

92   The supreme, stainless cause
     is possession of the four reliances,
     which comes from contemplating how the Dharma of the two truths
     is established by the four types of reasoning.

93   From this comes forth the fruition—profound, timeless awareness,
     and when this fully manifests,
     the eight great treasures of confidence are released
     from concealment in the basic space of awareness.

94   The treasure of memory
     is not forgetting the teachings previously studied and contemplated.
     The treasure of intelligence
     is discerning the vast and profound meanings of those teachings.

95   The treasure of realization
     is internalizing the entire meaning of the sūtras and tantras.
     The treasure of retention
     is never forgetting anything one has studied.

96   The treasure of confidence is satisfying all beings
     by teaching well.
     The treasure of the Dharma is completely protecting
     the precious treasury of the sacred Dharma.

97   The treasure of bodhicitta
     is maintaining the unbroken lineage of the Three Jewels.
     The treasure of accomplishment is attaining acceptance
     of the true nature, the equality of the unborn.

98   Those who master the inexhaustible eight great treasures
     and never part from them
     are praised by the buddhas and their heirs,
     and become the protectors of the three worlds.

99   The teachings of the Buddha are valid
     since they are proven through valid cognition.
     One develops certainty through a valid path
     of valid teachings, so one sees the truth, which is the fruition.

100 Having completely purified his vision
     and perfected great compassion,
     the Sugata demonstrated the path
     and said, "Taste the deathless nectar I have found.

101 Experience it through the four reasonings
     and the four reliances."
     Even though he shared this nectar,
     it is difficult to experience its supreme taste

102 because of our degenerate era
     and the way it goes against the Dharma.
     Seeing this, my mind is filled with pure motivation
     and the greatest reverence for the teachings.

103 Through the virtue of expressing just a little
     of the way to develop the stainless wisdom,
     which comes from contemplating in this way,
     may all beings attain the state of Mañjuśrī.

104 When the lotus of my heart turned toward
     Mañjuśrī, the sun of speech, it blossomed with devotion
     and this honey pollen of excellent explanations came forth.
     May this increase the feast of fortunate bees.

In accord with my previous intention to write this, when the learned one Lhaksam Gyaltsen recently urged me to do so, I, Jampal Gyepé, wrote it in a single day, the 29th day of the third lunar month of the Sakyong year. Maṅgalam—may this be auspicious! There are 104 verses. May this be virtuous!

Radiant Light
of the
Sun and Moon

Khenchen Palden Sherab

I

Prelude

PRELIMINARY VERSES OF HOMAGE

———

THE HOMAGE TO MAÑJUŚRĪ AND PADMASAMBHAVA IN UNION

Namo śrī vajra padma tīkṣṇaye
Homage to the glorious and sharp vajra lotus!

THE HOMAGE TO ŚĀKYAMUNI BUDDHA[1]

With the chariot of the winds of the two accumulations,[2] you led the four divisions[3] of the troops of the ten powers[4] to victory in battle over the gods of desire.[5]

With the sharp fangs and claws[6] of the four fearlessnesses,[7] you swallowed all at once the elephant[8] brains of antagonistic proponents of eternalism and nihilism.

By abiding on the snow mountains[9] of knowing the nature and entire extent of phenomena, you destroyed the darkness of the two obscurations[10] through the two yogic disciplines.[11]

In the center of a thousand-spoke wheel, among humans you are exalted like a lion. You are called Siddhārtha, since you have accomplished all aims. Please bring forth auspiciousness![12]

THE HOMAGE TO PADMASAMBHAVA[13]

Shining with a thousand luminous marks of deathlessness,[14]
you sprang forth from a lotus blossom in the center of a lake.[15]
Nangsi Zilnön,[16] nirmanakāya who outshines all apparent existence,
please be the crown jewel that beautifies my head until I am fully
    enlightened.

THE HOMAGE TO MAÑJUŚRĪ[17]

On the tip of the anthers of a thousand-petal lotus of devotion,[18]
Lord of Dharma, I continue to reverently pay homage to you.
Mawé Sengé, ever-youthful Lion of Speech,[19]
please bestow the light of intelligence on all beings everywhere.[20]

THE HOMAGE TO SARASVATĪ[21]

With a hundred thousand melodious words of the noble Dharma,
you beautify a garden of lotuses in full bloom—the throats of all the
    buddhas.
Sarasvatī, graceful swan glowing with the luster of moonlight,
playfully cruise at this time through the lake of my mind.

THE HOMAGE TO THE VIDYĀDHARAS
OF THE THREE LINEAGES[22]

With one gulp of discernment, you retained in the belly of your
    intelligence a hundred thousand streams of the definitive and
    secret three sections[23] of the tantras,
which you disgorged, like the learned one Agastya,[24] as excellent
    explanations having the eight qualities.[25]
I praise you hundreds of times, genuine masters of awareness of the
    past.[26]

THE HOMAGE TO LONGCHENPA[27]

The teachings of the Buddha are like the Realm of the Thirty-Three
    Gods,[28] where many nonsectarian and learned authors assemble,
    like the vassal kings paying homage to Indra.[29]

In their center, like Indra, you sit majestically on the supreme yāna
of Dzokchen, which is like Sasung, the royal elephant,[30] and from
there you survey all phenomena with your thousand shining
eyes.[31]

Openly brandishing your thousand-pronged vajra[32] of explanation,
debate, and composition, you are crowned with the jewels of
many scriptures.[33]

Supremely learned lord Longchenpa, as renowned as Indra, never
before has there been someone like you. Please victoriously crown
the top of my head.

THE HOMAGE TO JAMGÖN MIPHAM RINPOCHÉ[34]

Your arrogant and vicious opponents, like a thousand elephants,
are overpowered, even without study or contemplation,
by your laughing roar of reasoning, O Lion of Speech.[35]
Mipham Choklé Namgyal, may you be victorious.

THE HOMAGE TO THE ROOT TEACHER[36]

With the sharp vajra weapon of scripture and reasoning
you overpower your opponents, who resemble arrogant, jealous
gods.
Gracious teacher who kindly helps me see the excellent, genuine
path,
like the king of the gods, may you be ever victorious.

These verses of homage are offered like the welcoming gesture of strewing
fresh, white lotus petals. It is as the *Root Mañjuśrī Tantra* states:

The letter A, the great nature itself,
holds the teachings of the teacher in the highest esteem.

THE QUALITIES OF JAMGÖN MIPHAM

Before going further, I want to discuss Mipham Rinpoché, the author of the
root text, who was predicted in several terma scriptures. First, there is a prediction of him in a terma discovered by Drodul Sang-ngak Lingpa:[37]

The emanation of Nupchen[38] named Mipham
will come forth as an especially powerful lord of mind terma.

Another prediction of Mipham Rinpoché comes from the terma discovered by Terchen Traktung Dudjom Trolö Tsal:[39]

Mipham Gyatso will turn back the flood of invading armies,
conquer the tenet systems of mistaken views,
and make the Vajrayāna teachings shine brilliantly, like the sun.

There are other predictions of Mipham Rinpoché, particularly in the vajra predictions of the King of the Sages, Buddha Śākyamuni himself, as well as the vajra predictions of Orgyen Padmakara, the Second Buddha of our time.[40] They greatly praise Mipham as the very embodiment of the wisdom of all the buddhas, or in other words, as Jetsun Mañjuśrī, the Lion of Speech, appearing in the form of a spiritual friend.

Being a master of the eight great treasures of confidence[41] and the four right discriminations,[42] Mipham Rinpoché wrote outstanding commentaries on the countless entrances to the common and uncommon scriptures, particularly the profound and vast intentions of the sūtras and tantras, which had been perfectly expounded by the Buddha. Jamgön Mipham showed especially sharp intelligence in that his analyses did not depend on what other scholars had said. He was truly inseparable from Jetsun Mañjughoṣa[43] in the sense that he was a siddha as well as a scholar; he was all-knowing about the definitive meaning. He was the Jetsun Lama, whose compassion was totally beyond reference points. It is with the utmost reverence that I repeat his name, renowned throughout the three levels[44] of the world: Mipham Jamyang Namgyal Gyamtso, or Jampal Gyepé Dorjé.[45] It was his voice that bestowed the teaching in *The Sword of Wisdom That Ascertains Reality*.

Now to begin explaining the root text, there are three parts: the title, the exposition of the subject matter, and the final conclusion.

THE EXPLANATION OF THE TITLE

The title *The Sword of Wisdom That Ascertains Reality* corresponds to the words of Nupchen Sangyé Yeshé[46] in the *Lamp of the Eye of Meditation*, his text elucidating the key points of meditation:

One gains certainty about reality from the wisdom of contemplation, which employs examples, arguments, and reasoning to become decisive. Reality is discovered by comprehending and analyzing with discerning wisdom.

The subject matter of the *Lamp of the Eye of Meditation* is the Buddha's teachings—the sūtras and tantras—along with their commentaries, whose meanings are both profound and vast.[47] The profound wisdom of fully ascertaining reality comes from properly using correct, unmistaken reasoning that accords with the nature of things. Since this kind of correct reasoning instantly cuts through the three nets of not understanding, misunderstanding, and doubt, it is like a sword. Therefore *The Sword of Wisdom That Ascertains Reality* is said to be a title that connects the metaphor with the meaning.[48]

Titles are said to be necessary in order to eliminate confusion on the conventional level. The *Sūtra of the Descent to Laṅkā* states:

> If one does not apply names,
> everything in the world will be confused.
> Therefore to clear away confusion,
> the Buddha designated things with names.

2

The Validity of the Teachings and the Teacher

―――――

The Sword of Wisdom has three sections: the start of the composition makes it good in the beginning, the main part makes it good in the middle, and the conclusion makes it good at the end. The beginning section includes a verse of homage followed by a verse stating the author's purpose.

THE VERSE OF HOMAGE

1. **This philosophy is unmistaken;
    all errors have been eliminated.
    The mind is free from doubt about three points.[49]
    I pay homage to Mañjuśrī, the treasure of wisdom.**

THE MEANING OF THE WORD "PHILOSOPHY"

The word *philosophy* is drawn from the Sanskrit word *siddhyanta*.[50] Philosophy is connected with ultimate reality. It refers to a system of assertions that are made with certainty because they come from investigating and analyzing through scripture and reasoning. It reaches a final conclusion for which nothing further need be posited. A philosophy is unmistaken if it accords with the true nature of things, and mistaken if it cannot be proven to accord with the way things are.

There are two basic types of philosophical systems: worldly and transcendent. In relation to these two types of philosophy, Orgyen,[51] the Second Buddha, says in his *Garland of Views*:

In this world there are countless mistaken views, but they
can be summarized into four main views: (1) materialism,
(2) hedonism, (3) fundamentalism, and (4) extremism.[52]

And:

There are two paths that transcend the world: the vehicle of
characteristics and the vajra vehicle.[53]

The great translator Kawa Paltsek comments in the *Explanation of the Levels of the View*:

Both the worldly and transcendent views
appear from one source, like things made of gold.[54]
They can be summarized into seventeen views.
Once you have understood them, then either accept them or leave
them behind.[55]

THE VALIDITY OF THE TEACHINGS

1:1.[56]   First, to establish the validity of the teachings, Buddhist philosophy is
valid because it hasn't the slightest defect in terms of being mistaken. This is
because the Buddha Bhagavān, the one who taught these tenets, eliminated
all errors, including the two obscurations and their seeds and habitual tendencies. Our teacher is called a great being because his vision came from valid
direct perception and he perfected the qualities of wisdom, compassion, and
power.

Buddhist philosophy is proven to be a pure and valid scriptural teaching
through the three types of investigation[57] and through reasoning that fulfills
the three criteria for valid evidence[58] in relation to the three aspects of a valid
inference.[59] These lead to doubtless certainty,[60] the essence of intelligence,
which is Mañjuśrī, the great treasure of wisdom. Alternatively, one could say
that profound intelligence comes from the blessings of Mañjuśrī. Either way,
respectful homage is paid with body, speech, and mind to Mañjuśrī as the treasure of wisdom.

This verse of homage shows the validity of the teachings primarily by using
the reasoning of causal efficacy.[61] To formulate this as a syllogism:[62] "The Buddhist teachings are unmistaken because they were taught by the Buddha, who
has eliminated all errors." The first criterion of a valid proof—the presence of

the reason in the subject—is that Buddhist philosophy was indeed taught by the Buddha. The second criterion of a valid proof—the positive pervasion—is that if these teachings are by the Buddha, then they are definitely unmistaken. The third criterion of a valid proof—the counter pervasion—is that if the teachings are mistaken, then they were certainly not taught by the Buddha. These constitute the logical proof.

Once one has eliminated all errors of the two obscurations and habitual patterns, then ultimate wisdom and love arise. Once one has ultimate wisdom,[63] one is capable of teaching an unmistaken path. The motivation to teach an unmistaken path depends on compassion alone, so it is said that great compassion is the extraordinary cause of attaining buddhahood.

In this regard, the glorious Dharmakīrti says:[64]

> The practice is to become accustomed to compassion.

And also:

> In order to overcome suffering,
> compassionate ones actualize the skillful means to do so.

The glorious Candrakīrti says:[65]

> Loving kindness is said to be the seed of the abundant harvest of the
>   victorious ones.
> It is like the water that causes the seed to develop,
> and like the ripening that is enjoyed for a long time.
> Therefore from the outset I praise compassion.

The *Ornament of the Mahāyāna Sūtras* states:

> Compassion gives rise to patience, reflection, and aspiration,
> and it causes sentient beings to fully mature.
> It begins as the root and ends as the supreme fruit.
> This is the great tree of compassion.

In more detail, compassion is the root, patience is the trunk, reflection on actions that benefit others are the branches, aspirations are the foliage, good rebirths are the flowers, and bringing sentient beings to maturity is the fruit. This is the tree of compassion.

The *Tantra of the Enlightenment of Vairocana* states:

O Lord of Secrets,[66] because the timeless awareness of the
wisdom of omniscience is rooted in compassion, it results
from bodhicitta and is the perfection of skillful means.

The Buddha Bhagavān fulfilled his own aim through perfecting the qualities of relinquishment and realization,[67] and to fulfill the aims of others he perfected the qualities of wisdom, love, and power. These qualities are the causes[68]
for establishing him as an unfailing, authentic, great being. If students practice,
just as the Buddha taught, whichever aspects of the noble Dharma fit their individual styles, capacities, and intentions,[69] they will attain the corresponding
results of the higher realms and liberation. This is how Buddhist philosophy is
established as unmistaken.

A great number of supporting scriptures could be cited. For example, it is
said in a sūtra:[70]

> Having become omniscient, they turn the wheel of the
> Dharma.[71]

It is also said:

> If one has not attained omniscience, one cannot turn the
> wheel of the Dharma.[72]

The glorious Dharmakīrti says in the *Commentary on Valid Cognition*:

> A tathāgata is someone with realization.

The regent Maitreya says in the *Ornament of Clear Realization*:

> Because of their omniscience, the buddhas, who have all the
> signs of full enlightenment, give a variety of teachings.

The great master Nāgārjuna says in his *Praise to the Unsurpassable One*:

> You alone clarify phenomena,
> and you alone detect all phenomena.
> No one is your equal in this.
> I pay homage to the lama, who is superior.

Ācārya Asaṅga says in the *Ornament of the Mahāyāna Sūtras*:

> Definitely freed from all obscurations,

> your wisdom encompasses all phenomena.
> Buddha, you outshine the entire world.
> I pay homage to you as fully liberated.

The great master Ashvagosha says in his *One Hundred Fifty Praises*:

> Some people's faculties are the very best; others' faculties are not the
>   best,
> or they are small, medium, or great.
> Only you and no one else can fathom
> the limitless distinctions among them.

He also says:

> Only your pristine wisdom
> encompasses all phenomena.
> Unlike you, all others' wisdom
> seems to leave out some phenomena.

And:[73]

> You behave well without being asked.
> You show kindness without any reason.
> You are friendly even if not previously acquainted.
> You want to treat those unrelated to you like family.

And:

> Since you gave your own flesh,
> you must have given other things as well.
> Doer of good, you gave even your life
> when ordinary beings requested it.

> Hundreds of times you ransomed,
> with your own body and life,
> the bodies and lives of ordinary beings
> when they were held for execution.

Panchen Vimalamitra says in his commentary to the *Litany of the Names of Mañjuśrī*:

You cause the bondage of all beings' emotional afflictions to be liberated in accordance with their intentions. All your teachings have the sole purpose of being an antidote that subdues emotional defilements.

SCRIPTURAL SUPPORT FOR THE VALIDITY OF THE TEACHINGS

Many Indian Buddhist masters have commented on the validity of the teachings. For instance, the great master Lalitavajra says in the *Parkhap*,[74] his commentary on the king of tantras, the *Guhyagarbha Tantra*:

> These are designated as teachings by being known and proven.
> Different teachings appear to fit individual minds.

The great master Dharmakīrti says in the *Thirty-Five Hundred Stanzas*, his autocommentary on the *Commentary on Valid Cognition*:

> In one way, the Buddha's teachings should be called *inference*
>   because they are unfailing words that eliminate errors.
>
> One can be certain about what to accept and what to reject
> and the methods to use
> because the Buddha's main points are unmistaken.
> This inference also applies to others.
>
> When the teachings on what to accept and reject, and the related methods are unmistaken, then they are unfailing. An example is the explanation of the four noble truths. To fulfill their aims, people rely on what they have previously known to be true, and they accept similar unmistaken things. There would be no point in a teacher giving a wrong explanation because it would be contradictory and counterproductive.

Dharmakīrti also says:

> Anyone's words that are verified through valid cognition
> as being unmistaken
> attain the status of scripture.

> It does not make sense for words to be scripture simply because they were not produced by a person.[75]

> Even though others similarly use the word "scripture," in general it is only because of valid cognition that a text is scripture. The definition of a "scripture" is unmistaken words verified through valid cognition.

And Ācārya Asaṅga said in his *Compendium of the Mahāyāna Teachings*:

> What does "truth" mean? Truth is defined as the teachings that are not discordant with reality. Knowing the truth is a cause of purification.[76] In other words, Buddhist tenets are free of six negative faults and possess three positive virtues; therefore the Dharma is unmistaken and established as valid scriptural teachings.

As for the six faults and the three virtues, the *Levels according to Yogācāra* states:[77]

> Being meaningless, having a wrong meaning, and being meaningful;
> studying, debating, and being devoted to practice;
> being deceitful, unkind, and eliminating suffering—
> the śāstras are free of the six and accept the three.[78]

To explain these six faults and three virtues, "meaningless" refers to something that does not accomplish liberation. "Wrong meaning" refers to falling into the extremes of eternalism or nihilism, or saying that causing harm is a religious activity, and so on. Since they are free of these two faults, the Buddhist tenets are meaningful. "Studying" refers to exclusively studying, and "debating" refers to debating solely to expose the faults of others. Buddhist philosophy, which is free of these two faults, is devoted to practice. "Deceitful" refers to the hypocrisy of pretending to be noble when one is not. "Unkind" refers to not having the compassion to protect sentient beings from suffering. Being free of these two faults, Buddhist philosophy is the noble Dharma that causes the suffering of saṃsāra to be eliminated.

In other words, through the cause—transforming the afflictions—one attains the result: protection from the sufferings of the lower realms among the

three realms of existence. This is how Buddhist philosophy is proven to be unmistaken, valid scriptural teachings.

Ācārya Vasubandhu says in his *Explanation of Reasoning*:

> It transforms all the kleśas, which are the enemy,
> and protects from the lower realms of saṃsāra.
> Because of these qualities of transforming and protecting, it is called
>   a *śāstra*.[79]
> Other philosophies do not have these two qualities.

The regent Maitreya says:[80]

> The Buddha's speech is closely connected with meaningful scripture
>   and realization.
> It causes the afflictions to be eliminated from the three realms and
>   teaches the benefits of peace.
> It is the speech of a genuine sage.[81]
> If a teaching goes against these points, it belongs to someone other
>   than the Buddha.

Also:

> Those who rely solely on the Buddha's teachings,
> and explain them with an undistracted mind,
> and whose explanations accord with the path of liberation,
> speak words just like the Buddha's words. They are worthy of
>   acceptance on the crown of one's head.

Also:

> The valid scriptural teachings of the Buddha are established as an
> unmistaken philosophy because they teach the unmistaken path
> that unites emptiness and interdependence as the true nature of all
> apparent, knowable phenomena in saṃsāra and nirvāṇa.

The great master Nāgārjuna says:

> I pay homage to Buddha Śākyamuni,
> whose speech is incomparably supreme,
> because he taught as the path of the middle way
> that emptiness and interdependence are identical.

The teachings of the Buddha consist of nine yānas that fit individual students' styles, capacities, and intentions. If students fervently practice the various philosophies of the noble Dharma exactly as the Buddha taught, they will attain the corresponding results. Since this will happen without fail, Buddhist philosophy is said to be unmistaken. For this reason, Orgyen, the Second Buddha, says:

> The tenets of all the yānas are true at their own level, so do
> not argue about them.

There are many more passages like these. When one has devotion and pure perception toward all the Buddhist philosophical systems without closing the eye of intelligence, then the great door of the path of liberation will start to open.

THE VALIDITY OF THE TEACHER

1:2.   The second line of the root verse establishes the validity of the teacher. Having analyzed and established Buddhist philosophy as the unmistaken and valid scriptural teachings of the noble Dharma, one goes on to establish the teacher, the Buddha Bhagavān, as one who has completely eliminated all mistakes and ignorance. He is a great being whose valid cognition knows and sees all phenomena without obscurations through direct perception.

Valid teachings are dependent on a valid teacher. The cause for becoming a valid teacher is the perfect intention of wanting to benefit beings. The perfect activity of teaching leads to the perfect effect—becoming a *sugata* for one's own sake and a protector for the sake of others.

SCRIPTURAL SUPPORT FOR THE
VALIDITY OF THE TEACHER

The great master Dignāga says:[82]

> I pay homage to the valid, great being who wishes to be of benefit,
> and is a teacher, a sugata, and a protector.

In his autocommentary to the *Compendium of Valid Cognition*, Dignāga says:

In order to generate devotion, the first chapter of this treatise praises the Bhagavān's genuineness because he had the perfect cause and the perfect result. The cause is his perfect intention and perfect activity. His intention is the wish to benefit others and his activity is giving the teachings. The result is the perfect benefit for self and others.

The benefit for oneself is to become a *sugata*, "one gone blissfully." *Sugata* should be understood as having three meanings: one meaning is being very beautiful, like someone with an excellent body; another meaning is being irreversible, like someone cured of smallpox; a third meaning is being complete, like a full vase.

These three meanings show the especially perfect benefit for oneself. A sugata is free from the attachments of non-Buddhists,[83] and has gone beyond the levels of those in training[84] and those beyond training.[85] The perfect benefit for others is being their protector[86] with the purpose of liberating them. To the teacher who possesses those qualities, I pay homage.

The great master Vasubandhu says:[87]

I pay homage to the one who has completely abandoned the darkness of ignorance,
who leads beings out of the mire of saṃsāra,
and teaches according to the true meaning.

Ācārya Udbhaṭa Siddhasvāmin says:[88]

I have given up other teachers,
and I take refuge in you, the Bhagavān.
Why? It is because
you have no faults and are full of qualities.

There are many other similar passages, but they will not be included here.

USING REASONING TO ESTABLISH VALIDITY

1:3.   Going on to the third line of the verse, by using the three types of investigation,[89] two points have been established: First, that the teachings are a pure, clear, and incomparable entrance to complete liberation. Second, that the teacher, the Buddha, is an incomparable, valid, great being on the basis of his perfect intention, activity, and result. The third point is that the previous two points are established through reasoning. By using the reasoning of a valid proof in which the three criteria for valid evidence are complete,[90] along with the three aspects of valid inference,[91] these points can be established without doubt.

To phrase this as a syllogism: "The teacher, the Buddha, is a valid, great being because his teachings are valid scriptures. A similar example is a genuine, great sage." The first criterion of a valid proof—the presence of the reason in the subject—is fulfilled because the philosophy of these valid scriptures is established as the words of our teacher, the Buddha. The second criterion of a valid proof—the positive pervasion—is fulfilled because if scriptural teachings are valid, then they are definitely taught by a valid, great being, which in this case is the Buddha. The third criterion of a valid proof—the counter pervasion—is fulfilled because if the teacher is not a valid, great being, then the scriptural teachings will certainly not be valid.

By using reasoning based on the three types of valid cognition—direct perception, inference, and valid scriptures—concerning the Buddha and his teachings, then the highest sort of devotion—unfailing, confident certainty—will arise in one's mind. This kind of devotion is the essence of the ultimate way of taking refuge and making supplications. It is the root of the path of liberation, the root of blessings entering one's mind, and the single root of hundreds of positive qualities. Therefore the Second Buddha, Guru Rinpoché, said:

> When your mind has the devotion of certainty, then blessings enter.
> When your mind is free of doubt, your wishes are fulfilled.

The omniscient Khenchen Śāntarakṣita says in his autocommentary to the *Ornament of the Middle Way*:

> The teachings of the Tathāgata are good in the beginning, good in the middle, and good at the end. Just like pure gold that is unharmed by being burned, cut, and rubbed, the Buddha's teachings are not contradicted by direct perception,

inference, or the Buddha's own words.[92] Through his pristine wisdom unmixed with saṃsāra, the Buddha has clearly seen the suchness of reality without even a trace of ignorance. As the guru of the whole world, his lotus feet are beautified by the crown garlands atop the heads of the leaders of gods and humans. Why wouldn't those who know this generate the kind of devotion that takes practice to heart in a way that is free from attachment?

Here is a related verse:[93]

> By relying on the lama and the Three Jewels
> all degeneration is overcome and one's certainty becomes unfailing.
> From now until reaching the essence of enlightenment,
> I take refuge from the depth of my heart.

MAÑJUŚRĪ AS THE TREASURE OF WISDOM

1:4.   Therefore, homage is paid to Mañjuśrī, the great treasure of wisdom. He embodies the precious, unfailing, heartfelt wisdom of certainty, the incomparable intelligence like the thousand light rays of the sun, free from the thick darkness of doubt. Also, intelligence free of doubt arises from the blessings of Mañjuśrī, the great treasure of wisdom, so homage can be paid from that perspective as well.

This verse of homage shows primarily that the teacher is valid, and does so mainly by using the reasoning of the dependency of an effect.[94] Another way of looking at this verse of homage is that the first line is about the jewel of the noble Dharma, the second line is about the jewel of the Buddha, and the third line is about the jewel of the Saṅgha. In this way homage is paid to Jetsun Mañjuśrī, the great treasure of wisdom, as the embodiment of the Three Jewels.

This homage has two purposes: the benefit of self and the benefit of others. By showing that the teacher is a noble being, Mipham accumulated merit, so this homage benefits him.[95] The homage benefits others when students generate devotion and interest in the teaching and the teacher. The *Sūtra of the Vast Display* states:

> Those who have merit can fulfill their intentions.

And the great master Nāgārjuna says:

> It is not fruitless to pay homage
> to a teacher who composed a commentary.
> This is because devotion and interest
> are generated for the teacher and the commentary.

The *Udānavarga: A Collection of Verses from the Buddhist Canon*, by the Buddha Śākyamuni, states:

> People who have accumulated merit
> are not harmed by others,
> and various types of gods and demons
> are unable to obstruct them.

THE AUTHOR'S PROMISE IN COMPOSING THE TEXT

2. The teachings of the Sugata
are profound, vast, and difficult to realize.
For those who wish to taste this deathless nectar,
I will bestow the light of intelligence.

2.   The absolute aspect of the teachings is profound by being free from all extremes such as existence and nonexistence. The relative aspect of the teachings is vast by encompassing the bodhisattva levels, the pāramitās, and so on. Since these profound and vast teachings are difficult to realize, the Mahāyāna teachings of the Sugata are like deathless nectar. For fortunate ones who wish to taste them and practice them, Mipham says he will bestow the light of excellent explanations that will bring forth flawless intelligence in their minds.

This is the author's promise in composing the text. In this context, Ācārya Nāgārjuna says:

> The noble ones do not make many promises.
> Because if one has made a difficult promise,
> it is like carving on stone;
> even death does not make it go away.

3

The Two Truths

The second section, which is good in the middle, is the subject matter of the composition. This will be explained in three parts: (1) the two truths, which are the topic to be comprehended,[96] (2) the two types of reasoning,[97] which are what does the comprehending, (3) and the result of comprehension. For the first of these, the two truths, the root text says:

> 3. **The Dharma taught by the buddhas**
> **is completely based on the two truths:**
> **the worldly, relative truth,**
> **and the supreme, absolute truth.**[98]

3.   The perfect buddhas gave a multitude of teachings, which are like 84,000 entrances to the noble Dharma. They can be summed up in the two truths, which are the subject matter here. What are the two truths? They are the relative truth of worldly beings and the absolute truth that transcends the world. As for what is meant by "the world," Candrakīrti says in his *Clear Words*:

> Worldly beings are known to be their aggregates.[99]
> The world definitely depends on the aggregates.
>
> It follows that "the world" refers to individuals who designate things on the basis of the aggregates.[100]

We need to understand that the highest possible realization is the realization of the nature of the two truths, just as it is. As one progresses through the yānas, one realizes how the two truths more and more profoundly express the way things truly are.

Here we will briefly examine the two truths by presenting them in five ways: according to their essence, definitions, characteristics, classification, and purpose.

THE ESSENCE OF THE TWO TRUTHS

First, the essence of the relative is the realm of objects conceptualized through the mind and the sense faculties. The essence of the absolute is the realm of self-knowing, discerning wisdom, free from the intellect and its fabricated extremes.

The *Way of the Bodhisattva* states:

> The absolute is not within the domain of the mind.
> The mind is said to be the relative.

And the *Entrance to the Middle Way* states:

> All phenomena have two natures,
> which are seen truly or falsely.
> What is seen truly is the ultimate nature.
> What is seen falsely is the relative nature.

THE DEFINITIONS OF THE TWO TRUTHS

Second, as for definitions, the word "relative" is illusory appearances with no real essence. However, temporarily from a deluded perspective, their specific characteristics[101] are unfailingly true. This is the relative truth. The *Entrance to the Middle Way* states:

> Because ignorance obscures the nature, it is the relative.
> Whatever is constructed is an untrue appearance.
> The Buddha called this the all-concealing, relative truth.

The *Two Truths* states:

> The relative obscures what is genuine
> for a person in relation to a thing.

The "absolute" is the ultimate goal, and because the path and result are unfailing, it is called "truth." The *Clear Words* states:

It is the ultimate and it is also excellent, so it is the absolute.
Since it is also true, it is called the absolute truth.

The *Light of the Middle Way* states:

> The unmistaken, subjective mind is all the wisdom aris-
> ing from hearing, contemplating, and meditating on the
> genuine meaning. It is called the absolute because it is the
> ultimate.

THE CHARACTERISTICS OF THE TWO TRUTHS

Third, as for their characteristics, the relative truth is characterized by phenomena that are not beyond the realm of the mind and cannot withstand analysis. The *Heruka Galpo Tantra* states:

> Being fallible and the objects of the mind—
> These are the general characteristics of the relative.

The absolute truth is characterized by the true nature that transcends the
mind; in the true nature all concepts are pacified. *Root Wisdom of the Middle
Way* states:

> It is not known through something other,[102] so it is peace.
> It is nonconceptual and not the different objects.
> It is not fabricated through conceptual constructs.
> These are the characteristics of suchness.

THE CLASSIFICATION OF THE TWO TRUTHS

Fourth, there are two classifications: the relative truth and the absolute truth.
The *Sūtra of the Meeting of the Father and Child* states:

> Knower of the World, there are two parts to your truth.
> You did not hear this elsewhere; it is your own knowledge.
> These two are the relative truth and the absolute truth.
> There is no third truth whatsoever.

The relative truth has two categories: the correct and the incorrect. The correct relative is the objects that appear to the mind through the unmistaken
six senses,[103] and knowledge of the words and terms that follow what worldly

people consider true and false. The incorrect relative is what appears to someone with defective sense faculties, like visions of falling hairs. The *Two Truths*
states:

> Although they appear similar, because some of them can perform
>   functions
> and others cannot perform functions,
> there are the categories of the "correct" and the "incorrect."
> These form the categories of the relative.

The absolute also has two categories: the "expressible absolute," which accords with the ordinary mind, and the "inexpressible absolute," which transcends the ordinary mind. The *Adornment of the Middle Way* states:

> Since it accords with the ultimate,
> it is called the absolute.
> In reality, there is freedom
> from the hosts of conceptual constructs.

THE PURPOSE OF THE TWO TRUTHS

Fifth, in relation to their purpose, the *Two Truths* states:

> Those who understand the classification of the two truths
> are not confused about the words of the Buddha.
> Since all of them have accumulated merit,
> they will go to the far shore of perfection.

And the master Candrakīrti says:

> Emptiness is the profundity,
> and the other qualities are the vastness.
> If one understands the ways of profundity and vastness,
> one will obtain these qualities.

4

An Explanation of Causality through Interdependent Appearances

————

Next is the second section of the main topic—the two types of reasoning that comprehend the two truths. This has two parts: a brief overview of the two types of valid cognition and a detailed explanation of the four types of reasoning. First, for the brief overview, the root text says:

> 4. **If one wants to know the nature of the two truths**
> **with a mind that ascertains them unerringly,**
> **one should thoroughly establish the good, clear eyes**
> **of the two types of flawless valid cognition.**

AN OVERVIEW OF THE TWO TYPES OF VALID COGNITION

4. If one wants to know with unerring certainty the nature of the two truths—the relative truth and the absolute truth—which are the topic to be comprehended, one must establish the two types of unmistaken, flawless, valid cognition. These are the valid cognition that investigates conventional reality and the valid cognition that investigates ultimate reality. These two are supreme; they are like having two good, clear eyes that see with certainty. The reason that these two need to be established is that all phenomena are included within the two truths and it is impossible to realize anything greater than the truth related with the way things really are. Therefore, in order to bring about correct comprehension, valid cognition and Madhyamaka philosophy are said to be like two lion heads joined at the neck.[104]

Next there will be a detailed explanation of the four reasonings as that which does the comprehending, the four reliances as the way the four reasonings function, and the eight great treasures of confidence as the result of comprehension.

In terms of the four reasonings, the first three reasonings will be explained together and the reasoning for a valid proof will be explained separately. The first three reasonings will be explained by means of a general teaching on the interdependence of appearances. This will be followed by individual explanations of the reasonings of cause, effect, and nature, and then the three reasonings will be summarized.

THE GENERAL EXPLANATION OF THE FIRST THREE REASONINGS THROUGH INTERDEPENDENT APPEARANCES

For the general teaching on the interdependence of appearances, the root text says:

> 5. **No matter how things appear,**
> **they arise interdependently.**
> **Nothing independent appears;**
> **that would be like a lotus appearing in the sky.**

5. Everything that appears in this world of saṃsāra and nirvāṇa definitely arises through the interdependence of causes and conditions. We never experience anything that does not depend on causes and conditions, such as a lotus in the sky.

The great master Candragomin says in the *Lamp of Proven Reasoning*:

> Phenomena are established as interdependent
> because they are pervaded by the factors
> of the nature, causal efficacy, dependency, and valid proofs.
> Whatever is shown and the means for showing it
> are established in this way:
> there is the nature, the act of production, and what is brought about.

Since all phenomena that are designated with names are interdependent, they are therefore emptiness. For "interdependence" to have the same meaning as "equality,"[105] unconditioned phenomena must be included as well, so interdependence cannot be characterized solely as "having arisen from causes."[106] In this regard, the great master Nāgārjuna says:

> Whatever arises interdependently
> is explained as emptiness.
> It is dependently designated;
> it is the path of the Middle Way.
> Apart from what arises interdependently,
> there are no existent phenomena.
> Therefore apart from emptiness
> there are no existent phenomena.

What exactly is "interdependent arising"? There are three parts to the explanation: the meaning of the term, its essence, and its categories.

THE MEANING OF INTERDEPENDENCE

First, in Sanskrit, interdependent arising is *pratītyasamutpāda*. The *Formation of Words in Two Volumes*[107] states:

> Interdependent arising is *pratītyasamutpāda*. *Pratītya* is "dependent" or "conditional." As for *sam*, the word *sambandha* is "related." *Utpāda* is "arises." Neither outer phenomena nor inner phenomena arise independently. Things arise from the gathering of causes and conditions. Something arises later in dependence on an earlier cause, unless it is obstructed by something else. This is what is called *interdependence*.

The glorious Candrakīrti says:

> That which arises as dependent and related
> is defined as "coming together and connecting."

THE ESSENCE OF INTERDEPENDENCE

Second, the essence of interdependence is that all phenomena, both outer and inner, do not arise without a cause. Things do not arise from a cause that is some other permanent creator, such as the ātman, time, or an almighty god like Īśvara; these are not causes. Things arise based on the coming together of their own interdependent causes and conditions, and so they are said to be interdependently arising.

THE CATEGORIES OF INTERDEPENDENCE: OUTER INTERDEPENDENCE

Third, there are two categories of interdependence: outer and inner. All outer phenomena arise interdependently, like a sprout arising from a seed. Inner phenomena, like the twelve links of interdependence, arise for all the aggregates of superior, average, or inferior sentient beings.

The commentary on the *Salu Sprout Sūtra* teaches outer interdependence in more detail through the example of a sprout coming from a seed, which has seven aspects related to the cause and six aspects related to the conditions. The seven aspects of the cause are the seed, the sprout, the leaves, the stem, the cavity inside the stem and the essential oil, the flowers, and the fruit. The earlier parts successively give rise to the later parts through the power of the perpetuating cause.[108] The six aspects of the conditions are earth, water, fire, wind, space, and time. They provide, respectively, the support, the cohesion, the ripening, the growth, the accommodation, and what makes the stages of change possible. These conditions work together to help the plant grow from the stage of the sprout to the stage of the fruit.

INNER INTERDEPENDENCE

On the inner level of dependent arising, there are twelve aspects related to the cause. A sūtra explains these:

> Interdependence is like this: Because this exists, then that arises. Because this arose, then that arises. Conditioned by ignorance, there are formations. Conditioned by formations, there is consciousness. Conditioned by consciousness, there are name and form. Conditioned by name and form, there are the six sense sources. Conditioned by the six sense sources, there is contact. Conditioned by contact, there is feeling. Conditioned by feeling, there is longing. Conditioned by longing, there is grasping. Conditioned by grasping, there is becoming. Conditioned by becoming, there is birth. Conditioned by birth, then aging, death,

anguish, lamentation, suffering, misery, and distress arise. This is how the aggregates of this whole great suffering arise.

In relation to this, by ignorance ceasing, formations cease. By formations ceasing, consciousness ceases. By consciousness ceasing, name and form cease. By name and form ceasing, the six sense sources cease. By the six sense sources ceasing, contact ceases. By contact ceasing, feeling ceases. By feeling ceasing, longing ceases. By longing ceasing, grasping ceases. By grasping ceasing, becoming ceases. By becoming ceasing, birth ceases. By birth ceasing, old age and death cease. By old age and death ceasing, then anguish, lamentation, suffering, misery, and distress cease. It is only in this way that the great aggregates of suffering cease.

These twelve links conventionally arise since the latter links exist owing to the existence of the former links. Because the former ones arose, the latter links arise and function. If the former link does not exist or has not arisen, the latter link will not arise. The aggregate of suffering will cease if the previous link did not arise.

In terms of their conditions, the links associated with the afflictions, such as ignorance, arise with the assistance of perceived outer objects, the inner sense faculties, and so on. It is similar for the links associated with karma and the seven links associated with suffering, such as name and form.[109]

On the inner level,[110] the earth element is solidity; the water element is fluids; the fire element is heat; the wind element is the processes of breathing, digesting, and so on; the space element is the openings and cavities of the body; and there is also the element of consciousness. These six elements act together as conditions to make things happen. For example, the visual consciousness arises through the mutual functioning of five factors: the eye sense faculty is the support, a form is the perceived object, the object is visible, the space is unobstructed, and mental attention is present. These five factors should be adjusted to fit each of the other sense consciousnesses.

In terms of consciousness, a later moment of consciousness arises from the previous moment of consciousness as its perpetuating cause, and so it appears continuous. Without the previous moment of consciousness as the perpetuating cause, it would be impossible for consciousness to arise; it cannot arise from matter. That would be like a sprout coming from a stone or light coming from darkness.

Consciousness is defined as that which is clear and knowing. An example of the continuity of consciousness is the process of learning to read. Consciousness is seen to be an unbroken continuum in that the later moment of consciousness arises from the previous moment of consciousness. If the assembled causes of consciousness remain complete at the time of death, why would its continuity be cut? It wouldn't, because consciousness is not material.

Outwardly this sort of continuity is like the way a large river continues to flow, or the way a sprout irreversibly arises when an undefective seed has all the necessary conditions of water, manure, warmth, moisture, and so on.

Therefore, since all outer and inner things need their own exact causes and conditions to be assembled, if something suitable is lacking, the thing will not arise. On the other hand, if the causes and conditions are complete, then the thing will naturally arise through interdependence. This continuity of cause and effect has functioned from beginningless time; there has never been a creator such as the ātman or an almighty god. Causes, such as seeds, do not think, "These are my own effects; I gave rise to them." And effects, such as sprouts, do not think, "I arose from that."

THE FIVE SPECIAL FEATURES OF CAUSE AND EFFECT

There are five special features to the interdependence of cause and effect. As it is said:

> Know that causes and effects are not eternal, not annihilated, and
>   not transferred.
> Big effects can come from small causes,
> and effects are concordant with their causes.

To explain this in detail: (1) For as long as the seed has not ceased, the sprout will not arise. However, once the seed has ceased then the sprout will arise. This shows that they are not permanent. (2) If the seed has ceased and the continuity is broken, the sprout will not arise. The ceasing of the seed and the arising of the sprout are like the balance arms of a scale going down on one side and up on the other with no interval between them. This shows that the continuity is not cut. (3) The seed and sprout are two things; their essence and function are not the same. This shows that there is no transference from the former to the latter. (4) A small seed can produce a large fruit. This shows that a great result can be accomplished from a small cause. (5) In the same way that a wheat seed produces a wheat sprout, happiness comes from virtue. This demonstrates the continuum of similarity between a cause and its effect, or how an effect is concordant with its cause.

We need to understand the functioning of cause and effect in these five ways on both the outer and the inner level. More examples of these are extensively taught in the *Sūtra Connected with Questions on What Happens after Death*.

To conclude this discussion of the continuity of cause and effect, here is a quotation from the protector Nāgārjuna's *Essence of Interdependence*, first from the root verse and then from his autocommentary:

> Just like recitation, a butter lamp, a mirror, a seal,
> a magnifying lens, a seed, sour taste, and sounds—
> the aggregates are linked and not transferred.
> This the wise should know.

> A student learns how to recite prayers from a lama. A butter lamp comes from butter and a stick. A reflection comes from a mirror. The raised imprint of a seal comes from clay. Fire comes from a lens. A sprout comes from a seed. Saliva emerges from a sour taste. An echo comes from sound. Like these examples, the aggregates are linked, but the former do not transfer to the latter, and the latter do not arise without relying on the former. The wise should realize this.

5

Overview of the Four Reasonings and the Reasonings of Causal Efficacy and Dependency

———

Second[III] are the specific explanations of the first three reasonings, divided into two parts. The reasonings of causal efficacy and dependency will be taught together, and the reasoning of the nature will be taught separately.

The first of these—the reasonings of causal efficacy and dependency—also has two parts: what they are and what their purpose is. For the first of these, the root verse says:

> 6. **When the collection of causes is complete,**
> **it functions to produce an effect.**
> **Each and every effect**
> **depends on its own specific causes.**

THE FOUR REASONINGS

Before going into the specific explanations, we will look at the four reasonings in general. To begin with, what are the four reasonings? The Mahāyāna *Sūtra of the Definitive Explanation of the Intent* states:

> Reasoning should be known to have four types: the reasoning of dependency, the reasoning of causal efficacy, the reasoning of a valid proof, and the reasoning of the nature.

The śāstra, the *Compendium of the Abhidharma*, states:

> While endeavoring in the authentic Dharma and investigating phenomena, if one asks how many types of reasoning

are used for investigation, the answer is four: the reasoning of dependency, the reasoning of causal efficacy, the reasoning of a logical valid proof, and the reasoning of the nature.

THE MEANING OF *REASONING*

The general meaning of the four reasonings can be briefly described from several angles. First, for the meaning of the Tibetan term *rigpa*,[112] or the English *reasoning*, the emanated translator Kawa Paltsek says:

> What is called *reasoning* is exactly the way things exist in the world.

Jamgön Mipham says:

> If one asks why it is called *reasoning*, it is reasoning because it is the very nature of things; in other words, it is fitting and appropriate. Or it is reasoning in relation to comprehension that accords with the nature of things.

The lion of speech, Rongzom Dharmabhadra, says:[113]

> Reasoning is the term *nyāya*.[114] *Nyāya* means a thing's nature or its way of being. Since it is the way phenomena are in their nature, it is called *reasoning*. Reasoning is also a translation of *yukti* because it is factual. The term *reasoning* refers to two things: the way a thing is in itself and the mind that experiences it accordingly. One should understand that the term *reasoning* means both the defining characteristics of phenomena and the mind attuned to them. If one applies the main meaning of *nyāya*, which is "attainment," *nyāya* is what brings the attainment of fearlessness.[115] Therefore it is called *reasoning*.
>
> *Yukti* refers to a good argument; it means a well-stated syllogism. *Nyāya* also has the meaning of "harmless," as does the term *pratipadā*. Reasoning consists of the mind and language, and these have the ability to establish the correct meaning without impairing the object with contradictions. Reasoning also produces evidence concerning whatever

object is known. Of all the various aspects of reasoning, these are the main ones.

THE DEFINITIONS OF THE FOUR REASONINGS

Second is the general definition of reasoning, which is that reasoning is based on the power of facts and proves without overstatement or understatement that the nature of all phenomena is interdependence. Concerning this, the omniscient Rongzom Dharmabhadra says in *Entering the Way of the Mahāyāna*:

> In general, the system of the four reasonings establishes that all phenomena arise interdependently.

Third are the specific definitions of each of the four reasonings. (1) The reasoning of the efficacy of causes establishes the ability of a collection of causes to produce an effect. (2) The reasoning of the dependency of the effect establishes the ability of an effect to be produced from causes. (3) The reasoning of the nature establishes that all phenomena have their natures. (4) The reasoning of a valid proof establishes, through reasoning based on the power of facts, the way phenomena are in all three aspects of cause, effect, and nature.

Related to this, *Entering the Way of the Mahāyāna* states:

> The reasoning of causal efficacy establishes proof through the effect. The reasoning of dependency establishes proof through the cause. The reasoning of the nature establishes proof through the nature. The reasoning of a valid proof establishes proof by using unmistaken reasoning.

HOW THE FOUR REASONINGS ELIMINATE DOUBTS

The fourth point is the ways the four reasonings operate or eliminate doubts. (1) The reasoning of causal efficacy eliminates doubts about the functioning of causes because effects do not arise unless all the necessary causes are assembled. (2) Since effects are directly dependent on causes, the reasoning of dependency eliminates doubts about what has come about. This is because it is impossible for an effect to come about without depending on a cause. (3) The reasoning of the nature eliminates doubts about the nature because it establishes both the relative nature and absolute nature of things. (4) The reasoning of a valid proof eliminates doubts about reasoning because it unerringly establishes the nature of the two truths through the two types of valid cognition—direct perception and inference.

Entering the Way of the Mahāyāna states:

> In terms of what is eliminated by these four, respectively, there is the elimination of doubts about production, doubts about what is directly brought about, doubts about the nature itself, and doubts about reasoning.

The master Candragomin says in his *Lamp of Proven Reasoning*:

> Their purpose is to remove doubts
> about the nature itself, production,
> what is brought about, and reasoning.

THE OBJECT AND GAUGE OF THE FOUR REASONINGS

The fifth point is the objects and the ways to gauge the four reasonings. In order to debate, the subject of the debate must be unequivocally established in common for both the questioner and the respondent. If they disagree on the subject itself, then it is impossible to get to its basis in order to analyze and investigate it through the four reasonings. For example, if someone says the basic state of fire is not hot and burning, that opposes its actual basis. In this regard, Rongzompa says in *Entering the Way of the Mahāyāna*:

> As for the object and gauge of the four reasonings, it is appropriate to present the reasoning of the nature if it is unmistaken in relation to the basis of the thing's nature and it does not oppose the basis. It is similar for production, that which is brought forth,[116] and the actual bases of all reasonings. If they are unmistaken in terms of not being opposed to the basis, then it is suitable to present them as reasoning.
>
> Being unmistaken about the actual basis of the nature is like reasoning that sunlight through a crystal can start a fire.[117] The basis being opposed is like saying that fire washes deer; it opposes the actual basis of the nature of fire as heat. This applies to other examples as well.

In another passage from the *Lamp of Proven Reasoning* the great master Candragomin says:

> The gauge for comprehending whether the four reasonings are
>   present
> is that the actual basis of the reasoning is flawless
> and that what appears does not contradict the actual basis.

EXCESSIVE APPLICATION OF THE FOUR REASONINGS

Sixth, there can be an excessive application of the four reasonings. When someone becomes stubborn about using only logical reasoning to comprehend objects of consciousness, it goes too far and becomes absurd. One also incurs the fault of regressing into materialism.[118]

Entering the Way of the Mahāyāna states:

> As for the excessive use of the four reasonings: When the
> reasoning of the nature is applied excessively, then all sub-
> stantial things are not annulled, and one ends up asserting
> the nature as a cause.[119] When the reasoning of causal ef-
> ficacy is applied excessively, all creation and effort are not
> annulled, and one ends up asserting an agent as the cause.
> When the reasoning of dependency is applied excessively,
> all powerful ability is not annulled, and one ends up as-
> serting an almighty god like Īśvara as the cause. When the
> reasoning of a valid proof is applied excessively, then one's
> reasoning is flawless in every situation and one ends up be-
> coming conceited. Also, when the materialists establish sub-
> stantial reality, they establish it mainly in two ways: through
> the reasoning of the nature and through direct perception.
> This is why the gauge and excessive use of these two reason-
> ings need to be taught.

In addition, in the *Lamp of Proven Reasoning* the great master Candrago-min says:

> The excessive application is that the nature becomes a substantial
>   thing,
> causal efficacy is asserted as the cause,

dependency necessitates dependence on an almighty god,
and valid proofs make one conceited.

The *Discourse on Valid Cognition* states:[120]

> One who explains the true nature through conceptual analysis
> is a long way from the Buddha's teachings and is impaired by logic.
> However, one who goes against the reality of the Dharma
> does need to investigate by using reasoning.

> Since the profound nature is not an object of conceptual analysis,
> whoever seeks the nature through logic alone is a long way from the
> Buddha's teachings and becomes impaired. However, incorrect or
> negative statements about the intended meaning of the Buddha's
> teaching of the profound nature should be disproved through logic.

What is the reason for this? The great master Nāgārjuna says in the first two
verses of *Root Wisdom of the Middle Way*:

> I prostrate to the one who teaches
> that whatever is dependently arisen
> does not arise, does not cease,
> is not extinct nor everlasting,
> neither comes nor goes,
> and is neither identical nor different.
> I pay homage to the perfect Buddha
> who is supreme among all who speak.
> By dissolving all fabrications, he teaches peace.

In accord with these verses of praise, the two truths should be understood
as the pith of the flawless speech of the supreme teacher Śākyamuni, who is
the sovereign of all proponents of reasoning in the three worlds. Concerning
the two truths, it is not the case that one of them is refuted and the other is affirmed. Appearance is interdependence, and interdependence is emptiness. The
two truths are inseparable, like fire and its heat. Unified appearance-emptiness
is free from the four extremes of existence, nonexistence, both, or neither. It is
free from the eight constructs of arising or ceasing, eternalism or nihilism, coming or going, and sameness or difference, which resemble the eight analogies of
illusion. When one realizes with deep certainty that the two truths are equal

and pervade the entire ground, path, and result, then one has a firm foothold in the profound and vital key points of the Buddhist view and practice.

However, if one does not understand this and falls into the excessive use of the four reasonings as explained above, then one will be far removed from the Buddhist view and practice. Therefore it is very important to understand the unity of appearance and emptiness.

SUMMARY OF THE FOUR REASONINGS

The object to be comprehended—the way functional things are—and the mind that accurately comprehends them are what constitute valid cognition, or reasoning. The first three reasonings of causal efficacy, dependency, and the nature are based on comprehending three aspects of objective phenomena—their causes, effects, and natures. The fourth reasoning, the reasoning of a valid proof, uses unmistaken ways of negating and affirming objects of comprehension by eliminating misunderstandings about them.

To do this there are two types of valid cognition: the valid cognition of direct perception, which comprehends overt, manifest phenomena, and inferential valid cognition, which comprehends hidden phenomena. Inference validly knows its subject matter by using logical reasoning to infer hidden phenomena. In the end, inference must depend on direct perception, and direct perception depends solely on the nature of things. In this way both causal efficacy and dependency are also the nature of things, so they are categorically included in the reasoning of the nature. The reasoning of the nature decisively settles the discussion of all reasonings and brings them to a close. Once a thing's nature has been reached, there is no need for more valid proof. For example, there is no need to logically show that fire is hot.

Concerning this, Rongzom Mahāpaṇḍita says in *Entering the Way of the Mahāyāna*:

> Although it is fine to formulate proofs with any one of the four reasonings—the reasoning of the nature, causal efficacy, dependency, and the valid proof—in order for realization to come easily for those who haven't studied much or those of lesser intellect, it is best to use only logical arguments connected with the nature.

The great master Candragomin says in the *Lamp of Proven Reasoning*:

> All compounded things have a nature,
> which is established as being however it is.
> This nature is shown through the reasoning of a valid proof
> established by the reasonings of causal efficacy and dependency.
>
> In making a proof, the reason is established
> as not separate from the subject's nature.
> All types of reasoning
> include establishing the presence of the reason in the subject.
>
> All reasoning includes direct perception, inference, and reasoning
>   based on the nature.
> A sign's defining characteristic must pervade the property to be
>   proven
> because a pervasion would be impossible if these properties were
>   unrelated.
> It is unfeasible for totally separate things to be in relationship.
>
> This is how cause and effect are related.
> Naturally a cause does not go beyond
> the causal efficacy of producing an effect.
> And naturally an effect does not go beyond
> being dependent on the cause of its arising.
>
> Learned ones never assert
> a relationship between totally separate things.
> Once the components of causal efficacy are assembled,
> it is impossible that dependency will not arise.
>
> When a single effect has arisen dependently
> it must have arisen from assembled causes.
> If causal activity is halted, then dependency is cut off.
>
> Without dependency, the activity of assembled causes
> would be fundamentally impossible;
> nothing would arise since relationships are dependent.
> The logical pervasions naturally incorporate this fact.

Therefore the mind that comprehends in accordance with the nature of things is what is called *reasoning based on the power of facts*. Because it unerringly comprehends the way things are, other reasonings can never disprove it. Both levels of valid cognition—conventional and ultimate—are called the *power of facts*. In other words, the fact that fire is naturally hot is its relative nature or relative state of being, and the fact that fire has no inherent nature is its ultimate nature or ultimate state of being. The true nature of things is established unerringly by bringing together and unifying both the relative and ultimate levels of valid cognition and not by either of them alone.

WHAT THE REASONINGS OF CAUSAL EFFICACY AND DEPENDENCY ARE

The Reasoning of Causal Efficacy

6:1–2. To return to the explanation of verse 6, for the reasoning of causal efficacy, the outer level of causality is like a seed, water, manure, and so on, and the inner level of causality is like the sense objects and sense faculties, and so on. When the numerous causes are assembled and complete, then results are produced, such as a sprout on the outer level or a consciousness on the inner level. Because there is the ability to produce something, it is called the reasoning of the causal efficacy.

This is stated in the *Sūtra of the Definitive Explanation of the Intent*:

> The reasoning of causal efficacy is like this: things are achieved, or established, or come into being through certain causes and conditions. This functioning is known as the reasoning of causal efficacy.

In discussing the level of the śrāvakas from the *Levels according to Yogācāra*, the great master Asaṅga says:

> The skandhas, which are produced by their own causes and conditions, form connections between themselves and their own objects. For example, the eye causes the seeing of forms, the ear causes the hearing of sounds, and it is similar with the other senses up to the mind causing the knowing of objects. Forms abide as the object of the eye, and it is similar with the other sense objects, up to phenomena abiding as the object of

the mind. The way these phenomena correspond and mutually support one other is the reasoning of causal efficacy, and their connections and ways of connecting are also the reasoning of causal efficacy.

The "handle"[121] Anuyoga tantra, the *Scripture That Embodies the Realization of All the Buddhas*, states:

> What is causal efficacy? It is the causes and conditions that function in order to achieve something, to be called something, or for something to arise and remain.

Also, the great Dharma King Trisong Detsen says in his *Compendium of Authentic Teachings on Valid Cognition*:

> The reasoning of causal efficacy is described as functioning and causes. Certainty about the causes and conditions of the producer and the produced is said to be the causal efficacy of producing effects.

The great, emanated translator Kawa Paltsek says in his *Dictionary of Dharma Terminology*:

> Arising from the visual consciousness, there is the causal efficacy of seeing a form; it is not the hearing of a sound. The eye sense faculty gives rise to the visual consciousness; it doesn't produce something else, like the hearing consciousness related to the ear. This is applicable to all the other consciousnesses as well. Barley seeds give rise to barley; they don't produce something else, like beans and rice. This is the reasoning of causal efficacy.

The emanated translator Chokro Lui Gyaltsen says in his *Extensive Commentary on the Sūtra of the Definitive Explanation of the Intent*:

> The reasoning of causal efficacy is taught through the fact that phenomena are causally effective.

And the omniscient Rongzom Dharmabhadra says in *Entering the Way of the Mahāyāna*:

The reasoning of causal efficacy is the knowledge of the causes of things through their effects, like perceiving the causal efficacy of medicine for life and poison for death. One knows the producer through that which is produced.

THE REASONING OF DEPENDENCY

6:3–4.   Next, for the reasoning of dependency, all the various effects, such as sprouts or consciousnesses, are necessarily dependent on their own specific causes, such as seeds for sprouts, or sense objects and sense faculties for consciousnesses. Ascertaining this constitutes the reasoning of the dependency of effects.

The *Sūtra of the Definitive Explanation of the Intent* states:

> The reasoning of dependency is the fact that compounded things arise from causes and conditions, and terminology comes from making designations.

And from the *Levels according to Yogācāra*, in the section on the level of the Śrāvakas:

> The reasoning of dependency is like this. In brief there are two aspects to dependency: that which dependently arises and that which is dependently designated. Dependent arising refers to aggregates arising through certain causes and conditions, and in dependence on those causes and conditions. Dependent designation refers to a collection of aggregates that are designated as aggregates by a collection of names, words, and letters, and that are dependent on that collection of names, words, and letters. This is the dependency of aggregates that arise and are designated.

The "handle" Anuyoga tantra, the *Scripture That Embodies the Realization of All the Buddhas*, states:

> Lord of Laṅkā, what is dependency? It is that whatever comes together has causes and conditions because it has arisen or has been designated.

The *Compendium of Authentic Teachings on Valid Cognition* states:

> The reasoning of dependency explains the reasoning of phenomena and effects. Every compounded thing is dependently designated, and every effect arises and is dependent on its own causes and conditions.

The great emanated translator Kawa Paltsek says:

> The visual consciousness is incapable of arising by itself; it arises in dependence on the eye faculty and the form of the object. This reasoning applies to all the other consciousnesses as well. A sprout arises in dependence on a seed and mental formations arise in dependence on ignorance. This is the reasoning of dependency.

The great translator Chokro Lui Gyaltsen says:

> The reasoning of dependency is a teaching on the dependency of cause and effect.

And the omniscient Rongzom Dharmabhadra says:

> The reasoning of dependency brings understanding that for functional things effects come from causes. Things are caused to arise or be born, like a sprout comes into existence in dependence on a seed. Also, the reasoning of dependency shows how conventional designations are caused to exist, like the designation "good" exists in dependence on the designation "bad."

There are many more passages like that.

6

The Six Causes, Five Effects, and Four Conditions

———

THE SIX CAUSES

As an addendum to explain the system of causes and effects, here are the classifications of causes, conditions, and effects in three sections: the six causes, the five effects, and the four conditions.[122]

First, for the six causes, the *Treasury of the Abhidharma* states:

> The active cause, the co-arising cause,
> the cause of equal status, the concurrent cause,
> the omnipresent cause, and the ripening cause
> are asserted as the six main types of causes.

THE ACTIVE CAUSE

From among these six, the first is the active cause. The *Treasury of the Abhidharma* states:

> The active cause is other than the thing itself.

The Vaibhāṣikas assert that the active cause is all phenomena other than the effect itself, and in this way all causes and noncauses are included in it. There are two types of active cause: effective and ineffective. The effective active cause is illustrated by the way a seed benefits a sprout. The ineffective cause is posited as a cause merely from the perspective of not obstructing something's arising. Examples of the ineffective active cause are uncompounded things in relation to a sprout, or the aggregates of a hell-being in relation to the arising of a formless mind.[123] Although it could be said that it is sometimes possible for an ineffective active cause to indirectly aid the process of arising, only the effective active cause should be considered an active cause. In general all causes are included in the effective, active cause.

In order to eliminate confusion about how active causes work within the system of causes, a number of them are taught. There is the producing cause, which has two parts: the perpetuating cause and the cooperating condition. The perpetuating cause is like a seed that gives rise to a sprout, and the way a previous moment of consciousness gives rise to a later moment of consciousness. The cooperating conditions are like water, fertilizer, and so on, for a seed, and the observed object condition and the sense faculty for a consciousness. Another way of explaining this is that the producing cause is like a seed in relation to a sprout, and the clarifying cause is like a butter lamp in relation to a vase in a dark room.

Active causes can also be taught according to ten types. *Distinguishing the Middle and the Extremes* states:

> The ten active causes are arising,
> abiding, supporting, revealing,
> changing, separating, transforming,
> convincing, understanding, and attaining.
>
> Examples of these are the eye,
> sustenance, the earth, a butter lamp,
> fire, a sickle, artistry,
> smoke, the cause, and the path.

The arising active cause is like the visual consciousness arising from the eye sense faculty. The abiding active cause is like maintaining the body through the four types of sustenance.[124] The supporting active cause is like the earth supporting sentient beings. The revealing or clarifying active cause is like a butter lamp illuminating a form in a dark room. The changing active cause is like fire cooking or burning something. The separating active cause is like a sickle reaping grass. The active cause that transforms into something else is like the knowledge of artistry or a skilled smith who turns gold into a gold box or jewelry. The active cause that convinces is like being certain there is fire from the evidence of smoke. The active cause of understanding is like logical reasoning giving rise to conviction about some topic, such as "the cause" in the second verse quoted above. The attaining active cause is like attaining nirvāṇa through the path.

THE CO-ARISING CAUSE

For the co-arising cause, the second of the six main causes, the *Treasury of the Abhidharma* states:

> Those that arise together produce a mutual effect.
> Examples are the four elements, the mind and what accompanies it,
> and the defining characteristics and the object defined.

The co-arising cause refers to things that mutually support one another to produce an effect. Examples are spear poles that hold each other up,[125] the four elements within the same conglomerate, the mind and what accompanies it, and characteristics with the thing characterized.

What is meant by "that which accompanies the mind"? Some examples are the mental states or the undefiled vows of meditative stabilization.[126] If the mind and what accompanies it are there at the same time, then they produce the same effect and have the same nature, such as being virtuous.

Generally speaking, there are two ways of positing the co-arising cause. The first is the cause-and-effect relationship between a thing produced and what produces it, for example, water, a seed, and so on, in relation to a sprout.

The second is the cause-and-effect relationship of one thing not existing without the other. For example, the designations "short" and "long" depend on each other, as do the designations "near" and "far." In this context a cause-and-effect relationship is posited only in that one cannot exist without the other. It is not a matter of one producing the other; they are present simultaneously because they arose together. If one of them is not there, then the other does not exist. This aspect is defined as a cause merely in relation to reasoning.

THE CAUSE OF EQUAL STATUS

For the third main cause, the cause of equal status, the *Treasury of the Abhidharma* states:

> Causes of equal status are similar.

The cause of equal status is presented in terms of the cause and the effect being the same type. For example, virtue arises from a virtuous mind, and barley arises from barley. It is categorized as a cause because it arises before its effect and it belongs primarily to its own type.

THE CONCURRENT CAUSE

For the fourth, the *Treasury of the Abhidharma* states:

> The concurrent cause is the primary mind and the mental
> states having the same support.

The concurrent cause is mentioned only in relation to mental states and as a particular type of co-arising cause. It refers to the primary mind and mental states being concurrent in five ways: (1) they have the same support—the same sense faculty, which is their ruling condition; (2) they perceive the same observed object; (3) they happen simultaneously and not sequentially; (4) they are the perception of the same aspect, such as blue; and (5) they are one entity for each specific functional thing.

This cause is the mutual and concurrent way that the primary mind and mental states arise. The way it is presented is similar to what was said earlier about the mind and what accompanies it, and it is taught for further clarification.

THE OMNIPRESENT CAUSE

For the fifth, the *Treasury of the Abhidharma* states:

> The "omnipresent" is related to mental afflictions. There are
> five omnipresent mental states for each of the realms.[127]

The omnipresent cause is the mental afflictions. This is just a separate explanation of how afflicted phenomena are produced. Since afflicted phenomena arise from an afflicted mind, this is a particular type of the cause of equal status. The mental afflictions arise before their effects, and their effects are produced by the arising of the mental afflictions pertinent to specific realms.

THE RIPENING CAUSE

For the sixth cause, the *Treasury of the Abhidharma* states:

> The ripening cause is only nonvirtue or contaminated virtue.

The ripening cause is explained separately from the perspective of resulting samsaric experiences. These are either unpleasant or pleasant owing to their arising solely from nonvirtue or contaminated virtue, respectively.

THE FIVE EFFECTS

Second in the group of causes, effects, and conditions is the five effects. The *Verse Summary of the Gateway to Knowledge* states:

> The five effects are enumerated as
> the ripened effect, the ruling effect,
> the effect that corresponds with its cause, the effect of personal
>   activity,
> and the effect of separation.[128]

THE RIPENED EFFECT

For the first of these five, the *Treasury of the Abhidharma* states:

> The ripened effect is the final result.

The ripened effect refers to the aspects of effects that support the production of mundane, samsaric happiness and suffering.[129] The ripened effect is essentially unobscured and neutral, but its neutrality changes in accord with its own cause being virtuous or unvirtuous. It arises from its own ripening cause and belongs to phenomena that are related to the mind or that comprise the mindstream of a sentient being.

THE RULING EFFECT

Second, for the ruling effect, the *Treasury of the Abhidharma* states:

> The ruling effect is the first.

The ruling effect refers to all effects of the active cause, the first of the six causes.

THE EFFECT THAT CORRESPONDS TO ITS CAUSE

Third, for the effect that corresponds to its cause, the *Treasury of the Abhidharma* states:

> The effect that corresponds to its cause is related to the two causes
>   that gave rise to it—
> the cause of equal status and the omnipresent cause.

The effect that corresponds to its cause is the effect of two types of causes—the cause of equal status and the omnipresent cause. It is named thus because the effect is concordant with its own cause.

THE EFFECT OF PERSONAL ACTIVITY

Fourth, for the effect of personal activity, the *Treasury of the Abhidharma* states:

> The effect of personal activity
> is whatever has arisen through someone's power.

The result of personal activity is the effect of two causes: the co-arising cause and the concurrent cause. It is like a pot produced by a person—the object produced and the one who produced it are two individual things. This effect gets its name from the similarity with its producer, like a pot from a potter.

THE EFFECT OF SEPARATION

Fifth, for the effect of separation, the *Treasury of the Abhidharma* states:

> Separation is extinguishment by the mind.

The effect of separation is cessation. It is the absence of what has been eliminated through the mind's discerning, analytical wisdom. Even though its own nature is uncompounded and not generated by a cause, it is posited as an effect because cessation occurs when the obstructions to cessation have been removed. Once there are no more obstructions, this effect arises owing to the "cause" of the obstructions not arising.

THE FOUR CONDITIONS

The third part of the group of causes, effects, and conditions is the four conditions. The *Verse Summary of the Gateway to Knowledge* states:

> The four conditions are the causal condition, the similar, immediate condition, the observed object condition, and the ruling condition.[130]

THE CAUSAL CONDITION

For the first of these, the causal condition, the *Treasury of the Abhidharma* states:

> The causal is the five other causes.

The causal condition is defined as comprised of the five causes other than the active cause.

THE SIMILAR, IMMEDIATE CONDITION

For the second, the similar, immediate cause, the *Treasury of the Abhidharma* states:

> The primary mind and mental states that have arisen
> are not final, but are similar to and immediately precede what
>   follows.

The similar, immediate condition is whatever previous moment of mind or mental factor generates its own ensuing moment of mind or mental factor. All moments of the primary mind and mental states are immediate conditions except for the final mental instant of someone on the verge of entering arhathood without remainder.

THE OBSERVED OBJECT CONDITION

Third, for the observed object condition, the *Treasury of the Abhidharma* states:

> The object is all phenomena.

The observed object condition is all phenomena. Cognitions arise from perceiving them.

THE RULING CONDITION

Fourth, for the ruling condition, the *Treasury of the Abhidharma* states:

> The active cause is explained as the ruler.

The ruling condition is the active cause, the first of the six causes. Among these four, the observed object condition and the immediate condition are exclusively causes for cognition. The other two conditions—the causal condition and the ruling condition—generate all composite things.

THE PURPOSE OF THE REASONINGS OF CAUSAL EFFICACY AND DEPENDENCY

In the joint presentation of the reasonings of causal efficacy and dependency we have completed the first part, what they are. Now for the second part, their purpose, the root text says:

7. **Therefore by understanding correctly or incorrectly
how causes and effects function,
one engages in or refrains from activities.
All the philosophical systems and fields of knowledge, like artistry,**

8. **are also rooted in this.
This is why cause and effect encompass all worldly training
and the training that transcends the world.**

7, 8.   For the reasons explained above, the efficacy of causes and the dependency of effects are correct—causes do give rise to effects and effects do depend on causes. What is incorrect is to think that causes do not give rise to effects and effects do not depend on causes. By understanding how cause and effect works, one either engages in or refrains from actions in the world. This applies to worldly knowledge, such as artistry, as well as the other four of the five major fields of knowledge: healing, language, reasoning with valid cognition, and the Buddhist teachings. The reasonings of causal efficacy and dependency also apply to the five minor fields of knowledge: synonyms, performance, astrology, poetics, and composition. These ten fields of knowledge, along with all the Buddhist and non-Buddhist philosophical systems, are all rooted in investigation based on causal efficacy and dependency.

Therefore these two reasonings should be understood to encompass all training in worldly activities, as well as all training that transcends the world, such as the various philosophical systems.

THE TEN FIELDS OF KNOWLEDGE

Before going on to the reasoning of the nature, I want to insert some quotations and comments about the ten fields of knowledge—the five main fields plus the five minor fields. The great translator Chokro Lui Gyaltsen says in the fortieth chapter of his vast twelve-thousand-verse commentary on the Mahāyāna *Sūtra of the Definitive Explanation of the Intent*:

> When the subjects that bodhisattvas cultivate are combined, they comprise the five fields of knowledge: the Buddhist teachings, healing, reasoning, language, and artistry. When bodhisattvas thoroughly pursue these five fields of knowledge as the main subjects of study, they see that the five fields of knowledge cover a wide variety of specific topics. These five fields are taught so that the specific topics will be understood.

And the great, emanated translator Kawa Paltsek says in his *Dictionary of Dharma Terminology*:

> What are the five fields of knowledge? These are the Buddhist teachings, causality, language, healing, and artistry. These five fields sum up the objects of knowledge, which is why there are five main topics.
>
> First, knowledge of the Buddhist teachings is knowledge of the twelve branches of the Buddha's speech.[131] Second, knowledge of causality is expertise in *tarka*, or non-Buddhist philosophy, as well as the reasoning of internal and external interdependence, such as the fact that specific results occur based on specific causes and conditions. Third, the knowledge of language is expertise in language, or *vyākaraṇa*. This is like citing the ten meanings of a single word. Fourth, the knowledge of healing is expertise in medical diagnosis of the 404 sicknesses of the body and their respective antidotes. Fifth, the knowledge of artistry is expertise in all sorts of skills and activities, such as construction and archery.

The purpose of mastering the fields of knowledge is taught in the *Sūtra on Repaying Kindness* by the Buddha and the *Ornament of the Mahāyāna Sūtras* by the regent Maitreya. It is said in Maitreya's autocommentary:

> Without making the effort to learn these five fields of knowledge, even bodhisattvas will not reach enlightenment. This

is because they need to know these topics in order to cut through others' wrong views and also to take care of others. Therefore make effort in this!

To explain this a little more, causation and language, or *tarka* and *vyākaraṇa*, enable us to defeat our opponents in debate. Artistry and healing enable us to benefit others and take care of them. The Buddhist teachings enable us to eliminate the afflictions in our own minds. Wisdom arises from knowing the twelve branches of the Buddha's speech, and through this we can become *āryas*, or sublime beings.

It is also stated in the *Sūtra on Repaying Kindness*:

> If bodhisattvas have not trained in the five main topics of knowledge, they will never be able to attain the wisdom of omniscience in unsurpassable, perfect, complete enlightenment. Therefore in order to attain unsurpassable enlightenment, they should train in the five topics of knowledge.

There are extensive quotations like this. As the regent Maitreya says:

> Without making the effort to learn these five fields of knowledge, even bodhisattvas will not reach enlightenment. Since all these topics must be mastered in order to cut through the wrong views of others and also to take care of others, one needs to make the effort.

The Ācārya Asaṅga says in the *Levels according to Yogācāra*:

> What are the five fields of knowledge? They are the knowledge of artistry, the knowledge of healing, the knowledge of reasoning, the knowledge of language, and the knowledge of the Buddhist teachings. In general, the main purpose of the five great fields of knowledge is to take care of one's disciples. One takes care of them through artistry and the knowledge of healing, and particularly through knowledge of the Buddha's teachings. The main purpose of knowing language is to clarify contradictions and connections of words, and the purpose of valid cognition is to clarify contradictions and connections in the meaning. By knowing the meaning of the

Buddha's teachings, one can attain liberation by freeing one's own mind and attain omniscient buddhahood for the sake of others.

As for the five minor fields of knowledge, the *Tantra of Deliverance* states:

> In order for bodhisattvas and sentient beings to tame their minds, they should train in the treatises on poetics for the sake of others; the treatises on synonyms, which apply many meanings to one word or use many words for the same meaning; the treatises on written composition that use techniques such as changing heavy and light accents and alternating verse and prose; the treatises on performance, which please people by broadcasting the news, or by making people laugh, or by changing the language or the tone of one's voice into other ways of speaking; and the treatises on astrology, which show amazing things by using mathematical calculations.

As for their purposes, if we know poetics, we will not be confused about elegant wording. If we know synonyms, we will not be confused about terminology. If we know composition, we will not be confused about writing verse. If we know performance, we will not be confused about using language. If we know astrology, we will not be confused about mathematics.

7

The Reasoning of the Nature

————

Next, the third reasoning, the reasoning of the nature, has two aspects to its explanation: the relative nature, which is appearance, and the ultimate nature, which is emptiness. First the relative nature will be explained in two parts: what it is and its categories.

WHAT THE RELATIVE NATURE IS

To explain what the relative nature is, the root text says:

> 9. **Every interdependent thing**
> **has its unique defining characteristics,**
> **like solidity, wetness, or heat,**
> **because that is its own individual nature.**
> **This nature cannot be denied.**

9. Every phenomenon included in saṃsāra, nirvāṇa, or the path has arisen interdependently owing to causes and conditions and has its own individual nature not created by something else. Because of this, a phenomenon is defined on the basis of its own specific characteristics that are not shared with anything else. For instance, earth is solid, water is wet, fire is hot, wind is moving, space is unobstructed, and so on. No one can deny a thing's conventional nature, which is said to be established by the reasoning of the nature.

The *Sūtra of the Definitive Explanation of the Intent* states:

> The reasoning of the nature is like this: The true nature abides and the basic space of phenomena abides, regardless of whether or not the tathāgatas of the past appeared in this world. This is the *reasoning of the nature.*

From the *Levels according to Yogācāra*, in the section on the level of the śrāvakas:

> The reasoning of the nature is like this: Why are the aggregates the way they are, and why is the world the way it is? Why is solidity the defining characteristic of earth, and why is wetness the defining characteristic of water? Why is fire hot? Why is wind motion? Similarly, why is form defined as that which is suitable to be form? Why is feeling defined as experience, and perception as knowing all the distinguishing features? Why are mental formations defined as fully manifest formations? Why is consciousness defined as cognition of an object? The reason is that this is reality. This is the nature of these phenomena, and since it is like their very essence and their reality, it is called the *reasoning of the nature.*

The great Anuyoga tantra *Scripture That Embodies the Realization of All the Buddhas* states:

> Lord of Laṅkā, what is the nature? It is that which is unfabricated.

The *Compendium of Authentic Teachings on Valid Cognition* states:

> The reasoning of the nature is a description of the nature of things. Phenomena have a nature according to the relative truth and a nature according to the absolute truth, and this reasoning explains whatever their natures are.

The emanated translator Kawa Paltsek says:

> Things have their own general and specific characteristics, like the way water runs downhill, the sun rises in the east, the earth is solid, water is wet, fire is hot, wind is lightweight, or like things being empty and devoid of a self. The fact that things are primordially that way is called their *nature.*

And the great emanated translator Chokro Lui Gyaltsen says:

The reasoning of the nature reveals the nature; it distinguishes with certainty the characteristics of phenomena in terms of the way they are and the way they are not.

THE CATEGORIES OF THE RELATIVE NATURE: FUNCTIONAL THINGS AND DESIGNATIONS

For the two categories of the relative nature—functional things and designations, the root text says:

10. **In a single thing there are a variety of attributes,**
    and there are numerous facts and classifications
    of terminology that establish or exclude those attributes.
    Each thing has its own specific nature.

11. **An object is thoroughly apprehended by direct perception.**
    Then the conceptual mind—that which distinguishes and
        combines—
    uses terminology
    to label it as a separate thing.

12. **Objects of knowledge will be thoroughly understood**
    by categorizing them into two groups:
    substantial things and designations based on terminology.
    There are many further classifications that elaborate on this.

10.   A single thing, like a vase, has various attributes. Some attributes are affirmed and included as what the object is and what features it has. For example, a vase is impermanent and material. For the same object, other attributes are negated and excluded as what the object is not and as what it does not have. For example, a vase is not permanent and not conscious. On the basis of conventional terminology, there are numerous facts and classifications. Each thing has its own specific nature that is not created by something else.

11.   Specific things, like a substantially existent vase, are thoroughly apprehended through direct perception. Then, by using terminology such as being produced, being impermanent, having arisen, and so on, the object's characteristics are designated through terminology. This is done by the conceptual mind, which grasps a thing by mixing a name with an object. Conceptualization distinguishes and combines things by using terminology.

12.   Here objects of knowledge[132] are organized into two groups: substantial existents that are functional things and designations through terminology. In this way phenomena are correctly negated or affirmed, accepted or rejected, and engaged in or refrained from. This is how things are thoroughly and unmistakably understood.

There are a large number of classifications that elaborate on this, such as functional things and nonfunctional things, subjects and objects, universals and particulars, conditioned phenomena and unconditioned phenomena, permanence and impermanence, matter and consciousness, cause and effect, substantial existents and nominal existents, conceptual and nonconceptual, contradictory phenomena and connected phenomena, objects defined and their definitions, attributes and the basis for the attributes, topics and their explanations, what appears and what is not there, negations and affirmations, general phenomena and specific phenomena, and so on. On the basis of making various classifications that fit the facts, one will not be confused about objects of knowledge.

THE ULTIMATE NATURE

Next, to explain the ultimate, the root text says:

13.   **If one examines the true reality**
of causes, effects, and the nature of things,
one cannot find any production
and nothing that arises through dependency.

14.   **By its own very nature,**
appearance is essentially emptiness.
The basic space of phenomena, having the three aspects of
liberation,
is the nature of the ultimate.

13, 14.   In relation to what was explained above—the efficacy of causes, the dependency of effects, and phenomena whose nature is cause and effect—if one examines and analyzes their true or absolute nature by using the reasoning that investigates ultimate reality, not even the tiniest particle of a nature can be established. The ultimate nature has the three doors of liberation as its defining characteristic.

THE THREE DOORS OF LIBERATION

What are the three doors of liberation? First, when one thoroughly investigates and analyzes knowable phenomena by using the reasoning of the "diamond fragments,"[133] which is an investigation of causes, one cannot find a creator or a cause that makes things arise. There are only four possibilities, or four extremes: a thing could arise from itself, from something other than itself, from both of these, or without a cause. Because one cannot find signs of any of these, it is called the *signless cause*.

For the second door, when one investigates using the reasoning of the "production and cessation of existence and nonexistence," which is an investigation of effects, one cannot find any effects that arise in dependence on causes and conditions, nor anything that is existent, nonexistent, both, or neither. Because one cannot find anything there to speculate about, it is called the *wishless effect*.

For the third door, on the conventional level, all the specific natures that appear have their own nature unshared with anything else. However, when their natures are investigated with the reasoning of "neither one nor many," those specific natures, which are not created by something else, are not truly singular or truly multiple. Because they are empty of being one thing or many things, this is the empty essence.

So conventionally there are the three—cause, effect, and nature—but on the ultimate level there is the basic space of phenomena with the three doors of liberation. This is the reasoning of the ultimate nature.

SUMMARY OF THE FIRST THREE REASONINGS

Now to sum up the first three reasonings, the root text says:

15. **Although there is causal efficacy and dependency,**
    the reasoning of the nature is the final reasoning.
    Once the nature of a thing has been reached,
    there are no further reasons to be sought.

15.   As explained previously, on the conventional level, there is the causal efficacy that produces effects, and there are specific effects generated in dependence on their own causes. In addition, there is the reasoning of the nature of

specific things. Because this type of reason states the thing's nature, it is the final reasoning. Once one reaches the reasoning of the nature, there are no further reasons to be sought because one has reached the very nature of the thing, like the fact that fire is hot.

8

Valid Cognition

_____

THE GENERAL EXPLANATION OF A VALID PROOF

Next, we come to the fourth of the four reasonings, the reasoning of a valid proof. This will be explained in brief and then in detail. For the brief overview, the root text says:

> 16. **As was just explained, valid comprehension of a thing**
>   **accords with the nature of the two truths**
>   **and is established through the power of fact.**
>   **This is the reasoning of a valid proof.**
>
> 17. **Similarly, the way things appear and the way they are**
>   **are comprehended according to their natures**
>   **either by direct perception, or by inference of something else,**
>   **which is unmistaken because it relies on what directly appears.**

16.   As was just explained, valid comprehension of something happens in accord with the nature of the two truths. This applies to the appearance of the object being comprehended, which is the nature of the relative truth, and to the emptiness of the object, which is the nature of the absolute truth. The subjective mind, which arises owing to an object appearing and comprehends according to the object's nature, is established through the power of the actual way things are. This is called the _reasoning of a valid proof_, or _valid cognition_.

The _Sūtra of the Definitive Explanation of the Intent_ states:

> The reasoning of a valid proof is what establishes the facts of
> what is stated or explained or thought, based on whatever

causes and conditions are involved, so that the facts are completely understood.

From the *Levels according to Yogācāra*, the section on the levels of the śrāvakas states:

> The reasoning of a valid proof shows that the aggregates are impermanent, interdependent, suffering, empty, and devoid of a self. The three aspects of valid cognition—trustworthy scriptures, direct perception, and inference—are what bring this kind of deep understanding. By using these three aspects of valid cognition, the reasoning of a valid proof captures the essence of the genuine Dharma. It posits and establishes that the aggregates are impermanent, interdependent, suffering, emptiness, and lacking a self. This is the reasoning of a valid proof.

The Anuyoga tantra *Great Embodiment of the Realization of All the Buddhas* states:

> What is a valid proof? It is the causes and conditions that make something certain.

The *Compendium of Authentic Teachings on Valid Cognition* states:

> The reasoning of a logical proof is applicable to everything, and it demonstrates the defining characteristics[134] of whatever object is being established.

THE DEFINITION OF VALID COGNITION

At this point I want to insert a brief, supplementary explanation on valid cognition. To begin with, the definition of valid cognition is the unmistaken, conscious mind. Dharmakīrti's *Commentary on Valid Cognition* states:

> Valid cognition is the unmistaken, conscious mind.

Dharmakīrti also says:

> In defining valid cognition as being unmistaken, there are three features. The first is the object. When valid cognition

is unmistaken about an object, the object determined in this way is a specific phenomenon. The second is the subject, the unmistaken mind, which consists of the two types of valid cognition.[135] The third is the way in which valid cognition is unmistaken. When determining that something exists, valid cognition is unmistaken about its existence, and when determining that something does not exist, it is unmistaken about its nonexistence. Similarly, when determining the identity of a thing, valid cognition is unmistaken about the way the thing is or the way the thing is not.

However, someone might ask, "Isn't valid cognition defined as that which reveals something unknown?" Yes, but this is merely saying the same thing in different words; there is no real difference in the meaning. A cognition that reveals an unknown fact is a mind unmistaken about that fact, because an unmistaken cognition reveals something previously unknown.

One opinion is that the first way of defining valid cognition—as unmistaken conscious mind—applies to conventional reality, and the second definition—that it reveals something unknown—applies to ultimate reality. A second opinion is that the definition of valid cognition is complete only when the definition includes both the unmistaken conscious mind and the act of revealing something unknown. A third opinion is that the "unmistaken conscious mind" and the "act of revealing something unknown" mean the same thing. Mipham Rinpoché, the Jamgön guru, says that our Nyingma lineage agrees with the last position—that these two definitions have the same meaning in different words.

The general definition of mind is awareness. Consciousness is defined as clarity and experience. In terms of what is not valid cognition, the great Tibetan scholar Chapa Chöki Sengé condenses all types of nonvalid cognition into five types: analytical speculation,[136] inattentive perception,[137] subsequent cognition,[138] wrong consciousness,[139] and doubt.[140]

In terms of what constitutes valid cognition, there are two types. The *Discourse on Valid Cognition* states:

> Direct perception and inference are valid cognition.
> There are two because of their objects of comprehension.

There are many similar quotations. The *Commentary on Valid Cognition* states:

> Because there are two objects of comprehension,
> there are two types of valid cognition.

SPECIFIC AND GENERAL PHENOMENA

There are definitely two types of objects to be comprehended: functional, specific phenomena and nonfunctional, general phenomena. These two can be described from various points of view. In terms of having an effect, one type of phenomena is capable of performing functions, and the other is not capable of performing functions. In terms of their identity, one type has similar things in common, and the other type does not because its objects are unique. In terms of applying terminology to these objects, one type is stated directly, and the other is indirectly implied.[141] In terms of the subjective consciousness involved, the appearing objects of one type are known through concepts, and the appearing objects of the other type are known without concepts. In terms of the way the two types of objects appear, one is manifest phenomena and the other is hidden phenomena.[142]

Specific and general phenomena are the only two types of objects because there are only two types of mind that comprehend them: direct perception and inference. A manifest phenomenon as the object of comprehension is defined as that which is realized through valid direct perception. A hidden phenomenon as the object of comprehension is defined as that which is realized through valid inference.

THE DEFINITIONS OF DIRECT PERCEPTION AND INFERENCE

The definition of direct perception is nonconceptual and unmistaken consciousness. It has four categories: sensory direct perception, mental direct perception, self-aware direct perception, and yogic direct perception. The definitions of each of these will be given below.

The definition of inferential valid cognition is the mind that realizes its own hidden object as the object to be proven, and this is done on the basis of a sign that satisfies the three criteria for valid evidence.[143] When inference is categorized, it can have two categories: inference for oneself and inference for others. Inference can also have three categories: inference based on the power of fact, inference based on consensus, and inference based on trust.

A PREVIEW OF INFERENCE

There will be an extensive discussion below of the signs and reasons connected with inference, but here is a brief overview: Inference based on the power of fact is like realizing that sound is impermanent because of the logical sign of it being produced. Inference based on consensus is like realizing it is appropriate to use the word "rabbit-possessor" for the moon because that exists as a common notion.[144] Inference based on trust is the mind that realizes that the meaning one has been taught is unmistaken because it is supported by pure scriptures based on the three types of investigation.[145] For example, it is said:

> Wealth comes from generosity, and joy comes from discipline.
> Good looks come from patience, and confidence comes from joyful effort.
> Peacefulness comes from meditation, and liberation comes from insight.

17. Having inserted this overview of valid cognition, now we will go back to the main text and verse 17. The way things appear is the relative truth and the way things are is the absolute truth. Each of these has its own nature, which is realized either immediately through a direct perception, or inferentially through an unmistaken inference based on the directly appearing sign of another object.

DIRECT PERCEPTION AND INFERENCE IN RELATION TO THE TWO TRUTHS

The two types of valid cognition in relation to the two truths can be presented as four categories, which are illustrated here in sequence: (1) For the direct perception of the relative nature, an example is an undistorted visual consciousness directly seeing a blue utpala flower. (2) For direct perception of the ultimate nature, an example is the timeless awareness of meditative equipoise of sublime beings.[146] (3) For inference investigating the conventional level, an example is inferring from the presence of smoke that there is fire, or that because something is produced it is impermanent. (4) For inference investigating the ultimate level, an example is using the reasoning of "neither one nor many" to infer the emptiness nature.

Therefore the glorious Dharmakīrti says:

> When facts about things that are seen or unseen
> are not contradicted
> through direct perception or inference,
> then they are unmistaken.

9

Direct Perception

———

THE GENERAL EXPLANATION OF DIRECT PERCEPTION

The detailed explanation of the reasoning of a valid proof has two parts: direct perception and inference. First, for direct perception, there will be a general explanation, specific explanations, and a brief summary.

For the general explanation of direct perception, the root text states:

18. There are four kinds of direct perception:
     unmistaken sensory perception, mental perception, self-aware
       perception, and yogic perception.
     Since their objects are appearing, specific phenomena,
     direct perception is not conceptual.

19. Without direct perception,
     there would be no evidence, so there could be no inference.
     All appearances would be impossible,
     such as the way things arise from causes and then cease.

20. Therefore it is by relying on evidence
     that one understands emptiness and so forth.[147]
     Without relying on the conventional,
     one cannot realize the absolute.

DHARMAKĪRTI'S SYNOPSIS OF DIRECT PERCEPTION

18. First, to logically explain direct perception, the great master Dharmakīrti says in the *Essence of Reasoning*:[148]

Direct perception is nonconceptual and unmistaken. Conceptualization is the mixing of names with appearances in one's consciousness, and direct perception is free from that. Direct perception is consciousness free of the distortions produced by things like an eye disorder, spinning rapidly, being on a moving boat, or a bodily disturbance.[149]

There are four kinds of direct perception: (1) the sense consciousnesses; (2) mental direct perception, or the mental consciousness, which has a sense cognition as its similar and immediate condition for producing its own mental object immediately after the sense cognition; (3) self-aware direct perception, which is the primary mind and all the mental states; and (4) yogic direct perception, which is consciousness immersed in genuine being, which arises as the culmination of meditation on ultimate reality.

The object of a direct perception is a specific phenomenon, which means an object that appears differently when it is cognized nearby or at a distance. Specific phenomena ultimately exist;[150] they are causally effective things, which are defined as the only things capable of performing functions. Other things are generalities, which are the objects of inference.

The directly perceiving consciousness is established as the effect of valid cognition.[151] This is because a directly perceiving consciousness itself is identical with the ascertainment of an object.[152] It is valid cognition of an image or a semblance of an object because it is due to the image that the object is ascertained.

THE DEFINITION OF DIRECT PERCEPTION

Khenchen Śāntarakṣita, Kamalaśīla, and Vinītadeva[153] say that "nonconceptual" excludes inference, and likewise "unmistaken" excludes mistaken cognitions such as those due to an eye disorder. These two, by definition, exclude their dissimilar types.[154] Dharmottara[155] says that since perception is unmistaken in relation to its apprehended object, the term "unmistaken" automatically eliminates conceptualization.[156] Even so, the term "nonconceptual" is included in the definition of direct perception in order to eliminate the wrong understanding of some non-Buddhist schools, such as the Nyāya, Sāṃkhya, and Mīmāṃsaka, who assert that direct perception is conceptual. This is mentioned in Dignāga's autocommentary on *Discourse on Valid Cognition*:

> This distinction[157] is made on the basis of what others assert.

Generally in this context sensory and mental direct perception are recognized as having the nature of direct perception, but they are not always recognized as the direct perception that is valid cognition. It is important to understand that some scholars make a distinction regarding the statement "valid cognition is unmistaken." For instance, the great scholar Chapa distinguishes between direct perception and validly cognizing direct perception. He says that the definition of direct perception is consciousness that is nonconceptual and unmistaken, but for direct perception to be valid cognition it must eliminate misunderstanding through newly experiencing an object that was not ascertained before. However, the Nyingma tradition does not make this distinction.[158]

Going back to an overview of direct perception, validly cognizing direct perception can be illustrated by an unmistaken consciousness. The definition of valid direct perception is consciousness that is unmistaken and nonconceptual.

THE FOUR TYPES OF DIRECT PERCEPTION

There are four types of valid, or validly cognizing, direct perception. There is valid sensory direct perception that is not flawed by something like an eye disorder, as well as valid mental direct perception, self-aware direct perception, and yogic direct perception. Here are their definitions, one by one:

Valid sensory direct perception is defined as an unmistaken and nonconceptual consciousness that arises on the basis of a physical sense faculty as its ruling condition. There are five types of sensory direct perception: the unmistaken consciousnesses of seeing, hearing, smelling, tasting, and feeling. An example of a false direct perception is when the single moon appears as two moons because of a distortion caused by a defective sense faculty. This is not valid cognition.

Valid mental direct perception is defined as a nonconceptual and unmistaken consciousness that arises on the basis of the mental faculty as its ruling condition. An example of invalid mental direct perception is consciousness during a dream or a nonconceptual mental consciousness that ensues from a defective sense faculty.

Valid yogic direct perception is defined as nonconceptual and unmistaken consciousness that arises on the basis of śamatha and vipaśyanā meditation as its ruling condition. The vivid appearance of a skeleton when meditating on repulsiveness is not considered valid cognition because it is mistaken.

Valid self-aware direct perception is defined as nonconceptual and unmistaken self-awareness, which is the essential clarity of the primary mind and all mental states. No matter what type of consciousness arises, whether mistaken or unmistaken, the bare experience of its inherent clarity is unmistaken and nonconceptual.

DIRECT PERCEPTION IS NONCONCEPTUAL

Now in relation to the objects of those four types of direct perception, their objects are specific phenomena, which are perceived directly without being mixed with other objects or other times,[159] so direct perception is free of conceptualization, which is what perceives things by mixing objects with names.

In this context of direct perception being free of conceptualization, exactly what does conceptualization mean? Conceptualization is generally defined in three ways. In terms of its nature, *Distinguishing the Middle and the Extremes* states:

> Conceptualization is imputation;
> it is the primary mind and mental states of the three realms.

In terms of conceptualization being thought and analysis, the *Treasury of the Abhidharma* states:

> It is coarse thought and subtle analysis.

In terms of apprehending a thing by mixing an object with a name, the *Commentary on Valid Cognition* states:

> In relation to any kind of consciousness, conceptualization
> is what apprehends something by mixing an object with a name.

From among these three definitions of conceptualization—as imputation, as thought and analysis, and as apprehension due to the mixing of an object with a name—the last one is the conceptualization that direct perception does not have.

Another citation on this point comes from the *Discourse on Valid Cognition*:

> Direct perception is free from the conceptualization
> that applies names, classifications, and so forth.

UNDERSTANDING DIRECT PERCEPTION FROM VARIOUS PERSPECTIVES

There are four ways of positing the way sensory and mental direct perception arise: (1) sensory and mental direct perception arise in alternation, (2) after the first instant of sensory perception, there is only mental perception, (3) the sense perception continues for a while and mental perception arises only at the very end of that, and (4) sensory direct perception arises in the first instant, and then mental direct perception arises in association with that; they continue together and both end at the same time. From among these four, Jamyang[160] Lama Mipham says only the last option is correct.

The four kinds of direct perception can be understood from various perspectives. From the perspective of individual experience, there is the direct perception of ordinary beings and the direct perception of sublime beings. From the perspective of their support, both the sensory and mental direct perceptions rely on the support of the sense faculty to know their object. The support of self-aware direct perception is the "dependent nature."[161] The support of yogic direct perception is meditative absorption.

These four can also be discussed from the perspective of their objects. Whereas both sensory and mental direct perception know an object other than themselves,[162] self-aware direct perception knows itself, and yogic direct perception knows both itself and something other than itself.[163]

From the perspective of their objects, all four are different, yet they are not totally different from one another since all four are functional phenomena. Also, the three other than self-aware direct perception (sensory, mental, and yogic) have the same nature as self-aware direct perception, and yet all four are not identical. They are not merely different names for the same nature,[164] because from one perspective, the three types other than self-aware direct perception are a different substance. From another perspective, the other three are not a different substance because their nature is the same[165] as self-aware direct perception.

THE PURPOSE OF DIRECT PERCEPTION

The purpose of the four types of direct perception is to remove four types of wrong understanding. Valid sensory direct perception makes the Nyāya[166] view unacceptable. Valid mental direct perception makes the Vedānta view unacceptable. Valid self-knowing direct perception makes the views of the Vaiśeṣikas and the Vaibhāṣikas[167] unacceptable. And valid yogic direct perception makes the Cārvākas[168] view unacceptable.

To explain this, the great master Vinītadeva says:

> The four kinds of perception are taught in order to remove four wrong ideas. Some people think that the sense faculty itself is what sees, so sensory direct perception removes this misunderstanding by showing that what sees is the consciousness that arises based on the sense faculty. Others find fault with mental direct perception, so the second kind of direct perception eliminates their objections. Some others do not accept that the primary mind and mental states are self-awareness, so the third kind is taught. Others do not accept the valid direct perception of yogic practitioners, so the fourth kind is said to be for that.

Similarly, the great master Jayanta says:

> There are said to be four types of direct perception, and these are taught to remove particular wrong ideas, such as thinking that the visual consciousness based on the sense faculty is not that which sees. Others think that the direct perception of the mental faculty has another aspect as its essence, as I already explained. There are also the wrong ideas that self-awareness and yogic consciousness are impossible.

THERE IS NO INFERENCE WITHOUT DIRECT PERCEPTION

19.   Without the four types of direct perception, there would be no evidence, such as the appearance of smoke, and in consequence, there would be no inference of something, such as the presence of fire. Without inference, it would be impossible to comprehend all the phenomena of this world, including

conventional forms and sounds, and things like the way sprouts arise from seeds and then disintegrate and cease.

20.   Therefore it is by relying on evidence to provide proof that one will understand that the true nature of relative truth is emptiness and so forth.[169] Otherwise, if there were no evidence, there would be no understanding. It is said that without relying on the conventional truth of the appearances of the world as the method, there will not be realization of the absolute truth, emptiness, which arises from method.

In relation to this, the glorious Candrakīrti says in his commentary *Clear Words*:

> Therefore since it is the method for attaining nirvāṇa, without a doubt one must first accept the nature of the relative truth as it is, in the same way that a thirsty man must first accept something like a container to drink from.

In his autocommentary to the *Entrance to the Middle Way*, Candrakīrti also says:

> It is taught that the absolute abides only in the conventional truth. However, it is by thoroughly assimilating the teachings on the absolute that the absolute will be attained.

It is taught similarly in the *Treatise*:[170]

> Without relying on the conventional,
> one cannot realize the absolute.
> Without relying on the absolute,
> one will not attain nirvāṇa.

Next, here are the specific descriptions of sensory direct perception, mental direct perception, self-aware direct perception, and yogic direct perception. The root text begins with sensory direct perception:

SENSORY DIRECT PERCEPTION

21.   **The sense consciousnesses, which arise from the five sense faculties,**
       clearly experience their own objects.
       Without direct sense perceptions,
       one would not perceive objects, like someone who is blind.

21.   Sensory direct perception is the arising of one of the five sense consciousnesses based on one of the sense faculties as the ruling condition, such as the eye, ear, nose, tongue, or body. Each sense consciousness vividly experiences its own object, such as form, sound, smell, taste, or touch. If there were no sensory perception, then one would never perceive outer objects, just like the blind do not see objects or the deaf do not hear sounds.

MENTAL DIRECT PERCEPTION

Second, for mental direct perception:

> **22. Having arisen based on the mental sense faculty,**
> **mental direct perception clearly discerns outer and inner**
> **objects.**
> **Without mental direct perception,**
> **there would be no consciousness of all the phenomena that are**
> **commonly known.**

22.   Having arisen based on the mental sense faculty as its ruling condition, mental direct perception clearly discerns both external objects, such as forms, through the consciousness that knows objects, and internal objects, such as dreams, through the consciousness that knows itself.

A sūtra states:

> Monks, there are two aspects to being conscious of form:
> One is based on the eye and the other on the mind.

The *Discourse on Valid Cognition* states:

> The mind also has objects.

Dharmakīrti's autocommentary on the *Discourse on Valid Cognition* states:

> When the mind engages with form and other objects through the aspect of observing and experiencing them, it is exclusively nonconceptual.

Sherjung Bepa's *Ornament of the Commentary on Valid Cognition* states:

> Through familiarity, what is in front of oneself
> is designated as "this."

> The consciousness that directly perceives this
> is mental direct perception.

The great translator Ngok Loden Sherab says:

> It is the valid cognition of mental direct perception because
> it is tied to sensory direct perception.

To conclude, if there were no mental direct perception, then there would be no consciousness of all the internal and external things that are commonly known.

YOGIC DIRECT PERCEPTION

Third, for yogic direct perception, the root text says:

23. By meditating well according to the scriptures,
yogic direct perception clearly experiences its own object, the
ultimate.
Without yogic direct perception,
one would not see the ultimate, which transcends ordinary
objects.

23. Yogic practitioners, those who have meditated well according to the scriptures taught by the gurus, understand the ultimate nature, which is the absence of self. Their yogic direct perception also clearly experiences its own objects, such as seeing the two-thousandfold universe, the three-thousandfold universe, or countless universes, or all the atoms of the buddhafields fitting on top of one atom, or apparent existence appearing as the pure and infinite maṇḍala of the buddhas, and so on.

The great Ācārya Dignāga says:

> Yogic perception, as taught by the gurus,
> sees the ultimate, unmixed with ordinary objects.

And:

> Yogic direct perception, as previously explained,
> is what arises in their meditation.[171]

In this context, we will briefly investigate yogic direct perception, which is the clear realization of the absence of self, by looking at four aspects: the meaning of the term, its nature, its definition, and its categories.

The Meaning of Yogic Direct Perception

First, for the meaning of the term *yoga*, the *Formation of Words in Two Volumes* states:

> *Yojir* or *yoga* is the name of the meditation that unites śamatha and vipaśyanā.

Its Tibetan equivalent is the word *rnal 'byor*, which means that the mind abides or gains mastery (*mnga dbang 'byor*) in the natural state (*rnal*).

Pratyakṣa is the Sanskrit word for the Tibetan word *mngon sum*, or "direct perception." To break this down by syllables, *prati* has many meanings and is translated in many ways, such as "individual." *Akṣa* is an alternate word for the senses. Therefore it means "dependent on an individual sense faculty" or "dependent on the senses."

This terminology can be discussed according to the four permutations, or logical possibilities,[172] in correlating a term and its explanation. (1) *Pratyakṣa*, or *direct perception*, is "dependent on the senses," but there is no explanation of why this term is used. (2) The term *direct perception* is used for all consciousnesses that apprehend specific phenomena. Both sensory direct perception and mental direct perception fit the term as well as the explanation "dependent on the senses." (3) For self-aware direct perception and yogic direct perception, the term fits, but not the explanation.[173] (4) For mistaken sensory perception, the explanation fits, but not the term.[174]

In general the way the four logical possibilities work in correlating a term and its explanation can be illustrated by the term "lake born," which is an epithet for a lotus: (1) when something is born in a lake but is an insect, then the explanation "lake born" fits, but not the term; (2) when there is a lotus born on dry land, then the term fits, but not the explanation; (3) when there is a lotus born in a lake, both the term and the explanation fit; and (4) when there is a vase, neither the explanation nor the term fit.

THE NATURE, DEFINITION, CATEGORIES, AND PURPOSE OF YOGIC DIRECT PERCEPTION

Going back to the overall explanation of yogic direct perception, the second aspect is its nature, which is the mind that clearly perceives the absence of self in its object. Third, the definition of yogic direct perception is a nonconceptual, unmistaken consciousness that arises mainly by relying on meditation.

Fourth, the categories of yogic direct perception are generally based on the three types of sublime beings: the śrāvakas, pratyekabuddhas, and bodhisattvas, so there are three main categories. In relation to the pratyekabuddhas, the *Treasury of the Abhidharma* states:

> All have the same final support, which is a completely stable mind.

Because they do not train with a teacher, the pratyekabuddhas are considered to be beyond training, and the sublime śrāvakas and sublime bodhisattvas can be divided into those in training and those beyond training, so counting this way makes five categories. Then for each of these five, there is the yogic perception of meditative equipoise without appearances and the yogic perception of postmeditation with appearances, which makes ten categories of yogic direct perception.

To conclude this section, if there were no yogic direct perception, then there would be no way of seeing even a little of the extraordinary, noble objects that transcend the experiences of ordinary people's minds.

SELF-AWARE DIRECT PERCEPTION

Then for the fourth kind of direct perception, the root text says:

24. **The experience of direct perception clears away misunderstandings**
    about forms being the way they are.
    If it were the same in relation to one's own mind,
    this would entail another knower, and that would be endless.

25. **Therefore the mind, which is clear and knowing by nature,**
    knows itself in the same way that it knows objects.
    It illuminates itself without depending on anything else.
    This is called *self-awareness*.

26.   **Whatever the other direct perceptions experience
is ascertained as being direct perception
through self-awareness. Without self-awareness,
there would be no way to establish this.**

24.   In relation to the form of a white conch shell, direct perception
through the visual consciousness eliminates misunderstandings, such as the
conch shell being yellow. If the same relationship were needed to eliminate
misunderstandings about one's own mind, rather than the mind being aware of
itself, another knower would be needed. If a second knower were needed, then
a third knower would be needed to know that one, and this would be endless.
Whether the other knower was needed at the same time or at a different time,
there would still be infinite regress.

25.   For this reason, consciousness is the opposite of matter, like chariots
or walls, whose nature is not clear and knowing. Since the mind's nature is clear
and knowing, then just as the mind illuminates outer objects, it illuminates itself without depending on anything else. This is called *self-awareness*.

In relation to this, the great master Śāntarakṣita says in the *Adornment of
the Middle Way*:

> Consciousness arises
> with a nature opposed to matter.
> It is immaterial in nature
> and it knows itself.

When the three other direct perceptions experience their objects, that is
ascertained as direct perception through self-awareness. This is because one's
own mind is not hidden from oneself. One is certainly capable of knowing
when one is happy and when one is miserable.

26.   If there were no self-awareness, there would be no way or means to
establish that an experience of direct perception is direct perception. It can
be done only because the mind knows itself. For instance, if someone says: "It
is clearly established that the visual consciousness sees the color blue," then
this must be established by either direct perception or inference. First, for it
to be established by direct perception, another direct perception would have
to establish it at the same time or at a different time, but neither option is
feasible.[175] Second, there can be no establishment of the visual consciousness

through inference, because without a direct perception as its basis there is no inference. So that is also unfeasible.

Therefore since pots and other objects are made of matter, it is impossible for them to be "clear and knowing" about objects. Knowledge of the nature of objects must depend on a mind that is clear, knowing, and other than the objects themselves. Consciousness is not like matter because it knows its own nature without needing to depend on any other conditions.

Self-awareness is a very appropriate term to use because the mind experiences itself merely by arising. By nature, it is clear and knowing and free from the threefold reification of object, agent, and action. It is similar to a butter lamp, which illuminates itself.

Related to this, the *Discourse on Valid Cognition* states:

> Conceptualization is also posited as self-awareness.[176]
> Objects are not self-awareness, because self-awareness is what
>   realizes objects.

The *Adornment of the Middle Way* states:

> Being singular and partless by nature,
> it is illogical for it to have a threefold[177] nature.
> Therefore self-awareness
> is not a substantial thing with an agent and an object.
> Since it is the very nature of consciousness,
> it is appropriate for it to know itself.

SUMMARY OF DIRECT PERCEPTION

Now to summarize direct perception, the root text says:

27. **Inference is rooted in direct perception,
    and direct perceptions are ascertained by self-awareness.
    When the experience of an unmistaken mind is reached,
    nothing further is needed to establish that.**

28. **Therefore on the basis of direct perceptions
    that are nonconceptual and unmistaken
    misunderstandings are eliminated
    about manifest phenomena.**

27.   Inference is rooted in direct perception because it arises based on the power of a sign experienced by direct perception. Since direct perception is ascertained by self-awareness, it is necessary to classify self-awareness as direct perception. All experiences of the mind that are unmistaken—because of not being caused by delusion—come down to self-awareness. Once self-awareness has been reached, there is no need to search further for something to prove that, because self-awareness is the experience of an unmistaken mind. For example, is it like finding your elephant; once you have found it, you need not keep searching for its footprints.

So inferential valid cognition comes down to direct perception, which is what knows objects of consciousness. In the end, direct perception comes down to self-awareness, which clearly experiences itself. If one accepts the valid cognition of ordinary perception, one must also accept self-awareness. It wouldn't work for self-awareness not to be there, so the stance of denial is refuted. The way that self-awareness is established as being authentic is taught extensively in the scriptures of the two lords of reasoning, Dignāga and Dharmakīrti.

28.   Based on the four kinds of direct perception, all of which are unmistaken and are nonconceptual in terms of not mixing objects with names, it is the valid proof of direct perception that eliminates experiential misunderstandings about manifest phenomena, such as perceiving a vase as something other than a vase.

To sum up, inferential valid cognition comes down to valid direct perception, and valid direct perception comes down to the valid self-aware direct perception, which clearly experiences the mind itself as its object. Therefore all the classifications in the world of what is true and what is false would have no logical basis without self-awareness on the relative level. We should understand that the refutation of self-awareness in the Madhyamaka treatises uses reasoning on the absolute level only to refute self-awareness's true existence. Madhyamaka philosophy does not refute self-awareness on the relative level.

10

The Reasoning
of a Valid Proof

INFERENCE BASED ON EVIDENCE

———

Following direct perception, the second type of valid cognition is inference. This will be explained in three parts: its nature, its classifications, and a response to objections. First, the nature of inferential valid cognition will be presented from three perspectives: inference by the mind, inference based on evidence, and the ways in which inference is presented.

THE CONCEPTUAL NATURE OF INFERENCE

For inference by the mind, the root text says:

29. **Understanding happens through apprehending objects as mental images**
    and mixing those images with names.
    This is the activity of the mental consciousness and its concepts,
    which then develop all sorts of conventional terminology.

30. **Mental images appear in the mind**
    even for beings who do not understand language.
    By using concepts they have the ability to mix images with names
    to either engage or not engage with objects.

31. **Without the conceptual mind,**
     there would be no terminology, such as negation and
        affirmation.
     There could be no inference, no subjects to be learned,
     and nothing whatsoever could be taught.

32. **Through concepts one can comprehend and affirm**
     things that are not apparent, like goals for the future.
     Without inference and its concepts,
     everyone would be like newborn babies.

29.   As explained above in the overview of a valid proof, the definition of
inferential valid cognition is the mind that realizes its own hidden object as
the object to be proven, and this is done on the basis of a sign that fulfills the
three criteria for valid evidence. In brief, the inferential mind is the thinking
process with its concepts. The conceptual nature of inference is the mind's apprehension of a mental image of a specific object, like a vase. Then, by having
mistakenly[178] identified the appearance with a name, it mixes the object with a
word and calls it, for instance, a "vase." The thinking process and its concepts
are what understand things. In terms of how they function in this world, they
develop all sorts of conventional terminology that affirm and negate things.

30.   Even for beings who do not understand language, like small children
or animals, mental images of things like food and drink appear in their minds.
Even though they don't know the names, they have the ability to mix the images with names so that they either accept or reject objects, and they either engage with the objects or not.

31.   Without the thinking process and its concepts that mix objects with
names, there would not be all the conventional terminology of this world,
such as negating things and pushing them away or affirming them and pull-
ing them in. The faulty consequence would be that inference could not de-
duce hidden phenomena, so no subjects could be learned and nothing could
be taught about the things in the world.

32.   For this reason, it is by using concepts that we have a way to pursue
goals for the future and remember the past. And in the present, by applying
names and categories to objects, we can comprehend and affirm things that are
not apparent, like all the concepts about the conventional world and concepts
based on language. Therefore without conceptual inference there would be no

activity of accepting what is good and rejecting what is bad, since these are based on evidence. In consequence, the beings of this world would not know what things mean. We would all be like newborn babies.

INFERENCE BASED ON EVIDENCE

The second aspect of the nature of inference is inference based on evidence. The root text says:

33. **By relying on a sign, one can understand things.**
A sign is unmistaken if it fulfills the three criteria for valid
evidence:
The sign is present in the subject,
there is a positive pervasion, and a counter pervasion.

34. **An inference about a hidden phenomenon**
is proven through its relationship
with a sign
that is established by valid direct perception.

35. **To establish a proof there is the sign of being an effect, the sign**
of having the same nature,
and the sign of not being perceived, which refutes an object to be
negated
because the object is not perceived or something contradictory is
perceived.
These are the three types of signs.

33. How should the conceptual mind make inferences about phenomena that are hidden? There are two parts to this, which are called inference for one's own sake and inference for the sake of others. Inference for oneself has the same meaning as inferential valid cognition. So first of all, the essence of inferential valid cognition or inference for oneself is a mind that realizes the object to be proven based on a sign that fulfills the three criteria for valid evidence. As the *Discourse on Valid Cognition* states:

> Of these two types of inference, inference for oneself
> sees its object through a sign with the three criteria.

THE THREE CRITERIA FOR VALID EVIDENCE

Dharmakīrti says in the *Essence of Reasoning*:

> There are two types of inference: inference for oneself and
> inference for others. For oneself, that which is inferred is
> something known from a sign having the three criteria for
> valid evidence. Here the inference itself is presented as the
> effect of valid cognition, just as with direct perception.[179]
>
> A sign having the three criteria for valid evidence is ascer-
> tained to be present in that which is being inferred, and
> present in the similar class,[180] but not present in the dis-
> similar class.[181] "That which is being inferred" refers to the
> subject of the argument, which has a specific property that
> one wants to know about in this context. The similar class is
> the objects that are generally compatible with the property
> to be proven. The dissimilar class is the incompatible class;
> they are something other, something contradictory, or sim-
> ply absent.
>
> This conjunction of the three criteria for valid evidence
> has only three types of signs: the sign of not being perceived,
> the sign of having the same nature, and the sign of being an
> effect.

A sign is a phenomenon that someone relies on to understand another phenomenon. Among the three criteria for valid evidence, the first criterion is
called the *presence of the reason in the subject*. This means that the sign, which
is the reason, is established as a quality, or property, of the subject of the thesis.
If the sign cannot first be established in the subject, or locus,[182] of the logical
argument, then there is no point in going further to analyze the pervasions,
which are the second two criteria. To illustrate this, consider the traditional
syllogism "A pot is impermanent because it is produced."[183] One first investigates whether or not the sign exists in the locus of the argument: Is the sign
"being produced" a property of the subject "a pot"? Knowing this is true is the
first aspect: the presence of the reason in the subject.

The second criterion is the positive pervasion.[184] After establishing the presence of the reason in the subject, one goes on to investigate the relationship
between the sign and the property to be proven. The presence of the sign in

that which is being proven is the second aspect of valid evidence: the positive pervasion. In this example, if something is produced, it follows that it must be impermanent. If one ascertains this through valid cognition, then what is being proven, "impermanence," covers or pervades the sign, "being produced." This is an example of the positive pervasion.

The third criterion is the counter pervasion. If the property to be proven is the opposite of the sign or is absent, then the sign is contraindicated and cannot possibly be present.[185] For example, if a phenomenon is not impermanent, then production cannot happen. This opposition or absence is what is meant by the counter pervasion.

From the perspective of valid cognition, both of the last two aspects—the positive and counter pervasions—are expressed to ensure certainty. When these are taught with examples, the property to be proven exists in the entire similar class, and it is excluded from the entire dissimilar class.[186] Therefore, if the three criteria for valid evidence are complete, then there is a correct sign that is unmistaken in relation to the thesis to be proven.[187]

The great, emanated translator Kawa Paltsek explains in his *Dictionary of Dharma Terminology*:

> What is a sign with the three criteria for valid evidence? It is said to exist in the inference and the positive pervasion of the similar class, and not exist in the counter pervasion of the dissimilar class. A sign with the three criteria is directly related to the way unmanifest phenomena are part of the situation. For example, even though fire and water are not apparent, merely from the appearance of smoke and water birds one understands that fire and water are present, so there is an inference. Understanding that fire exists in a big cookhouse, a cookhouse exists in the similar class because a cookhouse is similar in possessing fire. Understanding that there is no fire in water, then places where fire does not exist are in the dissimilar class. The dissimilar class is like being the enemy of each other.

How are the three criteria for valid evidence defined? First, the presence of the reason in the subject is defined as the way of ascertaining through valid cognition that the sign is concordant with the subject someone wants to know about[188] in terms of the way the proof is stated. Second, the positive pervasion is defined as the way of ascertaining through valid cognition that the sign exists only in the similar class according to the way it is established in that proof. Third, the counter pervasion is defined as the way of ascertaining that the sign does not exist at all in the dissimilar class according to the way it is established in that proof.

THE USE OF EXAMPLES

Next we will look at the definitions of "examples." The definition of a correct example is a basis for ascertaining a pervasion, and that basis was previously ascertained to fit the thesis.[189] There are two types of correct examples: similar examples and dissimilar examples. The definition of a similar example is a basis for a previously ascertained positive pervasion that fits a previously ascertained thesis.[190] For the proof: "Sound is impermanent because it is produced," a similar example would be "like a pot." The definition of a dissimilar example is a basis for actually ascertaining a counter pervasion in order to ascertain the thesis to be proven. For the same proof, "Sound is impermanent because it is produced," a dissimilar example would be "like space."[191] The definition of a false example is that which is taken to be a basis for ascertaining a pervasion in order to ascertain a thesis, but the pervasion cannot be ascertained with that example.

THE RELATIONSHIP BETWEEN THE SIGN AND THE PROPERTY TO BE PROVEN

34. To return to the main point, a sign, or reason, is established by experiencing whichever of the four types of valid direct perception is suitable. By relying on the sign one makes an inference about some hidden phenomenon, which is the object to be comprehended. To establish an inference there must be a relationship between the sign and that which is to be inferred. Without that relationship, the inference cannot be proven.[192] On this, *Ascertaining Valid Cognition*[193] states:

> Without that, a relationship won't happen. A reason based
> on anything other than a relationship is merely a false reason.

Some non-Buddhists assert that there are many kinds of relationship, such as a relationship of possession, a relationship of inclusion, and so forth. However, the glorious Candrakīrti says that since any two phenomena must be either the same or different in nature, there are only two types of relationship. There could either be the relationship of having the same nature, or if things are different in nature, there could be the relationship of causality, which means that one of them arose from the other. Buddhists assert that these are the only types of relationship.

THE RELATIONSHIP OF THE SAME NATURE

To explain these further, first, there is the relationship of the same nature. A single basis, like a pot, is said to be impermanent by having eliminated the opposite aspect—permanent. And it is said to be produced by having eliminated the opposite aspect—unproduced. These aspects of being impermanent and produced are not substantial things, but they exist individually as aspects that exclude their opposite classes, which are mistaken. Each of them can be understood through its own name and cannot be understood through some other name. Being impermanent and produced are of the same nature in relation to the pot itself, but they are posited individually as words and objects of thought. This is called a relationship of the same nature, as applied to a pot. From the perspective of conceptually eliminating everything other than what is impermanent and produced, there is a relationship in that these aspects are conceptually distinct and yet combined in the object. However, since the object is a single entity, it is impossible for it to be in relationship to itself. It is similar to a sword being unable to cut itself.

THE CAUSAL RELATIONSHIP

The second relationship, the causal relationship, is based on the ways that cause and effect operate, such as the substantial cause and its cooperating conditions.[194] The causal relationship is taught in some texts through categories such as the six causes, the four conditions, and the five effects. However, the main point is that all causes are either productive active causes or dependently designated causes.[195]

Actually, a causal relationship is impossible in relation to an object; it exists only conceptually through relating an earlier cause with a later effect. If a thing does not exist, its effect does not arise. A *causal relationship* is just a term designated by that name.

The definition of a relationship is that, from the perspective of a mind that is unmistaken in mentally excluding everything other than the thing in question,[196] there is another phenomenon that is not discarded. There are two types of relationship: the relationship of the same nature and the causal relationship. The definition of a relationship of the same nature is that, from the point of view of exclusion, there is another phenomenon that is not discarded because it has the same nature.[197] The definition of a causal relationship is that, from the point of view of exclusion, there is another phenomenon that is not discarded because it arose from the thing in question.[198]

CONTRADICTORY PHENOMENA

An auxiliary point connected with related phenomena is contradictory phenomena, or opposites. Contradictory phenomena are defined as two things that are harmed by each other or that do harm to each other. There are two types of contradictory phenomena: those that are merely incompatible and those that are mutually exclusive. To define these, first, incompatible opposites are defined as phenomena that are functional things and that cannot stay together and continue with the same strength.[199] There are two divisions of incompatible opposites: factual opposites, like hot and cold, and mental opposites, like clinging to a self and the realization of nonself.

The second type of contradictory phenomena is mutually exclusive opposites. These are defined as phenomena that are in contradictory classes and that are not functional things. There are two types of mutually exclusive opposites: direct opposites, like permanent and impermanent, and indirect opposites, like being permanent and being produced.

11

Correct Signs
and False Signs

————

35.   When the three criteria for valid evidence are complete because of their relationship, it is through the sign, or reason, that a particular thesis is proven, and this is illustrated by a syllogism.[200] There are three kinds of reasons: the logical sign of being an effect, the sign of being of the same nature, and the sign of not being perceived. Not being perceived refutes an object to be negated either because that object is not perceived or because a contradictory object is perceived instead. All the reasons that comprehend a hidden phenomenon, which is the thesis to be proven, are subsumed under these three reasons. The *Commentary on Valid Cognition* states:

> There are only three correct reasons
> that have the presence of the reason in the subject and the
>   pervasion,[201]
> because it is certain that nothing occurs without their relationship.
> False reasons are the opposite of this.

It seems appropriate at this point to give a detailed presentation of the types of signs, or reasons. Generally speaking, the definition of a sign is that which is set forth as a sign. Anything that is a basic existent[202] could be a sign. There are two types of signs: correct signs and false signs.

CORRECT SIGNS

First we will look at correct signs, which will be explained in terms of their definitions and categories. The definition of a correct sign is one that fulfills the three criteria for valid evidence. When correct signs are divided according to the way syllogisms are set forth, there are three kinds: signs that are effects, signs that have the same nature, and signs that are not perceived.

SIGNS THAT ARE EFFECTS

The first of the correct signs is signs that are effects. The definition of an effect sign is an effect that has been set forth as a sign, and that is causally related to the thesis, and that fulfills the three criteria for valid evidence in establishing what one wants to infer.

THE FIVE TYPES OF EFFECT SIGNS

In terms of how effect signs are formulated in syllogisms, there are five types. First, a syllogism of an effect sign that establishes a direct cause is: "On that smoky mountain pass there is fire because there is smoke." Second, a syllogism of an effect sign that establishes a prior cause is: "That billowing blue smoke, which appears up in the sky, has a recent fire as its prior cause because there is still smoke." Third, a syllogism of an effect sign proving a general cause is: "The perpetuating aggregates[203] are accompanied by their own unique causes because they are functional things that arise only occasionally."

Fourth, a syllogism of an effect sign that proves a specific cause is: "A sense consciousness appearing as blue[204] is together with its own object condition because it is a sense consciousness." Fifth, a syllogism of an effect sign that infers causal properties is: "A lump of brown sugar in one's mouth exists as a form because its taste exists." In other words, one can infer from the present taste that a prior cause produced both the previous and the present taste, together with the form, as a single conglomerate.

In summary, there are many ways of establishing cause and effect, and many distinctions can be noted between them, such as inferring the presence of a stable basis from unmoving water, or the presence of water from water birds, or the presence of frogs from the sound of their croaking, or that it is going to rain from the sign of ants moving their anthill. One needs to understand that all these types of cause and effect are included within effect signs.

SIGNS WITH THE SAME NATURE

The second type of correct sign is the sign of having the same nature. The definition of a nature sign is a phenomenon set forth as a sign that is of the same nature as the thesis to be established and that fulfills the three criteria for valid evidence in establishing what one wants to infer. There are two types of nature signs: those categorized by the reason and those categorized by the thesis to be proven. These will be illustrated with syllogisms.

NATURE SIGNS CATEGORIZED BY THE REASON

First, nature signs categorized by the reason have two aspects: those that are qualified as dependent and those that are not qualified as dependent. First, in the syllogism "Sound is impermanent because it is produced or because it is created," the nature sign is qualified by being dependent on something else. In contrast, in the syllogism "Sound is impermanent because it is a functional thing," there is a nature sign free of qualification. The sign is not dependent on someone or something other because the reason merely describes the nature of sound. However, when it comes to the meaning of these two syllogisms, they are both correct nature signs and there is no real difference between them.

NATURE SIGNS CATEGORIZED BY THE PROPERTY TO BE PROVEN

Second, within nature signs categorized according to the property to be proven, there are those that establish the meaning and those that establish the term. The first is illustrated by the statement "Sound is impermanent because it is produced."[205] The second is illustrated by the statement "Sound is impermanent because it is momentary."[206]

SIGNS THAT ARE NOT PERCEIVED

The third main type of correct signs uses syllogisms with the sign that is not perceived. This sign will be defined and then categorized. The sign of not being perceived is defined as a reason that is set forth as a sign for refuting an object to be negated[207] and that fulfills the three criteria for valid evidence. It has two main categories: correct signs of not perceiving what does not appear and correct signs of not perceiving what is suitable to appear. These will be defined and illustrated with syllogisms.

A sign of not perceiving what does not appear is defined as a reason that fulfills the three criteria for valid evidence and that can definitely refute the presence of the property to be negated in the locus of the argument, but cannot definitely prove its absence.[208] The example is: "Consider this place in front, for a person whose perceptual capacity does not include ghosts,[209] it is uncertain whether ghosts are present because ghosts do not appear and therefore are not perceived."

In the context of proving the absence of something because it does not appear, there are two divisions: things that are not suitable to appear and things that are suitable to appear.

SIGNS THAT ARE NOT SUITABLE TO APPEAR

First, things that are not suitable to appear are those things that are beyond someone's perceptual capacity owing to their place, time, or nature.[210] For instance, ghosts or bardo beings might be present in a certain place, but since they do not appear to that person, they are said to be "not perceived." When this type of object is not perceived since it does not appear, there is no way to correctly guess whether it is there or not. However, if it is a different sort of object—an object that is suitable to appear, [211] then when it is not perceived, its presence is said to be refuted. This is the main distinction between objects that are or are not suitable to appear. Using this type of reason in a syllogism negates merely the statement that something is either definitely present or definitely absent. For example, the reason "because there is no valid cognition that perceives a ghost in the mind of someone for whom ghosts are beyond their perceptual capacity" is not what is meant by a sign of not perceiving what does not appear.[212]

In brief, the sign of not perceiving what does not appear is taught so that people will abide in equanimity and not exaggerate or disparage other people on the basis of qualities they are incapable of inferring. Just because someone is unable to perceive a hidden phenomenon because it does not appear is not a sufficient basis for deciding it is not there. Above all, people should not judge others.[213]

SIGNS THAT ARE SUITABLE TO APPEAR

The second division of proving something does not exist because it does not appear is the correct sign of not perceiving that which is suitable to appear. This is defined as a reason that fulfills the three criteria for valid evidence, which can prove that the phenomenon to be negated is definitely not present in the subject someone wants to know about.[214] This has two divisions: the first type is the sign of not perceiving a related object or an object that is suitable to be perceived, and the second type is the sign of perceiving what is contradictory, or opposite.

RELATED OBJECTS THAT ARE NOT PERCEIVED[215]

The sign of an unperceived related object is defined as a correct sign of not perceiving what is suitable to appear, and it is an existential negation[216] that refutes a related object as the object of negation. This type of sign has four categories, which will be illustrated with syllogisms.

The first of these categories is the sign of not perceiving a related object with the same nature: "In this house a pot does not exist, because a pot is suitable to appear and it is not perceived by valid cognition."[217] The second is a sign of not perceiving a cause because of not perceiving its related object: "On the ocean at night there is no smoke because there is no fire." The third is the sign of not perceiving the pervader: "On that rocky cliff, there are no aśoka trees because there are no trees."[218] The fourth is the sign of not perceiving a direct effect: "In the vicinity of the wall that is devoid of smoke, there is no direct cause of smoke because there is no smoke."[219]

CONTRADICTORY SIGNS

The second main category of correct signs of not perceiving what is suitable to appear is the perception of what is contradictory, or opposite. This is defined as the perception of a contradictory sign that proves that the object of negation is definitely not present in the subject that someone wants to know about, and it is a correct sign of not perceiving what is suitable to appear. This type of sign has two categories: correct signs of perceiving an incompatible opposite and correct signs of perceiving a mutually exclusive opposite.

SIGNS OF INCOMPATIBLE OPPOSITES

For the first category, the definition of a "correct sign of an incompatible opposite" is a correct sign that is a perceived opposite, for which one must ascertain a relationship pervaded by opposition between that sign and the property to be proven such that they do not abide together.[220]

There are three categories of signs of perceived incompatible opposites: perceptions of a contradictory nature, perceptions of contradictory effects, and perceptions of contradictory pervaded objects. Each of these has four subdivisions, which add up to twelve altogether, and will now be listed and illustrated with syllogisms.²²¹

The first group is the four perceptions of a contradictory nature. (1) There is perception of a sign's nature that contradicts the nature of the property to be proven: "In a place in the east covered by fire, there is no ongoing sensation of cold because that place is a thing covered by fire." (2) There is perception of a nature that contradicts the cause: "In a place in the east covered by fire, there is no effect of cold—no goose bumps on the skin—because that place is a thing covered by fire."²²² (3) There is perception of a nature that contradicts an effect: "In a place in the east covered by fire, there is no direct cause for a cold sensation because that place is a thing covered by fire."²²³ (4) There is perception of a nature that contradicts a pervader: "In a place in the east covered by fire, there is no ongoing sensation of snow because that place is a thing covered by fire."²²⁴

Second, there are four perceptions of a contradictory effect.²²⁵ (1) There is the perception of an effect that contradicts the nature of the property to be proven: "In a place in the east covered by strong, billowing smoke, there is no continuous cold sensation because that place is a thing covered by strong, billowing smoke."²²⁶ (2) There is perception of an effect that contradicts a cause: "In a place in the east covered by strong, billowing smoke, there is not the effect of cold—no goosebumps on the skin—because that place is a thing covered by strong, billowing smoke." (3) There is perception of an effect that contradicts an effect: "In a place in the east covered by strong, billowing smoke, there is no direct cause of a cold sensation because that place is a thing covered by strong, billowing smoke." (4) There is perception of an effect that contradicts a pervader: "In a place in the east covered by strong, billowing smoke, there is no ongoing sensation of snow because that place is a thing covered by strong, billowing smoke."

Third, there are four perceptions of a contradictory pervaded object.²²⁷ (1) There is perception of a pervaded object that contradicts another nature: "In a place in the east covered by a sandalwood fire, there is no continuous cold sensation because that place is a thing covered by a sandalwood fire." (2) There is perception of a pervaded object that contradicts a cause: "In a place in the east covered by a sandalwood fire, there is not the effect of cold—no goose bumps on the skin—because that place is a thing covered by a sandalwood fire." (3) There is perception of a pervaded object that contradicts an effect: "In a place in the east covered by a sandalwood fire, there is no direct cause of a cold sensation because that place is a thing covered by a sandalwood fire." (4) There is perception of a pervaded object that contradicts a pervader: "In a place in the east covered by a sandalwood fire, there is no ongoing sensation of snow because that place is a thing covered by a sandalwood fire."

Mutually Exclusive Opposites

The second type of sign of the perception of contradictory phenomena is the correct sign of mutually exclusive opposites being perceived. This is defined as a correct sign that is a perceived opposite, for which one must ascertain a relationship pervaded by opposition between that sign and the property to be proven in terms of their being mutually exclusive. It has two divisions that will be illustrated with syllogisms. First, there is the correct sign of being perceived as being contradictory to the pervader: [228] "Sound is devoid of being a permanent thing because it is produced." Second, there is the correct sign of being perceived as contradictory to the pervasion:[229] "A pot does not depend on another object to cause it to disintegrate because it definitely disintegrates by itself."

These two divisions of pervader and pervasion do not constitute the set number of mutually exclusive opposites; there are unlimited contradictions not covered by these two. Determining a definite number of divisions for this type of sign would depend on their purpose.[230]

FALSE SIGNS

In categorizing signs, we have finished discussing correct signs and now will look at false signs with their definitions, categories, and examples. To begin with, a false sign is defined as that which is set forth as a sign and does not fulfill the three criteria for valid evidence. It has three categories: unestablished signs, indefinite signs, and contradictory signs.[231]

Unestablished Signs

For the first of those, the definition of a false, unestablished sign is a sign that cannot be proven in the way the syllogism is stated in relation to what one wants to know. It has two categories: signs that are unestablished in relation to facts and signs that are unestablished from the perspective of someone's mind, which in this context refers to the respondent in debate.

Unestablished in Relation to Facts

The first subcategory, being unestablished in relation to facts, has four divisions: the sign is unestablished because (1) the subject does not exist, (2) the sign does not exist, (3) both the subject and the sign do not exist, and (4) even though the subject and the sign do exist, there is no relationship between them.

1. An example of a sign being unestablished because the subject does not exist is: "Consider the subject, absolute sound." Although a sign could be posited in relation to that, since the subject does not exist, the presence of the reason in the subject cannot be established.

2. An example of a sign being unestablished because the sign does not exist is: "Because it is a rabbit horn."

3. An example of a sign being unestablished because both the subject and the sign do not exist is: "Consider the subject, absolute sound, it is permanent because it is a rabbit horn."

4. For a sign that is unestablished because even though the subject and the sign exist there is no relationship between them, there are three subdivisions: (1) The sign is unestablished because it is impossible to have doubts[232] about it. For example: "Sound is impermanent because it is not an object of hearing," or "Sound is impermanent because it is taken as an object of the eyes."[233] (2) The sign is unestablished because there is an underpervasion; it is too narrow to encompass the subject.[234] For example: "Sound must have come from a previous moment of mind because it arose through human effort." (3) The sign is unestablished because the sign has aspects of both a pervasion and a nonpervasion.[235] The example is: "A sense consciousness in which two moons appear is valid direct perception because it is nonconceptual and unmistaken."[236] To explain this, although a sense consciousness in which two moons appear is established as nonconceptual, it cannot be established as unmistaken. Therefore the response in debate would be that this reason is unestablished. As for this sign being an indefinite sign[237] because of being an overpervasion,[238] the correct response in debate would still be that this sign is unestablished.[239]

In summary, altogether there are six[240] categories of signs that are unestablished in relation to facts.

Unestablished in Relation to Someone's Mind

The second category of false, unestablished signs are those unestablished[241] in relation to the respondent's mind. This has four categories: (1) the subject is unestablished, (2) the sign is unestablished, (3) both the subject and the sign are unestablished, and (4) the relationship between the subject and the sign is unestablished.

An example of the subject being unestablished is: proposing the jewels of ghosts as the subject of the syllogism to someone who does not ascertain the possessions of ghosts, such as their pots, jewels, or lamps. An example of the sign being unestablished is giving the reason "Because it is produced by an arhat."[242] Another example is setting forth smoke as a sign when someone doubts whether what is perceived is smoke or merely vapor. An example of both the subject and the sign being unestablished is "A ghost's pot exists here because a ghost exists." The relationship between the subject and the sign is unestablished has three categories: (1) The sign is unestablished because someone suspects that the relationship between the subject and the sign is impossible; for example, for a respondent who does not accept that sound is produced:[243] "Sound is impermanent because it is produced."[244] (2) The sign is unestablished because someone suspects there is an underpervasion; for example, for a respondent who asserts that sound is both produced by beings and not produced by beings: "Words[245] are not self-arising because they are produced by beings."[246] (3) The relationship is unestablished because someone suspects that the relationship takes both sides at the same time.[247] The sample syllogism applies to someone who accepts that although most functional things are impermanent, it is possible that some functional things are permanent, like the creator god Īśvara. The illustration is: "Īśvara is permanent because he is a combination of being impermanent and a functional thing."

The statements "Since there is virtue now, there was virtue previously" or "Hearing the cry of a peacock proves that there is a peacock in the central mountain valley" are not categorized as unestablished signs but as indefinite signs, since one cannot have certainty about these statements.

Other unestablished signs dependent on the respondent are included in the categories already given. For example, "Sound is impermanent because it arises through effort" is actually correct and not an unestablished sign for someone who thinks that sound arises only through effort. However, for someone who thinks that there are other sounds, like the sound of water, which do not arise through effort, then "having arisen through effort" is a false, unestablished sign.

Term generalities[248] are also categorized as unestablished signs in relation to someone's mind, but this would need a detailed explanation, which won't be given here. In sum, there are six[249] categories of signs that are unestablished in relation to someone's mind. Added to the six types of signs that are unestablished in relation to facts, this makes twelve types of unestablished signs.

INDEFINITE SIGNS

The second main category of false signs is the indefinite sign, or the sign that is impossible to ascertain. The definition of an indefinite sign is a sign that raises doubts as to whether the thesis is proven. There are two main categories: uncommon indefinite signs and common indefinite signs.

Uncommon Indefinite Signs

Uncommon indefinite signs also have two types. The first is the uncommon indefinite sign that is not different from the term being stated. This kind of uncommon indefinite sign has four categories. (1) The uncommon indefinite sign in which the subject of the argument and sign are the same; for example: "Sound is impermanent because it is sound." (2) The uncommon indefinite sign in which the property to be proven and the sign are the same; for example: "Sound is impermanent because it is impermanent." (3) The uncommon indefinite sign in which the subject of the argument, the sign, and the property to be proven are all the same; for example: "Sound is sound because it is sound." (4) The uncommon indefinite sign in which the entire thesis and the sign are the same; for example: "Sound is impermanent because sound is impermanent."

The second type of uncommon indefinite sign is the sign that exists in the subject, but there is a problem with the presence of the reason in the similar and/or dissimilar classes. It has four categories. (1) There is the uncommon indefinite sign that is not found owing to not existing in either of the two classes. For example: "Sound is impermanent because it is an object of hearing." "An object of hearing" is not found in either of the two classes.[250] (2) There is the uncommon indefinite sign because of doubts about knowing the two classes, since one is unable to perceive who would be in the two classes. An example is: "This person has transmigrated from being a god because he has eyes." Since the respondent is incapable of knowing who would or would not have transmigrated from the god realm, there are doubts that prevent one from knowing the two classes. (3) There is the uncommon indefinite sign that is not found even though it exists in the similar class. For example, from the perspective of a respondent[251] who accepts that the sound of the Vedas is permanent: "Sound is impermanent because it is produced." According to how sound is understood in the Vedas,[252] the sign is not found even though it exists in the similar class.[253] (4) There is the uncommon indefinite sign that is not found even though it exists in the dissimilar class. This is the opposite of the previous category. From the perspective of the Vedas: "The Vedas are permanent because they are produced." So the sign is not found even though it exists in the dissimilar class.[254]

Common Indefinite Signs

The second main category of the false indefinite sign is the common indefinite sign.[255] It has two categories: the indefinite reason related to facts and the indefinite reason with a remainder[256] in relation to someone's mind. There are four divisions of indefinite reasons related to facts, which will be explained with examples. (1) "Sound is impermanent because it is an object of comprehension." This sign is indefinite because the sign is found to pervade[257] both classes.[258] (2) "Sound arises through effort because it is impermanent." This sign is found to pervade the similar class,[259] and it is found partly inside and partly outside the dissimilar class.[260] (3) "Sound does not arise through effort because it is impermanent." This sign pervades the dissimilar class[261] and is found partly inside and partly outside the similar class.[262] (4) The fourth type is the false common indefinite sign that is partly inside and partly outside both classes. "The sound of a conch is an object of hearing because it arises through effort." Or for followers of the non-Buddhist Vaiśeṣika school who accept that things are a combination of permanent atoms made of the four elements[263] and tangibility: "The sound of a conch is permanent because it is intangible." Why would this example be a common indefinite sign that is found partly inside and partly outside both classes? For the similar class of permanence, intangibility is present in space but not present in an atom.[264] For the dissimilar class of impermanence, intangibility is present in lightning but not present in a pot.

The second type of false common indefinite sign is the sign with a remainder[265] in relation to someone's mind. It has two categories: the indefinite sign that possesses a correct remainder and the indefinite sign that possesses a contradictory remainder. For the first of those, the correct remainder,[266] the sign is found in the similar class but is not found in the dissimilar class. For example: "This being is not omniscient because he voices speech." Although one can ascertain that voicing speech exists in the similar class—those who are not omniscient—one cannot ascertain that voicing speech exists in the dissimilar class—those who are omniscient.

Second, for the contradictory remainder, the sign is found in the dissimilar class but is not found in the similar class. It is uncertain whether the sign exists in the similar class, so it is said to be an indefinite sign with a contradictory remainder. For example, "This being is omniscient because he voices speech." This is the opposite of the previous one. Although one can ascertain that voicing speech exists in the dissimilar class—those who are not omniscient—one cannot ascertain that voicing speech exist in the similar class—those who are omniscient.

CONTRADICTORY SIGNS

The third main type of false sign is the contradictory sign. The definition of a contradictory sign is that, because of the sign, one is certain that the thesis is erroneous. It has two categories: contrary to fact and contrary to someone's mind.

First, false signs contrary to fact have two divisions: those with erroneous negative phenomena[267] and those with erroneous positive phenomena. An example of the first, an erroneous negative, is: "Within a lump of clay without a bulbous form, a pot exists because it is not yet manifest."[268] Signs such as this are the complete opposite of the correct sign that is not perceived.[269] Second, for an erroneous, positive sign that is contradictory, an example is: "Sound is permanent because it is produced." This is a contradictory nature sign.[270] Another example is: "Sound is permanent because it arises through effort." This is a contradictory effect sign.[271] In sum, signs contrary to fact are the opposite of correct effect signs, correct nature signs, and correct thesis statements.

The second type of false sign is the contradictory sign in relation to someone's mind. For example, for someone who asserts that sound is permanent: "The sound of a conch is impermanent because it is sound" is a contradictory positive phenomenon. For someone who asserts that existence does not newly arise:[272] "A pot is not newly arisen because it exists" is a false, contradictory sign with a negative phenomenon. In debate a rebuttal would be made to both of these.

Even though a sign may be false in relation to someone's mind, that is not enough to make it an incorrect sign. Unless the sign is proven through evidence, it is not fitting for it to be a correct sign, whether or not the reason is correct or false according to someone's mind. One must always investigate the facts to determine whether it is a true or false sign.

Before concluding this section on signs, I would like to add this verse:

> If one were to ride the racehorse of these unrivaled types of signs
> that display the correct and false reasons taught here,
> why wouldn't one easily and instantly cover a great deal of ground
> toward reaching the most profound intellectual understanding?

12

The Ways Inference Is Presented

The third aspect of the nature of inference is the ways in which it is presented. There are three main ways of presenting inference: (1) in relation to the object being comprehended, in three parts, (2) in relation to the way inference is established, in four parts, and (3) in relation to how it is used, in two parts.

INSEPARABLE APPEARANCE-EMPTINESS

For the first of these, the three ways[273] of presenting inference in relation to the object being comprehended,[274] the root text says:

36. **When seen authentically**
    all appearances are primordially equal.
    When one's mindstream is pure, one's perceptions are pure.
    Everything is pure by nature.

37. **Functional things are based on their having arisen.**
    Nonfunctional things are based on having been designated.
    Therefore both functional things and nonfunctional things
    are empty of essence.

38. **Ultimately in the true nature, the empty basis**
    and its emptiness are not two different things.
    Appearance and emptiness are inseparable and ineffable.
    This is experienced by individual, self-knowing awareness.

36. The best way of investigating the absolute truth is by using Madhyamaka reasoning. When we investigate the authentic true nature, then all appearances of saṃsāra and nirvāṇa are found to be in a state of timeless equality beyond any categories of good and bad and so on. The best way of

investigating conventional truth is through Vajrayāna reasoning. When we investigate in this way, if our mindstream is pure we will see nothing but purity in the environment and the beings within it. Everything has a pure nature as its way of being.

37.   Functional things arise based on causes and conditions. Nonfunctional things do not arise based on causes and conditions; they are simply designations based on excluding everything that is eliminated by the designation. Therefore both functional things (like a vase) and nonfunctional things (like the emptiness that negates the vase) are unestablished in their true nature; they are empty of their own essence.

38.   Therefore in the ultimate true nature, the basis (like a vase), which is empty, and the emptiness, which negates the existence of that basis, are not separate, specific things. These two—the appearance (like a vase) and its being unestablished because of its emptiness—are inseparable. While appearing the thing is empty, and while being empty the thing appears. This is not an object of language or thought; it is inexpressible through words, names, or signs. If someone asks who realizes this, it is known only by yogins through their individual, self-knowing, timeless awareness. As it is said:[275]

> It is within the scope of individual, self-reflexive, timeless awareness.

AFFIRMATIONS AND NEGATIONS

Second, for the four ways[276] of presenting inference in relation to the way inference is established, the root text says:

**39.   All the aspects that are established
are encompassed by affirmation of their existence or what they are.
All the aspects that are refuted
are encompassed by negation, by showing their nonexistence or
what they are not.**

39.   In this world, all the myriad aspects that are established are encompassed by two types of affirmation: an affirmation of their existence or an affirmation of what they are. All the myriad aspects that are refuted are encompassed by two kinds of negation: a negation of their existence or a negation of what they are.[277]

As has been said, "Excluding everything other than functional things eliminates nonfunctional things." This refers to affirmations and its two classifications based on appearing objects and nonappearing objects.[278] An affirmation is defined as that which is detected by the mind. It has two categories: the appearing affirmation and the excluding affirmation. The definition of an appearing affirmation[279] is that which is detected by a nonconceptual consciousness, and it is illustrated by any specific thing that is an apparent object. The definition of an excluding affirmation[280] is an imputation that is detected by the conceptual mind, and it is illustrated by the elimination of another existent.

The definition of a negation is that which is excluded by the mind. It has two categories: the existential negation and the predicate negation. The definition of an existential negation[281] is that which is merely excluded by the conceptual mind; it excludes the presence of something. The term *existential negation* has the same meaning as the term *mere exclusion*. In an existential negation, nothing else is left behind after that aspect has been negated. The definition of a predicate negation[282] is that which is detected by the conceptual mind by excluding what something is not. In a predicate negation, or a negation of what something is not, after some aspect has been negated there is the suggestion of something else. The term *predicate negation* has the same meaning as the term *excluding affirmation*.

PROOF STATEMENTS AND REFUTATIONS

Third, for the two ways[283] of presenting inference in relation to how it is used the root text says:

40. **Having gained certainty about this way of using
     affirmations and negations based on valid cognition,
     one can then show others
     proofs and refutations according to reasoning.**

41. **In formulating refutations, one uses reasons with the three
         criteria for valid evidence
     to establish autonomous arguments,
     and one refutes others by showing the consequences,
     depending on what they assert.**

40.   Generally speaking, in relation to whatever we want to comprehend, we begin by relying on authentic valid cognition. To do so, we use unmistaken direct perception for objects that are not obscured and inference for objects that are obscured.[284] Certainty is gained by using inference for one's own sake,[285] which involves valid proofs that affirm what is reasonable and negate what is unreasonable.

Then for those who challenge one's position because they do not realize the nature of what is being comprehended or they have wrong ideas, one responds by showing them the facts one has seen in accordance with authentic reasoning. It is necessary to establish one's own position in a clear and reasonable way, and after that one criticizes and refutes the other's position by showing how it is unreasonable.

The *Discourse on Valid Cognition* states:

> Inference for the sake of others
> clearly presents the facts one has seen for oneself.

The *Essence of Reasoning* states:

> Inference for the sake of others
> is expressed through logical signs having the three criteria for valid
>   evidence
> because effects are designated in relation to their causes.
> Inference for others uses syllogisms with two classes of phenomena:
> Phenomena that are similar to the subject of the syllogism and
>   phenomena that are dissimilar to the subject of the syllogism.

CORRECT AND FALSE PROOF STATEMENTS

41.   Within the two broad categories of proofs and refutations, there are four points to be explained: valid proof statements, false proof statements, correct refutations, and false refutations. The first of these, a valid proof statement, has the same meaning as inference for others. The definition of a valid proof statement is a statement that demonstrates to the opponent, without adding anything or leaving anything out, the three criteria for valid evidence as they are established through the opponent's own valid cognition. Valid proof statements have two components: valid proof statements that apply to the similar

class of the subject of the syllogism, and valid proof statements that apply to the dissimilar class of the subject of the syllogism.

Here is a sample syllogism for the first of these two components, the similar class: "If something is produced, it must be impermanent, like a pot. Sound also is produced." A proof statement like this demonstrates the presence of the reason in the subject and the positive pervasion to the opponent. Here is a sample syllogism for the second component, the dissimilar class: "If something is permanent, it must be unproduced, like space. Sound, however, is produced." A proof statement like this demonstrates the presence of the reason in the subject and the counter pervasion to the opponent.[286]

The second type of proof statement is a false proof statement. It is defined as that which is set forth as a proof statement and has a relevant fault. There are three types of false proof statements: faulty in relation to the opponent's mind, faulty in relation to facts, and faulty in relation to the wording. First, in relation to the mind: "A happy feeling is not the mind because the feeling arises and perishes."[287] Second, a false proof statement in relation to facts would be: "Sound is permanent because it is whichever is suitable—either the presence of the reason in the subject or the similar class."[288] Third, a false proof statement in relation to wording: "Sound is impermanent because it is produced, like a pot. Also, sound is produced, and because of that, sound is impermanent." In a statement like this, the thesis, the reason, the example, the secondary syllogism, and the conclusion are all enmeshed.

CORRECT AND FALSE REFUTATIONS

The second main category here is refutations, which has two subcategories: correct refutations and false refutations. First, a correct refutation is defined as a statement that expresses a fault to a person with a faulty position such that the person is able to see the fault. In terms of how correct refutations are stated, there are two types. First, there are refutations that set forth reasons using autonomous arguments, as is done in inference for one's own sake, using reasons that have the three criteria for valid evidence. Second, there are refutations through consequence statements that rely on the assertion of the opponent to show that the three criteria for valid evidence are not complete.[289]

Here are illustrations of these two types of refutation. For an opponent who asserts that sound is permanent, an autonomous argument would be: "Sound is impermanent because it is produced." Second, to show the unwanted consequence to the same opponent: "Because of being permanent, sound would have to be unproduced." By making a proof statement using the sign that the opponent asserted, such as permanence, one throws back the unwanted consequences of their assertion. There are several ways of throwing back the consequences, depending on what seems fitting. It would depend on whether the sign is valid, or the pervasion is valid, or how the opponent's proof is stated, and so on.

The second type of refutation is a false refutation, which is defined as a statement of criticism that expresses a fault to a person with a faulty position, but the person is unable to see the fault.

Consequence Statements

An auxiliary point to add here is the definition of a correct consequence statement. This is a consequence statement that cannot be overridden by a rejoinder from the opponent. In other words, the opponent can no longer argue with the proponent. In contrast, a false consequence statement is defined as a consequence statement that can be overridden by a rejoinder from the opponent.

13

Conventional and Ultimate Valid Cognition

———

The second main section of inferential valid cognition is its classifications,[290] which have a main part and a summary. The main part has two aspects: the valid cognition of conventional reality and the valid cognition that investigates ultimate reality.

CONVENTIONAL VALID COGNITION

First, for conventional valid cognition, the root text says:

42. On the conventional level, since there are appearances that do
        not accord with reality,
     there are the way things appear and the way things are.
     In dependence on impure, ordinary perception
     or pure vision,

43. there are two types of conventional valid cognition,
     which resemble human eyes and divine eyes.
     These two have their own features
     and are categorized by their natures, causes, effects, and
        functions.

44. A mind that is unmistaken about ordinary facts
     arises from having correctly apprehended its objects.
     Valid ordinary perception eliminates misunderstandings about
        objects
     and fully apprehends the facts of a situation.

**45. Limitless, timeless awareness
arises from seeing suchness just as it is.
It eliminates misunderstandings about its objects, which are
inconceivable,
and results in knowing the entire extent of phenomena.**

42, 43.   The conventional, relative truth appears differently depending on
whether the way things appear accords with the way they truly are. There are
definitely two levels of conventional valid cognition, in that the relative truth is
comprehended as either impure or pure. Impure conventional valid cognition
is the ordinary, confined perception of worldly people, and pure conventional
valid cognition is based on the vision of sublime beings. Examples of these two
are human eyes, which merely see the objects on their own level, and divine
eyes, which see the human objects as well as their own objects.

44.   Each type of valid cognition has four distinguishing features by which
it is categorized: its nature, cause, effect, and function. First, for conventional
valid cognition of impure, ordinary perception: (1) its nature is a mind that is
unmistaken about the mere facts of its object, which is an ordinary object in a
particular context; (2) in relation to its cause, valid cognition arises from correctly apprehending the real way a functional thing is within a particular context; (3) its function is to clear away misunderstandings connected with the
ordinary perception of objects; and (4) its effect is that it fully and unerringly
apprehends the relevant facts.

45.   Second, the distinguishing features of conventional valid cognition
based on pure vision are that (1) its nature is the timeless awareness that is
unmistaken about its objects—limitless phenomena; (2) as for its cause, it
arises from unmistaken seeing within the meditative equipoise of unfabricated
suchness, just as it is; (3) its function is to eliminate misunderstandings about
its object, which is inconceivable for the mind of ordinary perception; and
(4) its effect is the timeless awareness that knows everything that can be known.

In this way, pure conventional valid cognition is the actual wisdom mind
of a buddha's three kāyas. It is the profound instructions of the vidyādhara
lamas of the three lineages. It is the key instructions of the lords of the three
families—Khenpo Śāntarakṣita, Lopön Padmasambhava, and the Dharma
King Trisong Detsen.[291] This is the core of the practice of the innumerable
learned and accomplished vidyādharas of the Early Translation tradition. It is
the third eye that sees very hidden phenomena—the profound meaning of the

sūtras, tantras, and śāstras. This understanding of the true meaning was revital-ized in Tibet by Jamyang Lama Mipham Rinpoché.

To sum up, I would like to express this in verse:[292]

> There are two valid cognitions that investigate conventional truth:
> the impure conventional valid cognition of ordinary perception
> and the pure conventional valid cognition that is the vision of
>   sublime beings.
> This classification is found only in the Early Translation tradition.

ULTIMATE VALID COGNITION

Second, for ultimate valid cognition, the root text says:

**46. There are also two approaches to the absolute truth:
the expressible and the inexpressible.
These are comprehended by the two types of valid cognition
that investigate ultimate reality.**

46. There is also a twofold division within the absolute truth. On the relative level there is the expressible ultimate, which says that the objects of consciousness that arise, abide, and cease in postmeditation do not actually arise, abide, or cease. Here emptiness is an existential negation. On the ulti-mate level, there is the inexpressible ultimate, which is characterized by the fact that within meditative equipoise the objects of timeless awareness arise, free of all constructed extremes such as arising or not arising and existing or not existing. So the ultimate truth has two types of valid cognition: the valid cognition that investigates the expressible ultimate and the valid cognition that investigates the inexpressible ultimate.

THE PRĀSAṄGIKA-SVĀTANTRIKA DISTINCTION CONCERNING THE ULTIMATE

In relation to establishing the view of the ultimate as expressible or inexpressible, two Madhyamaka schools arose: the Svātantrika and the Prāsaṅgika. The first one follows the gradual approach in postmeditation and the second uses the in-stantaneous approach within meditation. There are several ways of positing the defining characteristics of Svātantrika and Prāsaṅgika: whether conventional, specific phenomena are accepted or not accepted, whether logical reasoning is presented or not presented, whether the qualifier "ultimately" is applied or not applied to the object of refutation, and whether a commonly agreed-on subject for debate is accepted or not accepted. These and other distinctions are posited merely as subsidiary ways of classifying these two schools.[293]

Here are the main distinctions that define the two schools. The Svātantrika Madhyamaka begins, in the context of postmeditation, by emphasizing the insight that distinguishes the two truths. Temporarily, they establish the expressible ultimate truth and make assertions about it, and in the end they progressively engage in the inexpressible ultimate truth beyond all assertions.

The Prāsaṅgika Madhyamaka emphasizes the inseparability of the two truths, the union of appearance and emptiness, which is the inexpressible ultimate truth free of all assertions. They proceed this way from the very start, and do so within meditative equipoise. In this way the Prāsaṅgikas instantaneously engage in timeless awareness, which is beyond the intellect and inexpressible in thoughts or words.

The reasons why these two schools are designated as the Svātantrika or Autonomy school and the Prāsaṅgika or Consequence school will be described first in relation to themselves and then in relation to others. In relation to themselves, the Svātantrikas use valid cognition to comprehend the relative truth and the absolute truth, and accordingly make assertions about each of the two truths. In relation to others, the Svātantrikas undermine their opponents' confidence mainly by using syllogisms, which are logical, autonomous arguments that are proven by valid cognition. This is why they are called the Autonomy school. In relation to themselves, the Prāsaṅgikas are free from all assertions and the constructs of the four extreme views. In relation to others, they overturn their opponents' wrong understanding by showing the logical consequences of what their opponents assert. This is why they are called the Consequence school.

Here are the definitions of Svātantrika and Prāsaṅgika Madhyamaka in relation to the expressible and inexpressible absolute. The Madhyamikas who teach the absolute truth by emphasizing the expressible ultimate and making assertions about it are the Svātantrikas. The Madhyamikas who teach the absolute truth by emphasizing the inexpressible ultimate beyond assertions are the Prāsaṅgikas.

In summary, the Svātantrika and Prāsaṅgika philosophies arose as two different streams, since the Svātantrika masters teach the absolute truth by emphasizing the expressible ultimate and the Prāsaṅgika masters teach it by emphasizing the inexpressible ultimate. However, both of these streams flow into the great ocean of the same ultimate view. It is important to understand that they are of one taste, and not to mix them up or separate them into higher and lower views.

The Jamyang Lama, Mipham Rinpoché, extensively establishes this through reasoning based on the power of facts in his great commentary on the *Adornment of the Middle Way*. Also, the omniscient Rongtön Chenpo says:

> Explanations that separate Prāsaṅgika and Svātantrika into two distinct categories in terms of how they teach the intention of *Root Wisdom of the Middle Way*, and discriminate between them as having good or bad views, do not realize the meaning of what they are teaching. Those kinds of explanation are said to be overstatements or understatements of the pure view of the great Madhyamaka teachings of India, and these explanations should be discarded like spit.

I would like to add a verse about this:[294]

> There are two kinds of valid cognition that investigate the ultimate:
> the valid cognition that investigates the expressible ultimate
> and the valid cognition that investigates the inexpressible ultimate.
> This is the way the great scholars of India and Tibet distinguish
> them.

SUMMARY OF THE CLASSIFICATIONS OF INFERENCE

Second, to summarize the classifications of inference, the root text says:

47. By relying on the former, one engages in the latter.
It is like clearing one's eye of a flaw.
Once the eye of valid cognition is thoroughly cleansed,
one will see the reality of purity and equality.

47. There are two types of valid cognition for each of the two truths, so altogether there are four types of valid cognition. By relying on the former,

one engages in the latter. This means that for the valid cognition that investigates conventional reality, one temporarily relies on the conventional valid
cognition of ordinary perception—the impure way things appear—in order
to eventually engage in the conventional valid cognition based on the vision
of sublime beings—the pure way things really are. Then for the valid cognition
that investigates ultimate reality, one must start by temporarily relying on the
valid cognition that investigates the expressible ultimate in order to eventually
engage in the valid cognition that investigates the inexpressible ultimate.

For example, when someone has an eye disorder like cataracts, to the extent
that the flaw in the eye is cleared up the person will see forms clearly. It is similar for the eye of intelligence, the eye of valid cognition. By being thoroughly
cleansed, this eye will comprehend, just as it is, the reality of the two truths, the
true nature of all phenomena. This is not the object of the former two types of
valid cognition (ordinary perception and the expressible ultimate). It is the domain of the latter two types of valid cognition (pure vision and the inexpressible
ultimate). On the conventional level the ultimate way things are is great purity.
On the absolute level the ultimate way things are is great equality. Mipham is affectionately instructing us that if we want to attain liberation we must endeavor
to use the skillful means of the four types of valid cognition. This will enable us to
see the very profound view of the inseparable truth of purity and equality.

REFUTING OBJECTIONS TO VALID COGNITION

The third main section of inferential valid cognition is comprised of responses
that dispel objections. This has two parts: the general and the specific.

THREE GENERAL OBJECTIONS

First, there are responses to three general objections: that valid cognition is impossible, that it is not established, and that it is unnecessary.

VALID COGNITION IS IMPOSSIBLE

First, to respond to the objection that valid cognition is impossible, the root
text says:

48. **Both the nonconceptual mind and the conceptual mind**
    have undeluded aspects as well as deluded aspects,

> like perceiving two moons, dreams, and a rope as a snake.
> Therefore the two categories of valid cognition and nonvalid
> cognition are established.

49. **Without both valid cognition and nonvalid cognition**
> **it would be impossible to distinguish what is false owing to**
> **delusion**
> **from what is true and undeluded,**
> **and there could be no philosophy.**

48.   Someone might think that even if there is valid cognition it is impossible not to be deluded. Our tradition would respond that both the nonconceptual mind and the conceptual mind can be either undeluded or deluded. On the one hand, the sense consciousnesses can be undeluded, as can the two kinds of mental consciousnesses—the nonconceptual type that does not mix objects with names and the conceptual type that does mix objects and names. On the other hand, they can be deluded. A deluded sense consciousness is like the eye consciousness seeing two moons instead of one. A deluded nonconceptual mental consciousness is like experiencing a dream. And a deluded conceptual mental consciousness is like apprehending a multicolored rope as a snake.

49.   An undeluded consciousness is unmistaken, so it is valid cognition, but a deluded consciousness is mistaken, so it is not valid cognition. These are established as distinct categories through the reasoning based on the power of facts. If one could not clearly distinguish valid cognition from nonvalid cognition, it would be impossible to divide what is false because of being deluded from what is true because of being undeluded. Consequently it would be impossible to establish the falsity of non-Buddhist philosophy and the truth of Buddhist philosophy.

VALID COGNITION IS UNESTABLISHED

Second, for the objection that valid cognition is not established, the root text says:

50. **When one investigates the authentic, absolute truth,**
> **one uses direct perception and inference, and valid cognition**
> **and nonvalid cognition.**

> **In the same way that these are classifications,**
> **they are conceptual constructs.**

51. **However, their nature is established as empty,**
    and therefore beyond all constructs.
    Emptiness is in all conventional constructs,
    just like heat is in fire.

52. **Therefore appearance and emptiness**
    abide inseparably in all phenomena
    as the means and what arises from the means,
    so one cannot affirm one of them and negate the other.

50. Someone might think that valid cognition is not established for the ultimate; that when authentic reality is investigated and logically analyzed through reasoning that investigates the ultimate, terminology is used like the "valid cognition of direct perception and inference," the "nonvalid cognition of direct perception and inference," and other classifications like "negating and affirming" and "subjects and objects." In the same way that these are classifications, they are conceptual constructs.

51. Our tradition would respond that by their very nature, all classifications are established as emptiness beyond constructed extremes. Because of being free of all constructs (such as existence, nonexistence, both existence and nonexistence, or neither existence nor nonexistence), suchness pervades all conventional constructs in the same way that heat pervades fire.

52. For this reason, both appearance (such as a pot) and emptiness (the fact that the pot is unestablished) are present in all conventional phenomena and can never be separated. It is said that appearance is skillful means and emptiness is what arises from skillful means.[295] So one cannot affirm only the ultimate and negate the conventional, or affirm only the conventional and negate the ultimate. The inseparable truth of emptiness and appearance is the reality of all phenomena. This is why the *Heart Sūtra* says:

> Form is emptiness; emptiness is form. Form is none other
> than emptiness; emptiness is none other than form.

This verse accords with the Buddha's words that negate constructs involving any of the four extremes of existence, nonexistence, both, or neither.

VALID COGNITION IS UNNECESSARY

Third, for the objection that valid cognition is unnecessary, the root text says:

> **53. If one asks whether someone can engage in the absolute truth**
> **merely by seeing the world**
> **without investigating it according to valid cognition or nonvalid**
> **cognition,**
> **indeed there is nothing to prevent that from happening.**

> **54. In seeing how "this" arose from "that,"**
> **worldly people use inference, which deduces the meaning**
> **by relying on direct perception.**
> **Even though they do not designate things with those words, the**
> **meaning is not forsaken.**

53.   Someone might ask, "People who see according to the conventions of
the world, like the Prāsaṅgikas, do not investigate by discriminating between
valid cognition and nonvalid cognition. Would merely accepting relative reality be enough for them to directly access the ultimate? If so, then the categories of valid cognition and nonvalid cognition are unnecessary." Our tradition
would respond that there is indeed nothing to prevent one from accessing the
ultimate without using the classifications of "valid cognition" and "nonvalid
cognition."

54.   However, ordinary people use valid cognition when, for example,
they see a seed as the cause that gives rise to a sprout as its effect, and that effect
is dependent on the seed as its cause. This entails the valid cognition of direct
perception as well as the valid cognition of inference, which deduces the existence or nonexistence of a hidden phenomenon by relying on the direct perception of evidence. Therefore even though worldly people do not specifically
designate things with the names "valid cognition" and "nonvalid cognition,"
the meaning of those terms is not lost. Worldly people rely on valid cognition
and nonvalid cognition when they accept or reject things, affirm or negate
them, or engage in or refrain from them, so the categories of "valid cognition"
and "nonvalid cognition" are highly necessary.

SPECIFIC OBJECTIONS ABOUT CONVENTIONAL AND ULTIMATE VALID COGNITION

Second, the response to specific objections about valid cognition has three parts: responding to objections about investigating conventional reality, responding to objections about investigating ultimate reality, and a summary of how these two types of valid cognition are concordant.

THE OBJECTION TO CONVENTIONAL VALID COGNITION

First, to respond to objections about investigating conventional reality, the root text says:

> 55. **Without both types of conventional valid cognition,**
>   **pure vision would be false,**
>   **and for the impure level of seeing something like a conch,**
>   **one could not tell which is true and which is false—the white**
>   **conch or the yellow one.**

Someone might think, "There is only one conventional truth, so one type of valid cognition should be sufficient. It makes no sense to have two types of valid cognition to investigate one conventional truth."

55.   Our tradition would respond that there must be two types of conventional valid cognition: the conventional valid cognition that relies on pure vision and the conventional valid cognition of impure, ordinary perception. If there were only the valid cognition of ordinary perception, then there would be no pure valid cognition on top of that, and it follows that pure vision would be false. There would be no valid cognition of things such as buddha nature, all the atoms of the buddha fields fitting within one atom, and apparent existence being the pure and infinite maṇḍala of deities, and so on. As well, there must be valid cognition on the level of impure, ordinary perception. Without that, one could not distinguish that a white conch is true and a yellow conch is false. So there cannot be only the one conventional valid cognition of ordinary perception; both types are needed.

THE OBJECTION TO ULTIMATE VALID COGNITION

Second, to respond to the specific objection about investigating the absolute truth, the root text says:

56. **Without both ways of investigating the absolute truth,**
   one would not know the unity of the two truths,
   and the absolute would be reduced to a fabricated extreme.
   In this way, ultimate valid cognition would destroy itself.

Someone might think, "There is only one absolute truth, so only one type of valid cognition should suffice. There is no need to have two types of valid cognition to investigate one absolute truth."

56.   Our tradition would respond that there must be two types of ultimate valid cognition: the valid cognition that investigates the expressible absolute truth and the valid cognition that investigates the inexpressible absolute truth. If one asserts that the final absolute truth is merely the expressible absolute, then one would not know the final reality, because the path of emptiness as a negation of existence is within the realm of concepts. One could never realize the meaning of the unity of the two truths, the inseparability of appearance and emptiness, free from the thirty-two ways of misunderstanding it. Also, since the negation of existence and so forth[296] is a conceptual construct, it follows that the absolute truth would be reduced to a constructed extreme. And because the absolute would be a conceptual construct, it could not withstand the reasoning that investigates the ultimate nature of things. The valid cognition that investigates the ultimate would destroy itself.

THE CONCORDANCE OF CONVENTIONAL AND ULTIMATE VALID COGNITION

Third, for the summary that shows how these two—conventional and ultimate valid cognition—are concordant, the root text says:

57. **Upon investigation, relative truth—the object being**
   comprehended—is not established,
   and neither are the mind and self-awareness, which do the
   comprehending.
   They are like the moon in water.
   Ultimately, the two truths are inseparable;

58. **they are a single truth, the final reality of nirvāṇa,**
   because the ultimate is in all phenomena.

**Consciousness and objects of knowledge are inseparable
from the appearance of the kāyas and wisdoms, which are
beyond notions of a "center" or "limit."**

57.   From the perspective of suchness, which is the ultimate reality of all
phenomena, the object of comprehension—the relative truth—is not established in fact. Nor is the comprehender—the mind comprised of the seven col-
lections of consciousness and self-awareness. When analyzed and investigated
with the reasoning that investigates the ultimate, the mind is unestablished by
its very nature. It is like a reflection of the moon in water.

58.   In the ultimate true nature, all conventional appearances are primordially empty and yet they still appear. The inseparability of the two truths is a
single truth, a unity. It is the final reality, primordial peace and nirvāṇa by its
very nature. In this state all phenomena are equal. All objects of knowledge are
in the state of emptiness endowed with all the supreme aspects. There are no
phenomena apart from the basic space of phenomena. Since nothing goes beyond this, it is the ultimate. Consciousness and the objects of knowledge are
inseparable from the appearance of the kāyas and wisdoms, which are naturally
beyond any notions of a "center" or "limit."

14

The Four Reliances

───────

Following the section on the four reasonings as what comprehend the two truths, next is a section on the four reliances, which are how the four reasonings function. This has two parts: the general teachings and the detailed explanation. For the general teachings on the four reliances, the root text says:

59. After opening wide the excellent eye of wisdom
    that is profound and vast, as explained above,
    one needs to see the excellent path taken by
    the highly intelligent ones,

60. the descendents of the Sugata.
    So do not let your actions be fruitless
    by playing around when you could train systematically
    in the vehicles of the sūtras and tantras that are so difficult to
       find.

61. Therefore those who exhibit intelligence
    possess the four reasonings as described above,
    and perform their investigations without depending on others.
    This is how they become certain about the four reliances.

62. Without a mind like this,
    it is like the blind leading the blind.
    Relying on consensus, literal words, or what is easy to
       understand
    goes against the understanding of the four reliances.

THE IMPORTANCE OF THE FOUR RELIANCES

59.   After having opened wide the excellent eye of wisdom, which is the flawless path of reasoning of the profound absolute truth and the vast relative truth, one should exert oneself in this method of seeing the excellent path taken by the Sugata Buddha Bhagavān and his heart children—the highly intelligent bodhisattvas—which leads to nondwelling nirvāṇa, which goes beyond both existence and peace.

60.   At this time in this Sahā[297] world, among the 1,002 buddhas of this good eon, the Buddha Śākyamuni, the son of Śuddhodana and the supreme guide of the Mantrayāna, is like a white lotus in terms of how he generated bodhicitta. It is very difficult to find an approach like his, which reveals the vast vehicles of the precious teachings of sūtra and mantra. Yet now we have encountered it; our actions and aspirations have coincided owing to our previous accumulation of great merit. Here Mipham affectionately instructs us that if we want to attain liberation we must not waste the freedoms and endowments of the precious human birth we now have. We need to fully taste these teachings in our being. As he says, "Do not let your actions be fruitless!"

61.   In reply, someone might ask, "Then how do I go about seeing this excellent path?" Our response is that those who exhibit flawless intelligence possess four kinds of reasoning: the reasonings of causal efficacy, dependency, the nature, and valid proofs. They do not depend on others; for instance, by simply following what other people tell them. Those with the ability to investigate for themselves do so by using flawless reasoning based on the power of facts. This is how they become certain about the four reliances, which are based on the four ways of reasoning. This kind of certainty is what is needed to see this excellent path.

62.   If one does not have the intelligence to investigate through one's own ability, as explained above, then it is like the blind leading the blind. Without investigation people might simply follow the consensus of the world or take words literally. Or people might use reasoning based on the provisional meaning or the ordinary sphere of consciousness merely because those are easier to understand. We must discard these four approaches because they oppose the understanding that stems from the four reliances.

WHAT ARE THE FOUR RELIANCES?

The four reliances are: rely on the Dharma rather than individuals, rely on the meaning rather than the words, rely on the definitive meaning rather than the provisional meaning, rely on timeless awareness rather than consciousness.

The Kālacakra commentary, the *Stainless Light*, states:

> As for the four reliances, rather than relying on individuals, one should rely on the Dharma. In relation to the Dharma, rather than relying on words, one should rely on the meaning. In relation to the meaning, rather than relying on the provisional meaning, one should rely on the definitive meaning. And in relation to the definitive meaning, rather than relying on consciousness, one should rely on timeless awareness.

In his *Dictionary of Dharma Terminology*, the emanated translator Kawa Paltsek says:

> What are the four reliances? Rely on the Dharma rather than the individual. Rely on the meaning rather than the words. Rely on the sūtras of the definitive meaning rather than the sūtras of the provisional meaning. Rely on wisdom rather than consciousness.
>
> "To rely on" means to become familiar with something based on practical application and certainty. For instance, in relying on the Dharma rather than on the individual, one can rely on an individual if that person teaches the Dharma of cause and effect in relation to saṃsāra and nirvāṇa without mistakes and without getting mixed up. Or one can rely on someone who teaches with certainty the ultimate meaning of phenomena not arising or really happening. No matter what a person is like, if their teaching does not contradict the Dharma you can rely on them. On the other hand, it is foolish not to examine an individual. If the person's conduct is not in accord with the Dharma, do not closely rely on him even if he is the son of the king. Therefore rely on the Dharma, not on the individual.

In relying on the meaning rather than the words, the right meaning is found in the Dharma teachings that transcend the world—the teachings on the result of endeavoring in activities directed toward enlightenment. At the instant the mind reaches fruition, the threefold reification of subject, object, and action is completely purified and the wisdom of omniscience manifests. This is the meaning one should rely on. In terms of the words, when engaging in the many activities of the world, or when studying and teaching any or all of the 84,000 gateways to the Dharma, there is very little significance in pursuing the letters and the words. So do not rely on them.

In relying on the definitive meaning rather than the provisional meaning, the sūtras of the definitive meaning are the teachings of the Dharma that bring deep understanding of the profound and vast meaning. The sūtras of the provisional meaning are those that depend on or lead to familiarity with the definitive sūtras, or those that teach weariness with saṃsāra, or those that apply to the relative truth. In comparison, the definitive sūtras never depend on or lead to familiarity with the provisional sūtras. Therefore rely on the definitive meaning, not the provisional meaning.

In relying on wisdom rather than consciousness, wisdom refers to knowing that the characteristics of all phenomena ultimately do not arise and cease, and that there is no self in phenomena and no self in individuals. This is what one should become familiar with and rely on. Consciousness is the understanding that ensues from the five desirable qualities of form, sound, smell, taste, and touch. Do not rely on consciousness by being attached to it or dwelling in it. Therefore rely on wisdom, not on consciousness.

RELY ON THE TEACHINGS, NOT ON THE TEACHER

Second, the detailed explanation goes through each of the four reliances in turn. For the first of these—relying on the Dharma rather than individuals—the root text says:

63. Therefore one should not rely on individuals;
    one should rely on the Dharma.
    One will be liberated by what is said about the path established
       through authentic reasoning,
    not by those who say it.

64. If what an individual says is correct,
    then it is suitable, no matter what the person is like.
    Even the sugatas have emanated in forms such as butchers
    in order to tame sentient beings.

65. However, if what the person teaches
    contradicts the meaning of the Mahāyāna,
    there will be no benefit, no matter how good the person looks,
    like the form of a buddha emanated by a demon.

63. If we don't have the intelligence and ability to investigate for ourselves, then we might not see that what we are taught contradicts the four reliances. This is why it is important not to rely on individual teachers, but to rely on the Dharma that is taught. A path established through evidence is an authentic approach to liberation; it uses reasoning based on the power of facts. We will become liberated by what is said about the unmistaken path, not by the ones who say it. So we need to rely on the Dharma rather than the individuals.

64. If individuals teach an authentic path established through reasoning, then that path is suitable no matter what sort of good or bad people they seem to be. Even the fully awakened ones have emanated in forms such as butchers in order to train disciples.

65. However, in relation to the essential meaning of the Mahāyāna, which is emptiness beyond conceptual constructs, someone might give a teaching that contradicts the Mahāyāna scriptures. For example, someone might criticize our Nyingma tradition as having the Hashang view,[298] or teach that the approximate absolute truth[299] investigated through reasoning is the supreme absolute truth. If their teaching contradicts the Mahāyāna scriptures, there will not be the slightest benefit from it, no matter how good the speaker looks or behaves. For example, evil demons can emanate as buddhas with perfect conduct and the major and minor marks, and yet their teachings contradict the Mahāyāna. So rely on the teachings rather than the teacher.

RELY ON THE MEANING, NOT ON THE WORDS

For the second reliance, the root text says:

66. **When intelligent ones hear and contemplate the Dharma,**
    they should rely on the meaning and not on the words.
    If the meaning is understood, there is no contradiction
    no matter how it is expressed in words.

67. **Things are named because of wanting to express an**
        understandable meaning.
    Once the meaning has been understood,
    if the speaker keeps trying to formulate it in words,
    it is like continuing to search for tracks after an elephant has
        been found.

68. **If one elaborates further because of attachment to words,**
    concepts proliferate endlessly.
    Wandering further and further from the meaning,
    immature beings just make themselves tired.

69. **For any single phrase, like "Bring me the wood,"**
    if wood is differentiated according to its locale, etc., the
        possibilities are endless.
    Once one has understood the meaning of the phrase,
    then the words have fulfilled their purpose.

70. **When a man points to the moon with his finger,**
    a childish person looks at the finger instead.
    Foolish ones who adhere to the words
    have difficulty understanding, even though they think they
        understand.

66.   When hearing and contemplating the Dharma in order to eliminate misunderstanding, one should rely on the meaning expressed rather than the words that express it. If one accurately understands what the subject matter means, then the words that express the meaning are acceptable and not contradictory regardless of whether the words are good or bad or grammatically correct, and so on.

67.   The purpose of words is to name things so that the desired meaning will be understood. Once the words have conveyed the meaning and the meaning is understood, if a speaker keeps elaborating with more words, it is like someone continuing to search for the tracks of an elephant that has already been found.

68.   If one keeps elaborating merely because one is attached to the words, the only thing that will increase are the words. Verbal constructs proliferate endlessly until conceptualization ends. Wandering further and further from the meaning that has not been understood, immature, foolish ones just make themselves tired.

69.   For instance, in relation to a single phrase like "Bring me the wood," if wood is differentiated according to its type, locale, and time, the possibilities are endless. However, the mere words "Bring me the wood" need not be understood that way. If one understands and merely brings the wood that is relevant in that situation, then the language has fulfilled its purpose.

70.   In order to show the moon to a child, when someone indicates the moon with his finger, the child will look at the finger, not understanding to look at the moon. Similarly, foolish people become attached to the words that are merely the means of expression. When they investigate only the words instead of investigating what the subject matter means, even though they think they understand the subject matter, they have a hard time understanding it.

In relation to this, the *Great Commentary on the Kālacakra Tantra* says:

> Whether the words are proper or slang,
> a yogin can grasp the meaning.
> Milk certainly mixes with water,
> yet a swan can extract and drink the milk.
>
> The absolute truth does not rely on language.
> Great beings do not rely on the words.
> If one knows what the words on the absolute truth mean,
> how could commentarial words go further than that?

And Nupchen Sangyé Yeshé says in his *Lamp of the Eye of Meditation*:

> In brief, the best way to study
> is to understand the meaning.

The *Mirror of the Dharma* states:

> It is better to truly understand one word
> than to hear a multitude of words.

The *Sūtra of the Descent to Laṅkā* states:

> What is called "being very learned"
> is being an expert in the meaning; it is not being an expert in the
>   words.

There are many similar scriptures that support this understanding.[300]

RELY ON THE DEFINITIVE MEANING, NOT THE PROVISIONAL MEANING

Next, for the third reliance, the root text says:

71. **When one engages in the meaning,**
    one should know the provisional meaning and the definitive
        meaning,
    and rely on the definitive
    rather than the provisional.

72. **Since the Omniscient One was all-knowing,**
    he taught the yānas in a sequence,
    like steps ascending a staircase,
    according to students' styles,[301] capacities, and interests.

73. **There are eight categories of intentions and indirect intentions**
    based on the Buddha's purpose regarding the basis for the
        intention.
    He spoke this way because it suited his purpose,
    whereas taking the words literally would impair valid cognition.

74. **Because of his intentions, there are various levels of teachings,**
    from the four Buddhist tenets up to the sublime Vajrayāna.
    The aspects that are not understood by the lower levels
    are clarified by the higher ones.

75. Having seen which teachings are closer to reasoning that accords
  with scripture,
  one holds to the definitive meaning.
  Like swans who can extract milk from water,
  those of the highest intelligence play in the ocean of the
  Buddha's speech.

76. The profound Vajrayāna teachings
  are concealed through the six parameters and the four styles of
  interpretation.[302]
  They are established through flawless reasoning
  along with the key instructions of the lineage.

77. All phenomena are a unity
  of primordial purity and great equality.
  The two types of accurate valid cognition
  establish exactly what this means.

78. Without contradiction, one penetrates the essence
  of the *Prajñāpāramitā*, the creation stage,
  the completion stage, and the great completion,
  by means of the four styles of interpretation through the literal,
  general, hidden, and ultimate meanings.

79. Through that, highly intelligent ones
  become confident through certainty about the meaning.
  These heirs of the Buddha hold the inexhaustible treasure of the
  Dharma
  and the victory banner of the teachings of scripture and
  realization.

GENERAL EXPLANATION OF THE PROVISIONAL AND DEFINITIVE MEANINGS

71. When studying and contemplating the meaning of the scriptures, one
needs to know how to distinguish the definitive meaning of the Buddha's
words from the provisional meaning. Once one knows this, one should rely on
the definitive meaning and not the provisional one.

72.   By means of direct perception, the Buddha knows the true nature and
the full extent of phenomena without the slightest obscuration. He is omniscient regarding the beings to be trained and the methods for training them.
In order to lead students step by step to the state of buddhahood according to
their styles, capacities, and interests, Buddha taught the sequence of the yānas as
the way to engage in training. Like the steps on a ladder, the yānas start with the
listeners, or śrāvakas, along with the followers of realism, or Vaibhāṣikas, and
extend up to the Vajrayāna and the most secret and unexcelled Atiyoga.

The *Mahāparinirvāṇa Sūtra* states:

> My profound teachings
> are like the steps of a ladder.
> Endeavor and train in them in succession,
> one after another, without jumping ahead.

The Anuyoga tantra, the *Overview of the Great Scripture of the Embodiment
of the Realization of All Buddhas*, states:

> The ultimate, definitive yānas
> certainly appear in three groups:
> the yānas that lead away from the cause of suffering, the yānas of
>   austerities,
> and the yānas of the skillful means of transformation.

The types of minds of all students can be summarized into three levels:
higher, intermediate, and lesser. Each of these three levels has three divisions,
and these correspond to the nine stages of the yānas. In his great commentary
on the *Litany of the Names of Mañjuśrī*, titled *The Radiant Light of the Sun and
Moon*, Orgyen, the second buddha of our time, says:

> Each of the three levels of students' minds—higher, inter-
> mediate, and lesser—have three subdivisions, which make
> nine in all. There is no need to explain this further since it is
> easy to understand.

The section on the characteristics is taught for the three lowest levels, the
section on yoga is taught for the three intermediate levels, and the section on
creation and completion stage practice is taught for the three highest levels.
Which level is taught depends on the capacities of different individuals. The
Precious Illuminator states:

The nine sequential yānas depend on distinctions in the students'
minds.
A particular view and conduct are taught for each yāna.

For the names of the nine yānas, the Dzokchen tantra *Self-Arising Awareness* states:

There are the Śrāvakayāna, the Pratyekabuddhayāna,
and likewise the Bodhisattvayāna.
Then Kriyāyogayāna, Upayogayāna,
and likewise Yogayāna are taught.
Then there are Mahāyogayāna, Anuyogayāna,
and likewise Dzokchen Atiyogayāna.
This is how the nine yānas are explained.

Many similar quotations could be cited. Among the teachings of the nine
yānas, the lower ones are provisional teachings and the higher ones are definitive. What are the provisional meaning and the definitive meaning? The omniscient king of Dharma Longchen Rabjam expressed them as follows in the
Precious Key for Assessing the Provisional and the Definitive. He says that the
definitive meaning is the true nature of all phenomena, just as it is. This nature
is pure, like space; it is realization of the mind's luminosity. Being naturally
pure and unchanging, its skylike nature transcends arising, abiding, and ceasing. Without exception, the sūtras and śāstras that teach this are included in
the definitive meaning.

On the other hand, the provisional meaning is all the phenomena that appear, that arise and cease, that come and go, and are pure or impure, with their
various parts such as the aggregates, sense sources, and constituents of a person.
These dreamlike appearances are assessed and imputed with words, thoughts,
and expressions. All the sūtras and śāstras that teach the provisional meaning
are part of the relative truth.

For example, speculating about the skylike nature of mind in words, expressions, and thoughts is the relative truth. The true nature, which is the absolute
truth, is the authentic, definitive meaning.

As it says in the *Praise of the Inconceivable Middle Way*:

The emptiness of all phenomena
is taught as the definitive meaning.

The teachings on whatever arises and ceases,
living beings, sentient beings, and so on,
are taught as the provisional meaning, which is the relative truth.

The Mahāyāna sūtra *King of Meditative Stabilization* states:

In accordance with the teachings of the Sugata,
know how the definitive sūtras are distinguished,
and know that the teachings on sentient beings, individuals,
   ordinary beings,
and all phenomena are the provisional meaning.

The Mahāyāna *Sūtra of the Teaching of Inexhaustible Intelligence* states:

Which sūtras teach the definitive meaning and which sūtras
teach the provisional meaning? Whichever sūtras are directed toward engaging in the path are called provisional,
and whichever sūtras are directed toward engaging in the
result are called definitive.

In more detail, whichever sūtras teach about the self, sentient beings, living beings, ordinary beings, persons, prehis-
toric beings, the personal self, those who act, those who feel,
those who vocalize different sounds, and a self where there is
no self are called the provisional meaning. Whichever sūtras
teach about emptiness, the signless, the wishless, inaction,
the unborn, the unarisen, no phenomena, nonself, and the
absence of sentient beings, life force, persons, or the self—
these teachings on nonexistence up to the doors of liberation are called the definitive meaning. In relation to all of
these, one should rely on the definitive-meaning sūtras and
not on the provisional-meaning sūtras.

In brief, the true nature and the sūtras that teach it are called the definitive
meaning. Teachings that lead the minds of sentient beings to the true nature
by means of many skillful methods, and teachings on what is impure and deluded, with all its categories, are called the provisional meaning and its sūtras.
This system of the definitive meaning and provisional meaning is taught first
in order to be like a mirror for looking at phenomena and a key that opens a
door.

15

The Definitive Meaning

THE EIGHT INTENTIONS

---

73.   So that the definitive and provisional meanings will be clear and the real meaning of "intention" will be understood, I will now explain the classifications called *intentions* and *indirect intentions*.

The Tathāgata teaches the Dharma to students according to their styles, capacities, and interests, and his purpose is connected with the system of intentions and indirect intentions. If a student doesn't accurately understand the intention of a teaching and instead apprehends it according to the words, then the student won't realize the true meaning. Since it is a mistake to apprehend an interpretable teaching according to its provisional meaning or its literal meaning, it is very important to distinguish these. This is why the four indirect intentions are taught.

THE FOUR INTENTIONS

First, among the categories of intentions and indirect intentions, drawn from the Sanskrit term *catvārābhiprāya* there are the "four intentions." To explain these, the *Ornament of the Mahāyāna Sūtras* states:

> One should know the four kinds of intention
> as related to equality, to another meaning,
> to another time,
> and to an individual's thoughts.

The main purpose of the four intentions is that they are related to what others need. First, having the intention related to equality, the Buddha Śākyamuni

said: "At that time I was the Buddha Vipaśyin."³⁰³ Having the intention related
to another meaning, there are statements such as "All phenomena are essenceless," and "There is no form, there is no feeling," and so on. This intention is
related to the absolute truth, and does not mean that conventional things are
nonexistent. Having the intention related to another time, the Buddha said:
"By merely saying the name of a buddha, one will be born in the realm of that
buddha." Here the Buddha's intention was that the person will certainly be
born there at some point in time, but it is uncertain whether that birth will
happen immediately after this life. An example of having the intention related
to an individual's thoughts is that if a person holds the idea that generosity
alone is sufficient, then that person is told that generosity is inferior and discipline is praised as superior.

Each of the four intentions therefore has its own particular purpose. To explain further, the great emanated translator Kawa Paltsek says in his *Dictionary
of Dharma Terminology*:

> What are the four intentions? They are the intention related
> to equality, the intention related to another time, the inten-
> tion related to another meaning, and the intention related
> to an individual. Although a different meaning is applied to
> what is immediately understood, the teachings are not con-
> tradicted by a single word. Taming beings by such skillful
> means is called the four intentions.
>
> For the intention related to equality, since neither the
> buddha of the past nor Śākyamuni Buddha was endowed
> with a greater or lesser degree of the dharmakāya, a greater
> or lesser accumulation of merit and wisdom, or greater or
> lesser enlightened activities that benefit beings, Śākyamuni
> Buddha said, "Previously I was the buddha of the past." This
> is the intention related to equality.
>
> For the intention related to time, it is said: "If you recite
> the name of one buddha, such as Amitābha or Avalokiteś-
> vara, you will become enlightened." This means that
> although one is not enlightened now, based on recitation
> practice as the cause, at some point one will become enlight-
> ened. A similar example is the saying: "Whatever aspira-
> tions are made will come to pass accordingly." Although it

isn't the case now, it will happen eventually because of the cause. This is an intention related to another time.

An intention related to another meaning is illustrated by the Buddha saying: "One will not hear the sūtras unless one has honored as many buddhas as there are sands in the Ganges River." This doesn't mean that we cannot perceive the sūtras right now. This is said so that someone will attain the first bodhisattva bhūmi. This is the intention related to another meaning.

The intention related to an individual can be seen from how praising devotion to, and strength in, a virtue such as discipline stimulates someone to practice it. Similarly, so that someone who thinks that guarding ordinary discipline is the highest virtue will practice other virtues as well, generosity is praised and discipline is criticized. This could be applied to any of the pāramitās, and demonstrates the intention related to an individual.

THE FOUR INDIRECT INTENTIONS

Second, drawing from the Sanskrit term *cātvābhisandhi*, there are what are called the *four indirect intentions*. The *Ornament of the Mahāyāna Sūtras* states:

> There is the indirect intention related to entry, the indirect intention related to characteristics, the indirect intention related to antidotes, and the indirect intention related to change.

The indirect intentions are roundabout ways of changing the meaning from the ordinary way of understanding the words. To begin with, the indirect intention related to entry has the purpose of getting śrāvakas to gradually engage in the Mahāyāna teachings. For example, śrāvakas know that the individual self does not exist. When the Buddha taught them that the aggregates comprising the self do exist, he meant that phenomena exist only on the relative level.

For the indirect intention in relation to characteristics, he used phrases like "there is no essence" in relation to the three natures[304] and primordial nirvāṇa, which apply to ultimate reality.

As for the indirect intention in relation to antidotes, the Buddha spoke in certain ways to eliminate students' misunderstandings that need to be relinquished. The indirect intention related to antidotes can be applied to the four intentions explained above: equality, another meaning, another time, and the thoughts of individuals. For instance, having the intention related to equality, he said, "I was Buddha Vipaśyin" so that someone holding him as inferior and another buddha as superior would relinquish their disparagement of him.

Having the intention related to the goal,[305] as an antidote for the disdain of someone who thinks, "It's easy to obtain the Dharma," the Buddha said, "Generating bodhicitta as taught in the Mahāyāna first arises only after having honored as many buddhas as there are grains of sand in the Ganges River."

Having the intention related to another time, as an antidote for the laziness of people who think they are incapable of training on the path, the Buddha said, "By making the aspiration to go to Sukhāvatī, you will be born there."

Having the intention related to an individual's thoughts, the Buddha criticized the idea that accumulating only a little bit of virtue is enough, and he praised other virtues. These were examples of the indirect intentions regarding antidotes using the four intentions mentioned above.

Here are several more examples related to antidotes. As an antidote related to a single individual rather than many people, which comes from some man's idea that his own family lineage, physical body, or wealth are superior, the Buddha praised other lands and other people so that the man would lower his opinion of himself. Similarly, as an antidote to attachment to mundane objects, the Buddha praised the qualities of transcendent riches.

As another example, for someone tormented by excessive regret because of having committed the negative action of harming a noble being, the Buddha said, "Harming a buddha or bodhisattva forms a joyful connection." The intention of this statement is that once the offense has been confessed or exhausted, that person would be joyful. For those whose bodhicitta is tentative and who want to turn back from the Mahāyāna, the Buddha said, "There is but one yāna." This does not mean that people do not temporarily attain separate results for the three yānas. The intention here is directed toward the ultimate result because all obstacles and faults will be removed by receiving Dharma teachings of the supreme yāna. As it says in the *Mantra of the Second Verse*:

> One will fully connect the words and the meaning by hold-
> ing the words in mind while contemplating their meaning.

Next, the indirect intention related to change refers to changing the usage of terms so that the intended meaning is different from the most common meaning. For example, when non-Buddhist extremists say that the Buddha's teachings are inferior because they are easy to understand, the Buddha coun-teracted this idea by saying:

> If one knows that the essence is essenceless,
> is afflicted with the afflictions,
> and fully abides in what is mistaken,
> one will attain perfect enlightenment.

Why did he say these things? To explain his intention, in the first line the Sanskrit word *sāra* can mean "distraction" as well as "essence." So one should know that the essence of training the mind is perseverance in nondistraction.[306] For the second line, since people have difficulties[307] while training in disci-pline, difficulties are produced. For the third and fourth lines, by fully abid-ing in the higher training of wisdom, which reverses[308] the notions of "purity," "bliss," "permanence," and "the self,"[309] one will attain perfect enlightenment.

Similarly, in the *Udānavarga: A Collection of Verses from the Buddhist Canon*, the Buddha said, "Kill your father and mother." Here these two states—the craving and grasping that propel us into saṃsāra—are like our father and mother. This intention related to relinquishment, and all types of similar in-tentions, are called the indirect intention related to change.

To augment this explanation of the four indirect intentions, here is what the emanated translator Kawa Paltsek says in his *Dictionary of Dharma Terminology*:

> What are the indirect intentions? They are the indirect in-
> tention related to entry, the indirect intention related to
> characteristics, the indirect intention related to antidotes,
> and the indirect intentions related to change. The indirect
> intentions are taught as a skillful means for the purpose of
> leading others with words that are not definitive, but provi-
> sionally suitable.

Here are two examples of the indirect intention related to entry. For non-Buddhists who question whether the self exists or does not exist, the Buddha explained that based on the momentary continuum of sentient beings or based on miraculous birth in general, the self exists. Another example relates to śrāvakas who question whether there is a self in phenomena. The Buddha explained that the aggregates, sense sources, and constituents do exist. He taught this way in order to lead ordinary beings to these teachings and the Mahāyāna without being frightened.

Next are examples of the indirect intention related to characteristics. For those who question whether all phenomena exist as functioning things according to the three natures, and for those who assert that phenomena do not exist based on Buddha's intention in relation to the imaginary nature, phenomena are taught to be nonexistent. For those who assert that phenomena do exist, based on the Buddha's intention in relation to the dependent nature and thoroughly established nature, phenomena are taught to be existent.

For the indirect intention related to antidotes, it is said that there are eighty-four thousand doors of the Dharma for the eighty-four thousand types of behavior of sentient beings. Teaching filthiness as an antidote of desire demonstrates the indirect intention related to antidotes.

Then there is the indirect intention related to change. "If you kill your father, kill your mother, cause discord in the Saṅgha, kill an arhat, and maliciously cause a tathāgata to bleed, then you will awaken into enlightenment." These statements are not to be taken literally. "Kill your mother" means knowing that the phenomenon of ignorance does not exist. "Kill your father" means knowing that the phenomenon of hatred does not exist. "Cause discord in the Saṅgha" means the five aggregates do not exist or are eradicated in emptiness. "Kill an arhat" means knowing that the phenomena of the ground-of-all consciousness and habitual patterns do not exist. "Causing a tathāgata to bleed" refers to the wisdom that realizes emptiness, the basic space of phenomena. These are examples of changing the term.

Another example is the quotation: "If one realizes the essence in the essenceless, abides in what is mistaken, and is afflicted by the afflictions, then one will attain ultimate enlightenment." For each line, respectively, the meaning is that if one meditates without distraction, abides in the opposite of what is mistaken, and practices austerities with various difficulties, one will become enlightened. Changing the terms in this way shows the indirect intention related to change.

SUMMARY OF THE INTENTIONS AND INDIRECT INTENTIONS

For the distinguishing features of intentions and indirect intentions, the great translator Ngok Loden Sherab taught:

> For the "intentions," the listener should not understand the meaning intended by the speaker from the speaker's words alone; instead he should understand a different meaning. For the "indirect intentions," the listener should understand the meaning that the speaker intends.

From the connected explanation of the *Compendium of the Mahāyāna Teachings*:

> The "intentions" are formulated merely in relation to the mind. One should not accept and rely on them in terms of what is apprehended externally. For the "indirect intentions," one can rely on what is apprehended externally.[310]

Therefore, having an intention toward an objective basis, such as the aggregates,[311] there are the four indirect intentions and the four intentions, which make eight altogether. These intentions are taught because there could not be correct valid cognition if the statements were taken literally, and because the purpose of the statements is to benefit specific individuals.

16

The Definitive Meaning in the Vajrayāna

---

74. The four Buddhist philosophical schools, or tenet systems—Vaibhāṣika, Sautrāntika, Cittamātra, and Madhyamaka—culminate in the resultant vehicle, which is the secret mantra Vajrayāna with its three outer tantras, three inner tantras, and its apex—unsurpassable Atiyoga. Whatever is not understood by the lower schools through investigation and analysis is clarified by the higher ones.

75. The Vajrayāna is also greater in terms of what is experienced and realized, which is the topic of its faultless scriptures. This superiority is also established through reasoning.[312] Seeing this, one holds purely to the definitive meaning and does not base one's confidence on the provisional meaning. Just like swans who can extract milk when it is mixed with water, those of the highest intelligence are victorious over the warfare of the four māras and playfully enjoy the great ocean of the Buddha's speech.

THE SIX PARAMETERS OF THE VAJRAYĀNA

76:1–2. In relation to the Vajrayāna being very profound and difficult to realize, the *Heruka Galpo Tantra* states:

> In the extensive explanation, the six parameters are
> the provisional meaning and the definitive meaning,
> the intentional and the unintentional,
> and the literal explanation and the nonliteral explanation.

The six parameters consist of three contrasting pairs: the meaning is either provisional or not provisional, there is either an implicit intention or no implicit intention, and the words should be taken either literally or figuratively.

In terms of practicing the secret mantra Vajrayāna in general, there is another way of listing the six parameters, which is found in the *Eight Herukas Fortress, Ravine, and Life Force*:[313]

> Be decisive with the view,
> cross over with the conduct,
> establish the basis with samaya,
> progress in stages with the empowerment,
> practice with deep meditation,
> and accomplish your goal with the key instructions.
> These are the six parameters.

Also related to Vajrayāna practice, Padmasambhava says in *Guru Rinpoché's Response to the Questions of the Lady*:[314]

> The six parameters are the parameter of Vajrayāna practice,
> the parameter of guru yoga practice,
> the parameter of the guru's instructions,
> the parameter of experiencing the instructions,
> the parameter of practicing the experience,
> and the parameter of accomplishing the result.

The tantras of the secret mantra Vajrayāna are explained through these six parameters because its statements and meanings never go beyond these six limits.

THE FOUR STYLES OF INTERPRETATION

As for the four styles of interpretation, the *Heruka Galpo Tantra* states: "These are the literal, general, hidden, and ultimate." So the literal way, the general way, the hidden way, and the ultimate way are the four styles of interpreting the meaning.[315]

The literal meaning breaks down the sentences into words and explains the words according to the grammar texts.

The general way of interpreting the Vajrayāna can be illustrated with examples. If one regrets that one has not entered the blissful and quick path of tantra, but instead has entered the slow and difficult path of sūtra, then the sūtra path is explained as a way to ascend to the path of tantra. On the other hand, one might regret having entered the tantric path, thinking that a statement like "the tantric path transcends the notions of 'dirty' and 'clean'" means that one would become like dogs and pigs that have no discrimination. Or one might think that a statement like "ritual intercourse and ritual killing within the practices of union and liberation are the Dharma" is the doctrine of heretics. However, unless one relinquishes attachment to the Sūtrayāna way of discriminating between clean and dirty, one will not understand the meaning of equality. Also, if one has the right motivation, then anything can be meritorious, as in the story of the Buddha's previous life as a ship captain who killed an armed criminal that was about to murder five hundred merchants.

The hidden meaning refers to the practices of the creation stage, karmamudrā, and the subtle body practices such as holding tightly, which are connected with the channels, wind energy, and essence element.

The ultimate meaning refers to the realization of absolute luminosity and the unity of the two truths being the ultimate nature just as it is.

Another way of stating these four styles of interpretation is that the literal meaning is like the syllables *oṃ āḥ hūṃ hrīḥ* or *evaṃ mayā*, indicating the four kāyas or the four cakras. The general meaning is like the Mantrayāna understanding of teachings, such as the paths and bhūmis, which are held in common with the Pāramitāyāna. The hidden meaning is like the subjects of the higher yānas that are not included in the lower yānas. The ultimate meaning is like the timeless awareness of the buddhas, which cannot be improved on by any yāna or view.

76: 3–4.   From the perspective of the six parameters and the four styles of interpretation, the meaning of the tantras exists in a hidden way by concealment so that it does not appear to unfortunate ones with wrong views. The valid key instructions of the lineage, which have come down from the dharmakāya Samantabhadra to one's own root guru, are necessary for realizing the meaning of the Vajrayāna.

VAJRAYĀNA REASONING

Along with the lineage instructions, the intended meaning of the profound and secret Vajrayāna is unerringly established by reasoning, such as the four kinds of reasoning[316] that investigate flawlessly or the special reasonings of the four realizations.[317]

These four special reasonings or logical statements are not held in common with the lower yānas but are taught in the *Māyājāla Guhyagarbha Tantra*, the glorious *Secret Essence of the Magical Net*. Of all the definitive tantras about reality, this is the king. It is the pinnacle of all the yānas, the source of all the teachings, a general commentary on all the scriptures, and the great, direct path of all the buddhas. It is the highest, real intention of all the tathāgatas and is full of magnificent, marvelous qualities.

These special reasonings have three aspects: the reasoning of the Buddha's valid speech, the reasoning of a higher meaning that is concordant with the words,[318] and the reasoning in which the words and the meaning do not concur.

To elaborate on these, first, the reasoning of the Buddha's words as valid cognition has its own four aspects: the reasoning of the four realizations, the reasoning of the three purities, the reasoning of the four equalities, and the reasoning of the great nature itself.

The Reasoning of the Four Realizations

The four reasonings are: the reasoning of the single cause, the reasoning of the principle of the syllables, the reasoning of blessings, and the reasoning of direct perception.[319] The *Root Guhyagarbha Tantra* states:

> By realizing the four aspects
> of a single cause, the system of seed syllables,
> blessings, and direction perception,
> everything is the great, truly perfected king, Ngöndzok Gyalpo.[320]

The earlier tenet systems use the four reasonings to comprehend the dualistic, confused perceptions of saṃsāra and nirvāṇa as their object of comprehension. The weakness of the earlier schools is overcome by the later schools, which use the four reasonings of realization to establish different objects of comprehension: (1) the reasoning of a single cause establishes the unborn nature, (2) the reasoning of the system of seed syllables establishes the unceasing display, (3) the reasoning of blessings establishes the indivisible nature, and (4) the reasoning of direct perception establishes that characteristics are beyond concepts.

The reasonings of the four realizations can be explained in syllogisms. First, regarding a single cause: "On the ultimate level, all phenomena of apparent existence have a single cause, which is the naturally occurring timeless awareness, the unity of space and wisdom, because all phenomena are within this state and not beyond it." Second, regarding seed syllables:[321] "On the relative level, the appearances that arise from the basic space of phenomena appear as the kāyas and wisdoms, as illustrated by seed syllables. This is because nothing goes beyond the nature of the basic space of phenomena." Third, regarding blessings:[322] "The relative and the absolute are inseparable and mutually bless each other, because they could not be in union if they had different natures." Fourth, regarding direct perception:[323] "The true nature, which is inseparability, is not within the domain of the intellect because it is unfathomable by ordinary thought. The true nature is yogic direct perception, which is the domain of individual, self-cognizing, timeless awareness."

THE REASONING OF THE THREE PURITIES

Next, the second of the four aspects of the reasoning of the Buddha's speech as valid cognition is the reasoning of the three purities. The king of tantras, the *Guhyagarbha*, states:

> Realize that the world, its contents, and the mindstream are pure.[324]

To explain this in the form of a syllogism: "The five elements, the five aggregates, and the eight consciousnesses are in essence the three purities because they primordially abide as having the nature of the five female buddhas, the five male buddhas, and the five wisdoms."[325]

THE REASONING OF THE FOUR EQUALITIES

The third of the four aspects of the reasoning of the Buddha's speech as valid cognition is the four equalities. The king of tantras, the *Guhyagarbha*, states:

> With the two equalities that are superior to two equalities,
> there is the realm of the maṇḍala of Samantabhadra.

These four equalities can be expressed in syllogisms: (1) The expressible absolute truth, which cuts through a certain amount of conceptual constructs, and the inexpressible absolute truth, which cuts through all conceptual constructs, are equal only in being the absolute, because both of them reveal that nothing has inherent existence. (2) The correct relative truth, which can perform functions in relation to appearances, and the mistaken relative truth, which cannot perform functions in relation to appearances, are equal only in being relative, because although things appear, when they are analyzed they are

empty. (3) The two types of absolute truth—expressible and inexpressible—
are equal in spontaneously being the superior absolute, the very nature of the
seven riches,[326] because from the perspective of basic space, the absolute truth
is the natural state in which timeless awareness and the basic space of phenomena are indivisible. (4) Both the correct relative truth and the mistaken relative
truth are equal in being the maṇḍala of the kāyas and wisdoms, because the reality of appearances is the primordially pure nature.[327]

The Reasoning of the Great Nature Itself

The fourth of the four aspects of the reasoning of the Buddha's speech as valid
cognition is the reasoning of the great nature itself. The *Guhyagarbha Tantra*
states:

> Naturally occurring timeless awareness appears but does not
> dwell.

To phrase this in a syllogism: "In the great nature, which is the natural state,
although the phenomena of saṃsāra and nirvāṇa appear in many ways, they
are ascertained as being nothing but naturally occurring timeless awareness because they are established as such by timeless awareness, which is what investigates the ultimate natural state."

TWO MORE ASPECTS OF VAJRAYĀNA REASONING

The second main category of the special reasonings of the *Guhyagarbha Tantra* is the reasoning of using the same words but with a higher meaning. This
can be illustrated with a syllogism: "The Vajrayāna teaching that the five poisons are not to be abandoned uses the same words—the five poisons—but
with a higher meaning, because when conflicting emotions are not cleared
away through antidotes, and instead one uses the skillful means of realizing
their nature, then the five poisons arise as the five wisdoms."

The third main category of the special reasonings of the *Guhyagarbha Tantra* is the reasoning that does not have the same meaning as in the lower yānas.
As an example: "The true nature of phenomena is definitely not the nature
of conceptual constructs, because anything—all the various appearances of
saṃsāra and nirvāṇa—can arise." Another example is: "The appearances of
relative reality definitely arise, but in indefinite ways, because they have no

inherent nature whatsoever." Statements like these can be realized only through the special reasoning that is not held in common with the lower yānas.

THE THREE VIEWS OF THE NYINGMA LINEAGE

77: 1–2.   To summarize the profound key points of the view of both sūtra and tantra, the Nyingma lineage has its own terminology, which is called the three views. There is the view of phenomena, the view of the true nature, and the view of self-knowing awareness.

First, the view of phenomena is the superior relative truth. This view unmistakably establishes the reality of all apparent phenomena as primordially divine appearance, and this view establishes that timeless awareness knows things as they are. This reasoning, which establishes the relative as great purity, is the view of phenomena.

Second, the view of the true nature is the superior absolute truth. Primordially, all phenomena of saṃsāra and nirvāṇa are beyond all conceptual constructs. They are in the state of great emptiness, beyond the mind and its thoughts, words, and expressions. In this state, the fruition of all the buddhas, the seven riches of the ultimate—enlightened body, speech, mind, qualities, activities, space, and wisdom—as well as all notions of accepting what is good and rejecting what is bad, are equal. This reasoning, which establishes the ultimate as great equality, is the view of the true nature.

Third, the view of self-knowing awareness is the superior two truths. These two truths are established from the perspective of appearance as purity and from the perspective of emptiness as equality. These two truths are inseparably present as one taste in all phenomena. Complete purity and great equality are experienced in a way that is self-illuminating and not an object. They are combined as the single sphere of the dharmakāya, the uncompounded unity of awareness and emptiness, the great magical net.[328] This is what is known by noble beings through their individual, self-knowing wisdom. This view of self-knowing awareness is a unity, the way of the Great Completeness, or Dzokchen.

77: 3–4.   This understanding of reality is unmistakably established through the two types of valid cognition: the valid cognition that investigates authentic conventional reality and the valid cognition that investigates ultimate reality.

VAJRAYĀNA PRACTICE OF THE DEFINITIVE MEANING

78.   The meaning found through this investigation is applied in the secret mantra Vajrayāna, or the two stages: the creation stage and the completion stage. In teachings, when the creation stage of the relative level is illustrated in relation to the body, there are teachings such as the illusoriness of all phenomena. Teachings such as the pāramitās[329] and the illusory divine body also belong to the creation stage.

For the completion stage, the psychophysical aggregates are taught to be the illusory divine body, which is the energetic mind. The dynamic energy of suchness, which is the basis of appearance, is taught to be the fundamental ground. In relation to this, there are the very subtle timeless awareness channels, timeless awareness winds, and timeless awareness elements. In addition, there are the pairs of earth and water, fire and wind, and space and mind, which are sequentially in union as the three kāyas[330] and are spontaneously present as the essence of the three vajras of body, speech, and mind. All these are part of the completion stage with characteristics.[331]

Then there are the teachings on the completion stage of Dzokchen. Within the very subtle, fundamental mind, there is spontaneously present, radiant awareness. This is reflected outward as five lights having the aspects of the five wisdoms. All the coarse and subtle energies of the energetic mind expand and contract from this ground. The ground of mind is spontaneously present luminosity, awareness-emptiness, the Great Completeness, or Dzokchen.

Returning to the overall discussion of the four styles of interpretation, after determining the word meaning, the general meaning, the hidden meaning, and the ultimate meaning, one should apply them. For example, these four styles of interpretation can be illustrated by the luminosity of the ultimate completion stage. The meaning of the word "luminosity" is taught in the *Prajñāpāramitā Sūtra*. The general meaning is the practice of the creation stage as luminosity. The hidden meaning is the luminosity of the completion stage induced by the four levels of emptiness: empty, very empty, greatly empty, and universally empty. The ultimate meaning is luminosity in accordance with Dzokchen, the Great Completeness, which is the second part of the completion stage practice. This is the realization of the fundamental, natural state in which all phenomena are primordially empty, together with the realization of the originally pure timeless awareness of the fourth empowerment.

79. By practicing without contradiction the key points of profound meaning through these four styles of interpretation, one gains certainty in the profound meaning of the sūtras and tantras. One is confident and able to use one's own intelligence without relying on anyone else. Highly intelligent ones, who have reached the point where no one could rob them of their confidence, become the great heart children of the victorious ones, who inherit the kāya of the buddhas.

Having been taught the Dharma of the three yānas or the nine yānas, they hold the storehouse of the great treasure of the inexhaustible, sacred Dharma. These bodhisattva-mahāsattvas take care of all the remaining disciples of the Buddha by teaching them the Dharma of scripture, which is subsumed in the twelve branches[332] of the Buddha's speech and the six tantras. They also teach the Dharma of realization, which is subsumed in the three higher trainings and the two stages of Vajrayāna practice. In this way these individuals hold the great victory banner, which is all-victorious over whatever is not conducive to the precious teachings of scripture and realization.

17

Rely on Wisdom to Reach the Eight Great Treasures

———

RELY ON WISDOM, NOT ON CONSCIOUSNESS

For the fourth of the four reliances, the root text says:

80. When practicing the definitive meaning,
     do not rely on consciousness—
     the perceiving mind and what it perceives, which depend on
       words and concepts.
     Rely instead on nondual wisdom.

81. That which has reference points
     is the mind with a nature of apprehending the apprehended.
     Conceiving of things in this way is false.
     In reality, there is no actual contact.

82. Whether something is conceived of as an entity or a nonentity,
       or as both or neither,
     no matter how it is focused on, there are still reference points.
     The sūtras say that whatever is grasped through
       conceptualization

83. is the domain of demons.
     Conceptualization cannot be destroyed
     by negating or affirming.
     But if one sees without removing or adding anything, there is
       liberation.

84. Completely free from perceiver and perceived,
    naturally occurring, timeless awareness is natural luminosity.
    Since all fabrications of the four extremes are brought to an end,
    timeless awareness is said to be supreme.

85. Just like someone blind from birth looking at the form of
        the sun,
    immature beings have not previously seen this.
    No matter how they imagine it, they don't actually know it,
    so immature beings feel anxious.

86. However, by means of authentic scriptures,
    reasoning that refutes all extreme views,
    and the guru's key instructions,
    just like a blind man gaining sight, one will see it for oneself.

87. At this time, those with devotion taste the nectar
    of the Dharma of the Tathāgata,
    and their eye of increasing joy
    turns toward the wisdom body of the sugatas.

88. At this time, all phenomena without exception
    are resolved in the state of equality.
    One gains the inexpressible confidence of certainty
    and skill in explaining the inexhaustible treasure of the Dharma.

89. By gaining expertise in the way the two truths are,
    one sees the reality of the two truths in union.
    When this happens, it is like removing the husk to reveal the
        essence.
    One knows how to endeavor in all the skillful means.

90. Since the sugatas know about skillful means,
    all their methods are said to be a genuine path.
    This is why one gives rise to irreversible confidence
    in one's teachers and their teachings.

91. **By actualizing supreme, nondwelling, timeless awareness,
       one is naturally liberated from the extremes of cyclic existence
          and peace.
      Continuous, effortless, great compassion
      boundlessly pervades all directions and times.**

Why Dualistic Consciousness Is Deluded

80.   When practicing according to one's own realization of the definitive meaning, do not rely on consciousness, which has the nature of the perceiving mind and perceived objects that depend on words and concepts. Instead, rely on timeless awareness, which is beyond the duality of perceiver and perceived.

81.   The mind is deluded when it apprehends outer objects and uses reference points like empty, not empty, both, or neither. Conceiving of things in this way is false. In the reality of the true nature beyond concepts, duality cannot withstand analysis because subjects and objects never actually connect or make contact.

82.   Why is this so? Whether one conceives of something as an entity, or negates that and conceives of it as a nonentity, or as both an entity and a nonentity, or as neither an entity nor a nonentity, there is movement of the mind and conceptual reference points.

83.   The *Sūtra of the Manifold Display of Mañjuśrī* states:

> By having reference points, whatever is conceived of as an
> entity or a nonentity is an object of grasping, which places it
> in the domain of demons.

The same sūtra also says:

> To whatever extent there are reference points,
> to whatever extent there are mental formations,
> to that same extent there is demonic activity.

The habitual way that the mind grasps at reference points cannot be destroyed by concepts of affirming or negating, such as refuting an entity and establishing a nonentity. However, when one sees the true nature, in which all constructs of dualistic perception can appear without anything being removed on the one hand, or added or affirmed on the other, then one is free from all complexity and reference points.

SEEING WITH NONDUAL WISDOM

In regard to seeing the true nature, both the regent protector Maitreya and the protector Nāgārjuna say with one intention and one voice:

> In this there is nothing at all to be removed
> and not the slightest thing to be added.
> Look genuinely at the genuine.
> When the genuine is seen, there is liberation.

84.   In this context, since one is free from all the perceived objects and the perceiving subject, there is no more grasping and fixation. This is not a blank emptiness; it is luminosity, the knowing quality of spontaneous, naturally occurring, timeless awareness. It naturally brings to an end all conceptual constructs of the four extremes, like existence and nonexistence. Therefore the Buddha praised timeless awareness as supreme. For instance, the precious *Abridged Prajñāpāramitā Sūtra* states:

> No matter how many words for things are expressed in the universe,
> when one genuinely transcends the arising of all of them,
> what is attained is none other than sacred, deathless, timeless
>   awareness.
> This is *prajnapāramitā*, the perfection of wisdom.

85.   To give an example, people blind from birth have never been able to see the form of the sun. Similarly, immature, samsaric beings have not previously experienced seeing the true nature free from reference points. To whatever extent they lack that experience, to that same extent they are just imagining it. Without confidently knowing it, immature beings cannot access the true nature beyond fabrications, and this makes them anxious.

86.   However, when the true nature is resolved through the three types of genuine and special valid cognition, and then one meditates, one will realize the natural state just as it is. The *Vajra Mirror Tantra* states:

> Whoever comprehends something
> by means of valid cognition, scripture, reasoning, and the key
>   instructions,
> will internalize what is to be known.

To enlarge on this verse, there is the valid cognition of the authentic scriptures, which are the definitive meaning of the Buddha's words. There is the valid cognition of reasoning, which refutes all extreme views that differ from the positions taught by the great masters. And there is the valid cognition of the key instructions of a genuine guru with the lineage instructions. These bear witness to the fact that when wise beings practice these instructions and meditate on them, they give rise to uncontrived devotion for these instructions and attain liberation. Just like the blind gaining sight, transcendent, timeless awareness arises in their minds.

It is similar to comparing metaphoric wisdom—a conceptual semblance of experiencing the true nature when one is still an ordinary person—with the extraordinary certainty that arises when one actually sees the truth. At that point, one has a direct perception of the true nature, which clearly appears.

THE RESULTING REALIZATION

87.   At this time those with confident devotion taste the nectar of the excellent Dharma of the Tathāgata, and their eye of increasing joy sees the true nature in the heart. This is not the ordinary eye, which is as fragile as a bubble, but the supreme eye of timeless awareness, which one-pointedly turns toward and sees the dharmakāya wisdom body of the sugatas.

88.   Also at this time one perfects the realization that all phenomena with all their differences—saṃsāra and nirvāṇa, happiness and suffering, good and bad, and so on—are inseparable in the state of equality. One gains the confidence that comes from certainty, which is inexpressible in words and cannot be suppressed by anyone in the world, even the gods. From this point on, one becomes more and more proficient in explaining the entire treasure of the Dharma, the inexhaustible teachings of the three yānas. As it is said:

> When one gains the confidence of certainty in reality,
>   a hundred thousand Dharma treasures burst forth from one's heart.

89.   Therefore by gaining expertise through hearing, contemplating, and meditating on the way the two truths actually are, one finally sees for oneself the ultimate—the unity of the two truths, in the sense of seeing that which cannot be seen. When this happens, just as the outer husks of beans and rice are removed in order to obtain their essence, one knows how to endeavor in all the skillful means to attain the liberation spoken of by the Buddha. Ultimately

one attains the unity of the two truths, and what one realizes is the single basic space of phenomena. There is nothing that is not included in this single, ultimate realization.

The *Supplement to the Guhyagarbha Tantra* states:

> Just like all the rivers flow into the great ocean,
> all aspects of the yānas that lead to liberation
> are encompassed by self-knowing awareness, the king that realizes
> equality.
> It is the great skillful means that realizes the unsurpassable ultimate.

The Dzokchen tantra *The All-Creating Monarch* states:

> Actually, there is only one yāna,
> but it arises as nine yānas,
> all of which are encompassed by Dzokchen, the Great
> Completeness.

90. Therefore the sugatas—the holy buddhas who have reached lasting happiness—know which skillful means to use for systematically taming students according to their styles and capacities. By endeavoring in all the methods of the teachings, one reaches the end of the path—omniscient buddhahood—so these skillful means are said to be a genuine path. This is the reason one experiences irreversible devotion for one's teachers and their teachings, to the point where an army of a billion demons could not steal one's confidence away.

91. Essentially the fundamental, natural state is the union of emptiness and compassion. By truly realizing what this means, one attains and actualizes the fruition, which is supreme, naturally occurring timeless awareness, free from dwelling in either cyclic existence or peace, as it says in the *Prajñāpāramitā Sūtra*. For one's own sake, one is liberated in a state of being where there is no need to end saṃsāra on the one side and remain in nirvāṇa on the other.

As the Vidyādhara Garab Dorjé says:

> Awareness, which is not established as anything,
> arises in various ways and is completely unobstructed.
> All apparent existence arises in the sphere of the dharmakāya,
> and the arising itself is liberated in its own space.

Then for the sake of others—the beings who have not realized this—unending great compassion effortlessly arises and naturally pervades all directions and times without limit. One's enlightened activities are spontaneously present, all-pervasive, and everlasting, causing sentient beings to be established on the path, to actualize the path, and to reach the end of the path.

FRUITION: THE EIGHT GREAT TREASURES OF CONFIDENCE

The third main section of this text describes the fruition, which will be explained in terms of the eight great treasures of confidence:[333]

92. The supreme, stainless cause
     is possession of the four reliances,
     which comes from contemplating how the Dharma of the two
       truths
     is established by the four types of reasoning.

93. From this comes forth the fruition—profound, timeless
       awareness,
     and when this fully manifests,
     the eight great treasures of confidence are released
     from concealment in the basic space of awareness.

94. The treasure of memory
     is not forgetting the teachings previously studied and
       contemplated.
     The treasure of intelligence
     is discerning the vast and profound meanings of those teachings.

95. The treasure of realization
     is internalizing the entire meaning of the sūtras and tantras.
     The treasure of retention
     is never forgetting anything one has studied.

96. The treasure of confidence is satisfying all beings
     by teaching well.
     The treasure of the Dharma is completely protecting
     the precious treasury of the sacred Dharma.

97.　The treasure of bodhicitta
　　　is maintaining the unbroken lineage of the Three Jewels.
　　　The treasure of accomplishment is attaining acceptance
　　　of the true nature, the equality of the unborn.

98.　Those who master the inexhaustible eight great treasures
　　　and never part from them
　　　are praised by the buddhas and their heirs,
　　　and become the protectors of the three worlds.

How to Release the Eight Great Treasures

92.　As explained above, the topic to be comprehended is the Dharma of the two truths. This is comprehended by means of the four reasonings that unerringly establish the way the two truths are. Contemplating this thoroughly produces the supreme cause—the possession of the four reliances, unstained by any faults.

93.　This brings forth the fruition—timeless awareness, which is so profound that its depth is hard to fathom. When fully manifest, it becomes as vast as space, and the eight great treasures of confidence are released. It is as if they had been concealed within timeless awareness, the basic space of the fundamental ground, which ordinary people do not realize.

What Are the Eight Great Treasures?

The eight great treasures are found in the *Sūtra of the Vast Display*:

> (1) Not forgetting is the treasure of memory, (2) having a discerning mind is the treasure of intelligence, (3) internalizing the meaning of all the sūtras is the treasure of realization, (4) holding everything one has studied is the treasure of retention, (5) satisfying everyone by teaching well is the treasure of confidence, (6) completely protecting the noble Dharma is the treasure of the Dharma, (7) maintaining the unbroken lineage of the Three Jewels is the treasure of bodhicitta, and (8) accepting the unborn nature of phenomena is the treasure of accomplishment. These are the attainments of the eight great treasures.

94.   The treasure of memory is never forgetting the words and meanings of the scriptures one previously studied and contemplated. The treasure of intelligence is discerning through wisdom the meaning of what one has memorized, as well as the meaning of profound emptiness, which is so difficult to realize, along with the vast details, such as the paths and bhūmis.

95.   The treasure of realization is internalizing the entire meaning of what has been realized concerning the sūtras and tantras. The treasure of retention is never forgetting even the slightest aspect of what one previously studied because of having obtained the four doors of retention.[334]

96.   The treasure of confidence is satisfying all beings through excellent explanations that accord with the meaning. The treasure of the Dharma is completely protecting the precious treasury of the sacred Dharma. This is done by fortunate ones who adhere to the Dharma and defeat its opponents through reasoning.

97.   The treasure of relative bodhicitta is maintaining the unbroken lineage by being heirs of the succession of the Three Jewels, through ascertaining the Awakened One, the Dharma he teaches, and the Saṅgha that arises from that. The treasure of accomplishment is attaining acceptance of the true nature, the equality of all phenomena in being unborn. This acceptance comes from having meditated on the Dharma established through study and contemplation. These are the attainments of the eight great treasures.

Why They Are Connected with Confidence

Why are these called the eight great treasures of confidence? The first four treasures—memory, intelligence, realization, and retention—are the causes of confidence, and the last four—confidence, Dharma, bodhicitta, and accomplishment—are the result of confidence. The reason these eight are generally labeled as "confidence" is that fearless confidence arises from possessing memory, intelligence, realization, and retention, and the protection of the Dharma, bodhicitta, and accomplishment occur because of having confidence. Since confidence is the primary quality among them, they are called the *eight great treasures of confidence*.

98.   By gaining mastery of these eight great treasures of confidence, one is never separate from any aspect of the words or the meanings. Those who gain mastery of the limitless, inexhaustible, eight great treasures become noble beings, praised by the buddhas and their heirs as supreme descendents of the buddhas,

and they become protectors of the three worlds—the nāga realm below the earth, the human realm on the earth, and the god realm above the earth.

THE RESULT OF COMPREHENDING THE TWO TRUTHS

The third section of the main part of the text teaches the result of comprehending the unity of the two truths in this way:

> 99.　**The teachings of the Buddha are valid**
> **since they are proven through valid cognition.**
> **One develops certainty through a valid path**
> **of valid teachings, so one sees the truth, which is the fruition.**

99.　All the teachings presented by the completely perfect Buddha Bhagavān for the benefit of beings are valid. And using valid cognition not contradicted by reasoning to investigate conventional and ultimate reality has proven these teachings to be superior, especially in relation to the tenet systems of non-Buddhists. The great Buddhist masters, such as glorious Dharmakīrti and the glorious protector Nāgārjuna, teach a valid path in their treatises, which investigate the two truths and other topics. The path they teach gives rise to certainty, which is the highest type of devotion, and so their teachings are valid.

The renowned scholars of this world, including the gods, as well as the noble ones—the śrāvakas, pratyekabuddhas, and bodhisattvas—do not fully see the truth as it is, the unsurpassable fruition, through the nectar of the Dharma. However, once they complete the process of relinquishment and realization on the five paths and ten bhūmis, they will see it. They will attain the essence of the four kāyas and five wisdoms of a perfect buddha for the benefit of self and others.

18

Conclusion

———

The conclusion, which is good at the end, has two parts: an explanation of the manner in which this text was composed and the dedication of virtue.

WHY MIPHAM COMPOSED THIS TEXT

100. **Having completely purified his vision**
and perfected great compassion,
the Sugata demonstrated the path
and said, "Taste the deathless nectar I have found.

101. **Experience it through the four reasonings**
and the four reliances."
Even though he shared this nectar,
it is difficult to experience its supreme taste

102. **because of our degenerate era**
and the way it goes against the Dharma.
Seeing this, my mind is filled with pure motivation
and the greatest reverence for the teachings.

100.   Having first purified his own vision of the wisdom that knows the true nature of everything as it is, then for the sake of others, the Sugata perfected the great compassion that lovingly protects infinite sentient beings from suffering and its causes. The great being Śākyamuni, son of Śuddhodana, taught the path by demonstrating the three yānas or nine yānas to disciples in ways that are suited the capacities of their individual minds.

101.   The perfect Buddha said again and again in the sūtras and tantras: "Taste the deathless nectar of the sacred Dharma that I have found. Experience it unerringly through the four reasonings and the four reliances." By sharing

with this world the nectar he had found, numerous fortunate ones have experienced the taste of the sacred Dharma.

102.   However, in this era of the five degenerations, people's understanding goes against the teachings explained above, especially in terms of their mental afflictions and views, and they do not gain certainty through the four reasonings. This makes it hard for them to use the method of the unerring four reliances to experience the sublime taste of scripture and reasoning that was taught by the supreme guide Gautama.

Having clearly seen this, Mipham composed this treatise with the pure motivation of solely wanting to benefit others. He realized, based on the great reason of total conviction in the teachings that are so difficult to find, that the Buddha's teachings are more valuable than anything else. So he wrote this with the greatest reverence and clear, aspiring, and confident devotion.

THE DEDICATION OF VIRTUE

**103.   Through the virtue of expressing just a little
of the way to develop the stainless wisdom,
which comes from contemplating in this way,
may all beings attain the state of Mañjuśrī.**

103.   Mipham expressed some of the ways and means by which fortunate beings can develop in their minds the stainless, faultless wisdom that comes from contemplation, which is one of the three wisdoms of hearing, contemplating, and meditating. This faultless wisdom is the essence of a vast subject, so Mipham aspires that the limitless virtue arising from having composed this text will cause all infinite beings to attain swiftly and without delay the state of the wisdom being Mañjuśrī, who personifies the inseparability of basic space and timeless awareness.

JAMGÖN MIPHAM'S CLOSING VERSE AND COLOPHON

Third, for the conclusion, which makes the text complete:

**104.   When the lotus of my heart turned toward
Mañjuśrī, the sun of speech, it blossomed with devotion**

and this honey pollen of excellent explanations came forth.
May this increase the feast of fortunate bees.

In accord with my previous intention to write this, when the
learned one Lhaksam Gyaltsen recently urged me to do so, I,
Jampal Gyepé,[335] wrote it in a single day, the 29th day of the
third lunar month of the Sakyong year.[336] Maṅgalam—may
this be auspicious! There are 104 verses. May this be virtuous!

Here is a further concluding verse, which Mipham Rinpoché wrote at the
end of his annotated commentary on the root text:[337]

When one sees this excellent explanation of mine,
all one's large and small doubts are self-liberated,
clear intelligence arises and ascertains reality,
and the inexhaustible great treasury of confidence is found.

This was written on the fourth day of the fourth month of the
Fire Horse year.[338]

104.   With single-pointed, intense feeling for the exalted one Mañjuśrī,
the sun of speech, the lotus of Mipham's heart turned in Mañjuśrī's direction.
When the three types of devotion drew forth the sharp rays of the sunlight of
his blessings, this lotus opened and fully blossomed. Then the honey pollen of
these excellent explanations came forth from a hundred flower petals of intelligence. For the assembly of fortunate ones, like a swarm of bees who desire to
experience the supreme taste of the Buddha's teachings, may a festival of realization increase further and further until saṃsāra ends, in accord with the Buddha's intentions in his words and their commentaries.

Mipham's colophon, which begins, "In accord with my previous intention
to write this," is easy to understand and needs no further explanation.

KHENCHEN PALDEN'S CLOSING VERSES

To conclude, I, Khenpo Palden, would like to add these words:

1. The Buddha, the supreme teacher and leader of mankind,
    was not confused about the natural state of all knowable things.
    This is the great maṇḍala of the two wisdoms that know the true nature
        and extent of all things,
    and radiates nonconceptual compassion like a hundred thousand rays
        of light.

2. When the 84,000 Dharma teachings are proclaimed
    in accord with the styles, capacities, and intentions of disciples,
    this causes the beings of the three worlds to instantly arise
    from their sleep in thick, dark ignorance.

3. Teachings like this are good in the beginning, the middle, and the end.
    The learned and accomplished masters of India and Tibet
    play, like a hundred thousand nāgas, in the vast ocean of nectar of well-
        spoken teachings,
    endowed with twofold excellence[339] and the four precepts of pure
        conduct.[340]

4. In the country surrounded by a garland of snow mountains
    the supreme and ordinary siddhis were perfected by millions of
        vidyādharas
    led by the golden chariot of the aspirations
    generated by the three ancestral kings[341] and the Abbot, the Master,
        and the Dharma King.[342]

5. Subsequently, the Vajrayāna teachings of the tantras make it easy to
        understand
    the difficult, vital points of the profound and vast sūtras, tantras, and
        key instructions,
    which show the path followed by millions of learned and accomplished
        vidyādharas
    of the Early Translation school endowed with six special features.

6. The single circle of the profound meaning, like the powerful orb of the
    sun,
    fully emerged from the ocean of wisdom
    of Jamgön Mipham, the Dharma lord of the three realms,
    who is the Lion of Speech[343] emanated in monk's robes.

7. There is the splendid white umbrella[344] of the Buddha, the genuine
    teacher, and his teachings,
    which unfailingly shows the path to liberation and omniscience.
    The wheel of Dharma of the 84,000 teachings
    turns in the circle of the two truths of the nine sequential yānas.

8. In the center of the fully blooming thousand petals of the flawless
    Buddhist teachings,
    is displayed the anthers of the lotus possessing the four types of
    reasoning.
    The great excellent vase possessing the two valid cognitions that
    investigate ultimate reality
    is beautifully filled with the elixir of dependently arising phenomena.

9. The auspicious golden fish possessing the two types of valid cognition
    that investigate conventional reality
    dart swiftly through the ocean of the Buddha's teachings.
    Coiling to the right, the sweet-sounding Dharma conch of the four
    reliances
    resounds with the instructions of the nine lineages.[345]

10. The glorious knot of the eight treasures of confidence swirls without
    end
    owing to the timeless awareness of the purity and equality of the
    magical net.[346]
    The sword of wisdom that ascertains the profound meaning of the
    sūtras and tantras
    raises the victory banner over the entire world.

11. If you want to instantly cut through
    the hundred nets of not understanding, misunderstanding, and doubt
    about the ocean of profound and vast aspects of the Dharma,
    take hold of the sharp sword of wisdom born of contemplation.

12. In this way, in the holy place of Varanasi,
    at the Institute of Higher Studies formed by the Tibetan government,
    this text was shamelessly composed by Palden Sherab,
    a conceited Nyingma khenpo who follows the Early Translation
    tradition.

13. Affectionately intending to benefit some new students,
    and because the root text represents my own tradition,
    I used Mipham Rinpoché's word commentary and my teacher's[347] oral
    instructions as the foundation,
    and ornamented it with commentaries from genuine masters.

14. Their excellent explanations are as vast as the sky,
    but my intelligence is as small as the eye of a needle.
    Therefore in the presence of the unbiased masters,
    I confess my lack of understanding, my misunderstanding, and the
    uncertainty found here.

15. May the stainless virtue that arises from this
    illuminate the dark ignorance in all beings,
    and through this virtue, may they have the great wisdom that sees the
    true nature of phenomena,
    so that they reach the level of omniscience.

16. Throughout the surrounding area of this world
    may thick rainclouds of the authentic view
    send down a gentle rain of benefit, happiness, love, and affection.
    May this form an auspicious connection for the new sun of the golden
    age to dawn.

ADDITIONAL ASPIRATION PRAYERS BY JAMGÖN MIPHAM

To reinforce the magnificence of Mipham's blessings, here is a truthful and poetic aspiration prayer by the great sage Ajita,[348] with a sound as playful and charming as that of young celestial maidens:

> May the ray of the sun of virtuous actions
> banish far away the darkness of the degenerate age,
> so that this garden full of fresh utpala flowers of genuine intelligence
> will experience this festival that expands without end.
>
> Through all my lives, may I be endowed with the light of discerning
> intelligence
> concerning the treasury of the Buddha's teaching.
> And with pure motivation, free from pride,
> may I increase the benefit and happiness of the teachings and beings
> throughout the universe.
>
> May the lords of the Dharma prophesied by the king of the
> Dharma,[349]
> such as Dharmakīrti who was victorious in all directions,
> increase the ways in which the Dharma cuts off non-Dharma at the
> root,
> by attaining the Dharma eye that discerns the highest Dharma.
>
> The sunlight of Mañjughoṣa radiates within the heart,
> so the petals of well-explained words bloom throughout the ten
> directions
> and the honey pollen that benefits others spreads to the limits of
> space.
> May all beings be cared for in this way.
>
> Having cleared away the cataracts of the view,
> the eye of wisdom sees the very nature of phenomena.
> May the sun that shines from within
> forever beautify all the beings of this world.

Having touched the top of my head to the lotus feet of the Lion of
  Speech,
may the eye of far-reaching investigation
and proclamation of the lion's roar of reasoning
extend throughout space and beautify the universe.

KHENCHEN PALDEN'S COLOPHON

This commentary was composed in 1967 and was taught and studied according to our scriptural tradition in the Ngagyur Nyingma department in the
Central Institute of Higher Tibetan Studies. However, there was no published
book. Many diligent students of mine urged me again and again to make a
clear and complete edition of these teachings, but I was too busy.

Recently I was asked again to publish this for the welfare of the Nyingma
tradition, principally by the thirteenth chairman of the department, Khenpo
Rigzin Dorjee. In accordance with his wishes and the wishes of others, I finished writing the commentary in New York, and it was prepared for publication
at the Boudhanath Stupa in Nepal by the principal copyists, Lopön Orgyen
Tenzin, Tsering Tenzin, and Tashi Delek. Later I made a few corrections.

The text was compiled by the Nyingma khenpo Palden Sherab on the tenth
day in the eighth Western month, 2,530 years[350] after the passing of our teacher,
the Buddha, in the area of Deer Park near Varanasi. May this be a cause for the
arising of the new golden age, an era of joy and goodness throughout space and
time. *Sarva Maṅgalam*! May everything be auspicious!

ASPIRATION PRAYERS INCLUDED
FOR THE PUBLICATION

May these Dharma teachings be renowned in every corner of the
  universe,
like the maṇḍalas of the sun and moon.
May the lotus of good intellect open wide
and the Buddha's teachings spread and flourish.

By the victorious one, Longchenpa

Fearlessly raising the victory banner of the Early Translation
    tradition,
the victory drum of the Dharma of scripture and realization
    resounds in all directions.
May the lion's roar of reasoning extend above, below, and on the
    earth,
and the appearance of unequaled signs of goodness increase.

> By Jamgön Mipham

The limitless entrances to the Dharma
are like rivers flowing into the one taste of the ocean of liberation
    and peace.
Every bit of its words is the nectar of excellent explanations,
which thoroughly cleanse the stains of the three poisons.

Through the heaps of pure virtue from this publication,
may a hundred thousand doors of the genuine Dharma
open wide for everyone in the five states of being,[351]
so they acquire mastery of the jewel treasury of ultimate goodness.

> By the Dalai Lama, Tenzin Gyatso

Appendix A

Jamgön Mipham's Annotated Verses

The Sword of Wisdom That Ascertains Reality

1. **This philosophy** (the teachings, valid scriptures) **is unmistaken;**[352]
   all errors have been eliminated (the teacher, valid direct perception).
   The mind is free from doubt about three (through fulfilling the three
   criteria for valid evidence) **points** (the method of proof is valid
   inference).
   I pay homage to Mañjuśrī, (because he is the essence of all these) **the
   treasure of wisdom.**

2. **The** (Mahāyāna) **teachings of the Sugata**
   are profound (emptiness, the absolute)**, vast** (such as the bhūmis and
   pāramitās, the relative)**, and difficult to realize.**
   For those (fortunate ones) **who wish to taste this deathless nectar,**
   I will bestow the light of (excellent explanations which give rise to)
   intelligence.

3. **The Dharma** (in its multiplicity) **taught by the buddhas**
   is completely based on the two truths (the entire subject matter):
   (What are these?) **the worldly, relative truth**
   and the supreme, absolute truth (that transcends the world).

   (It should be understood that it is impossible to have any higher
   realization than the realization of the nature of the two truths, just
   as it is. As one progresses through the yānas, one realizes more and
   more profoundly how the two truths are the very nature of things.)

4. **If one wants to know the nature** (the natural state) **of the two truths**
    (which is the object to be comprehended)
    with a mind (which is what does the comprehending) **that** (properly)
       ascertains them unerringly,
    one should thoroughly establish the good, clear eyes
    of the two types of flawless (faultless) **valid cognition** (which
       investigate conventional and ultimate reality).

5. **No matter how things appear** (in the world),
    they arise interdependently (in relation to causes and conditions).
    Nothing independent (in relation to causes and conditions) **appears;**
    this would be like a lotus appearing (within our experience) **in the**
       sky.

6. **When the collection of causes** (like a seed, manure, heat, and
       moisture) **is complete,**
    it functions to produce an effect (like a sprout).
    Each and every effect
    depends on its own specific causes (because it will not arise without
       them).

7. **Therefore by understanding correctly** (that causes produce effects
       and effects depend on causes) **or incorrectly** (that causes do not
       produce effects and effects do not depend on causes),
    how causes (causal efficacy) **and effects** (dependency) **function,**
    one engages in or refrains from activities (in the world).
    All the (Buddhist and non-Buddhist) **philosophical systems and**
       (worldly) **fields of knowledge, like artistry,**

8. **are also rooted in this** (causal efficacy and dependency).
    This is why (there are two types of reasoning) **cause and effect**
       encompass all worldly training
    and the training that transcends the world.
    Every interdependent thing

9. **has its unique** (its own specific characteristics not shared with others)
       defining characteristics,

like solidity, wetness, or heat,
because of its own individual nature.
This nature (Who could say it is not so?) **cannot be denied** (on the
conventional level).

10. **In a single thing** (like a vase) **there are a variety of attributes,**
and there are numerous facts and classifications
of terminology that establish (what they are and their existence)
or exclude (what they are not and their nonexistence) **those**
attributes.
Each thing has its own specific nature (not produced by something
else).

11. **An object is thoroughly apprehended by direct perception** (like a
vase).
Then the conceptual mind (which grasps an object by putting
together language and a mental image)—**that which distinguishes**
and combines—
uses terminology (such as its function, being impermanent, being
something that has arisen)
to label it as a separate thing.

12. **Objects of knowledge will be thoroughly understood**
by categorizing them into two groups (of existents):
substantial (substantially existent) **things** (contradictory and related
phenomena, subjects and objects) **and designations based on**
terminology (which derive from the substance).
There are many further classifications (such as negative phenomena
and positive phenomena, what appears and what is not there,
definitions and objects defined) **that elaborate on this.**

13. **If one examines the true reality** (of these)
of causes (causal efficacy), **effects** (dependency), **and the nature of**
things,
one cannot find (even the cause) **any production** (causal efficacy)
and nothing (an effect) **that arises through dependency.**

14. **By its own very nature** (true nature),
     appearance is essentially (not that way through something else)
        emptiness.
     **The basic space of phenomena, having the three aspects of
        liberation** (the signless cause of causal efficacy, the wishless effect of
        dependency, and the nature which is essenceless),
     is the (reasoning of the) **nature of the ultimate.**

15. **Although there is causal efficacy and dependency** (on the relative
        level),
     the reasoning of the (its very own) **nature is the final reasoning.**
     Once the nature of a thing has been reached,
     (hereafter) **there are no further reasons to be sought.**

16. **As was just explained** (above), **valid comprehension of a thing
     accords** (through reasoning) **with the nature of the two truths
     and is established through the** (strong) **power of fact.**
     This is the reasoning of a valid proof.

17. **Similarly, the way things appear** (relatively) **and the way they are** (in
        their ultimate, natural state)
     **are comprehended according to their natures
     either by direct perception, or by inference** (which causes certainty)
        of something else (a fact),
     which is unmistaken because it relies on what directly appears (a
        sign).

     (Generally speaking, even though a sensory or mental direct
     perception is identified as having the nature of sensory or mental
     direct perception, it is taught that direct perception is not always
     valid cognition. However, the valid cognition mentioned above is
     said to be "unmistaken," and through study one will understand how
     to distinguish this.)

18. **There are four kinds of direct perception:
     unmistaken sensory perception** (not mistaken like being on a moving
        boat), **mental perception** (not mistaken like hallucinating when
        intoxicated), **self-aware perception, and yogic perception.**

Since their objects are appearing, specific phenomena (and not
general phenomena),
direct perception is not conceptual (concepts perceive things by
mixing objects with names through the three ways of defining
conceptualization).

19. **Without** (this) **direct perception,**
there would be no evidence (like the appearance of smoke), **so there
could be no inference.** (and if there were no inference)
All appearances (in the world) **would be impossible** (to see),
such as the way things (like a sprout) **arise from causes** (like a seed)
and then cease (in the end).

20. **Therefore** (without appearances, inference is impossible) **it is by
relying on evidence**
that one understands emptiness, and so forth.
Without relying on the conventional (the appearances in this world
as the method)
one cannot realize the absolute (which arises from method).

21. **The sense consciousnesses which arise from the five sense faculties**
(like the eye)
clearly experience their own objects (like form).
Without (there being) **direct sense perceptions**
one would not perceive (outer) **objects, like someone who is blind.**

22. **Having arisen based on the mental sense faculty,**
mental direct perception clearly discerns outer (like form) **and
inner** (like dreams) **objects.**
Without mental direct perception
there would be no consciousness of all the (outer and inner)
phenomena that are commonly known.

(Through direct perception the ultimate nature is comprehended
as the primordial awareness of sublime beings in meditative
equipoise. Through inference the ultimate nature is comprehended
as devoid of self by using the reasoning of interdependence. The
conventional nature is comprehended through direct perception,

for example, by the eye consciousness seeing a blue utpala flower.
The conventional nature is comprehended through inference, for
example, by inferring fire from the appearance of smoke that is
directly perceived.)

23. **By meditating well according to the scriptures** (taught by a guru who
     is a yogin),
     **yogic direct perception clearly experiences its own object, the
     ultimate** (such as seeing that objects are devoid of a self, or seeing
     the two-thousandfold universe, three-thousandfold universe, or
     innumerable universes).
     **Without yogic direct perception
     one would not see the ultimate** (objects of yogic perception), **which
     transcends ordinary objects** (seen by individuals).

24. **The experience of direct perception** (by the eye sense faculty) **clears
     away misunderstandings** (like a conch shell being yellow)
     about forms being the way they are.
     If it were the same (relationship of relying on something else to clear
     away misunderstandings) **in relation to** (experiencing) **one's own
     mind,**
     this (the mind not knowing itself through self-awareness) **would entail
     another knower** (which would need another knower to know it),
     and that would be endless.

25. **Therefore, the mind** (consciousness, which is opposite of things like
     chariots and walls), **which is clear and knowing by nature,
     knows itself in the same way that it knows** (outer) **objects.**
     It illuminates itself without depending on anything else (other than
     itself).
     This is called *self-awareness.*

26. **Whatever the other** (three) **direct perceptions experience
     is ascertained as being direct perception
     through self-awareness. Without self-awareness,
          there would be no way** (for direct perception) **to establish this.**

     (If the color blue is established by the visual consciousness, someone
     might question whether the visual consciousness itself is established

by a direct perception or by inference. For it to be established by direct perception, the sensory direct perception would be either the same or different as the consciousness that is its object, and neither of those is logically feasible. Nor could it be established by inference, because without a direct perception as its basis there is no inference.)

27. **Inference is rooted in** (it arises based on a sign experienced by) **direct perception,**
    and direct perceptions are ascertained by self-awareness (which therefore must be classified as direct perception).
    When the experience of an unmistaken mind (because not caused by delusion) **is reached** (one reaches self-awareness),
    nothing further is needed (to search for) **to establish that.**

28. **Therefore on the basis of** (sensory, mental, self-aware, and yogic) **direct perceptions**
    that are nonconceptual (in not mixing objects with names) **and unmistaken** (for sensory and mental direct perceptions),
    misunderstandings are eliminated
    about manifest phenomena (such as a vase).

29. **Understanding happens through** (the mind) **apprehending objects** (like vases) **as** (merely) **mental images**
    and mixing those images with names (such as "vases").
    This is the activity of the mental consciousness and its concepts,
    which then develop all sorts of conventional terminology (in the world, such as affirmation and negation).

30. **Mental images appear in the mind**
    even for beings (like small children and animals) **who do not understand language.**
    By using concepts they have the ability to mix (mere) **images with names** (even though they don't know the names)
    to either engage or not engage with objects (like following water and running away from fire).

31. **Without the conceptual mind** (that mixes objects with names),
    there would be no terminology (in the world), **such as negation** (of that there) **and affirmation** (of this here).

There could be no inference (of objects), **no subjects to be learned**
  (in terms of engaging and refraining),
and nothing whatsoever could be taught (by anyone).

32. **Through concepts one can** (mentally) **comprehend and affirm
  things that are not apparent** (now), **like goals for the future** (and
  thoughts of the past).
  Without inference and its concepts (without all the actions of
  accepting the good and rejecting the bad, which depend on
  evidence),
  everyone would be like newborn babies (and not know what
  anything means).

33. **By relying on a sign** (such as smoke), **one can understand things** (like
  fire, the object to be established).
  A sign is unmistaken (what is to be proven is established) **if it fulfills
  the three criteria for valid evidence:**
  the sign is present (established as being a quality) **in the subject, there
  is a positive pervasion** (of the sign with what is to be proven), **and a
  counter pervasion** (of the sign when what is to be proven is reversed).

34. **An inference** (is ascertained) **about a hidden phenomenon** (such as
  one hidden from a sense faculty)
  is proven through its relationship (whichever of the two is suitable—
  having the same nature or a causal relationship)
  with a sign
  that is established by valid direct perception (whichever of the four
  types is suitable).

35. **To establish a proof, there is the sign of being an effect** (which
  establishes the cause through being an effect in having a causal
  relationship), **the sign of having the same nature** (through having a
  relationship of the same nature),
  **and the sign of not being perceived, which refutes an object to be
  negated**
  because the object (that is suitable to be perceived) **is not perceived
  or something contradictory is perceived.**
  These are the three types of signs (which cover all reasoning).

(The best way of investigating ultimate reality is through the
reasoning taught in Madhyamaka and the Mantrayāna. If one
investigates in that way:)

36. **When seen authentically
all appearances** (of saṃsāra and nirvāṇa) **are primordially** (and
inseparably) **equal.**
(The best way of investigating conventional reality is through the
reasoning taught in the Vajrayāna. If one investigates that way:)
When one's mindstream is pure, one's perceptions (of the
environment and its inhabitants) **are pure.**
(In the natural state) **Everything is pure by nature.**

37. **Functional things are based on their having arisen** (through causes
and conditions).
Nonfunctional things (are determined as being the negative
of functional things because of not having arisen through
causes and conditions; they merely) **are based on having been
designated.**
Therefore both functional things (like a vase) **and nonfunctional
things** (like the emptiness that negates the vase)
are empty of essence (as neither of these is established in the true
nature).

38. **Ultimately in the true nature** (suchness), **the empty basis** (like a
vase)**and its emptiness** (which has been determined) **are not two
different** (specifically characterized) **things.**
(Both) **Appearance** (like a vase) **and** (its not being established,
which is its) **emptiness are inseparable** (since while appearing it is
empty and while being empty it appears) **and ineffable** (through
signs and terms since this is not an object that can be expressed or
conceptualized).
This is experienced by individual (the yogins who have realized this),
self-knowing (primordial wisdom) **awareness.**

39. **All the aspects that are established** (in the world)
are encompassed by affirmation of their existence or (affirmation
of) **what they are.**

**All the aspects that are refuted
are encompassed by negation, by showing their nonexistence** (a
negation with no implication of something else remaining) **or what
they are not** (a negation with an implication of something else
remaining).

40. **Having gained certainty** (through inference for one's own sake) **about
this way of using
affirmations** (of what is logical) **and negations** (of what is illogical) **based
on** (unmistaken) **valid cognition** (such as direct perception),
one can then (use inference for the sake of others to) **show others
proofs** (of one's own tradition as logical) **and refutations** (of the
other's tradition as illogical) **according to reasoning.**

41. **In formulating refutations** (of another's tradition), **one uses reasons
with the three criteria for valid evidence
to establish** (in one's mind) **autonomous arguments** (as in inference
for one's own sake),
and one (correctly) **refutes others by showing the consequences,
depending on what** (has been presented as a sign) **they assert** (which
does not fulfill the three criteria for valid evidence).

42. **On the conventional level** (as ordinarily seen), **since there are
appearances that do not accord with reality,
there are the way things appear and the way things are.
In dependence on impure, ordinary perception** (of worldly people)
or pure vision (of sublime beings)

43. **there are two types of conventional valid cognition,
which resemble human eyes** (which see their own objects) **and divine
eyes** (which see both human and divine objects).
These two (valid cognitions) **have their own** (unmistaken, individual)
**features
and are categorized** (differently) **by their natures, causes, effects,
and functions.**

44. (For the first of these, its nature:) **A mind that is unmistaken about
ordinary facts** (objects of knowledge)
(its cause: for example, a sense faculty for direct perception) **arises**

from having correctly apprehended (without error, like the true
nature of things) its objects (a nonconceptual sense consciousness
correctly apprehends the color blue as its object, and a conceptual
mental consciousness apprehends the presence of fire from the sign
of smoke).

(The way it functions:) Valid ordinary perception eliminates
misunderstandings (doubts) about objects
(its effect:) and fully (and unerringly) apprehends the (ordinary)
facts of a situation.

45. (For the second of these, its nature:) Limitless, timeless awareness
(the knower that is unmistaken about limitless objects of
knowledge)
(with its cause: the subjective mind in post-meditation) arises from
seeing suchness just as it is.
(The way it functions:) It eliminates misunderstandings (doubts)
about its objects, which are inconceivable (for the ordinary mind),
(its effect:) and results in knowing the entire extent of phenomena.

46. There are also two approaches to the absolute truth:
the expressible (such as being unborn and unceasing) and the
inexpressible (free from all conceptual constructs).
These (phenomena) are comprehended by the two types of valid
cognition
that investigate ultimate reality.

47. (In terms of these four approaches of valid cognition) By relying on
the former, one engages in the latter.
It is like clearing one's eye of a flaw (like cataracts).
Once the eye of valid cognition (which sees all phenomena) is
thoroughly cleansed,
one will see the reality of purity (the ultimate of conventional
investigation) and equality (the ultimate of ultimate investigation).

48. Both the (sensory and mental direct perception that are)
nonconceptual mind and the conceptual mind (that mixes objects
with names)

have undeluded aspects (like seeing a single moon while awake and
perceiving a rope as a rope), **as well as deluded aspects**
like (a sense consciousness) **perceiving two moons,** (the nonconceptual
mental consciousness seeing in) **dreams, and** (the conceptual mental
consciousness perceiving) **a rope as a snake.**
Therefore the two categories of valid cognition and nonvalid
cognition are established (as unmistaken and mistaken).

49. **Without both valid cognition and nonvalid cognition** (in their
entirety),
it would be impossible to (clearly) **distinguish what is false owing to**
delusion
from what is true and undeluded,
and there could be no philosophy (regarding the falsity of non-
Buddhist teachings and the truth of the Buddhadharma).

50. (To respond to someone who thinks valid and nonvalid cognition
are not established when investigating the ultimate:) **When one**
investigates the authentic, absolute truth (suchness),
one uses direct perception and inference, and valid cognition and
nonvalid cognition.
In the same way that these are classifications (just like affirmations
and negations, subjects and objects),
they are conceptual constructs.

51. **However, their** (specific) **nature is established as empty,**
and therefore beyond all constructs (existence, nonexistence, both,
and neither).
Emptiness is in (it pervades) **all conventional constructs**
(for example) **just like heat is in fire.**

52. **Therefore, appearance** (like a vase) **and emptiness** (its nonexistence)
(always) **abide inseparably in all phenomena**
as the means (appearance) **and what arises from the means** (its
emptiness),
so one cannot affirm one of them (like conventional reality) **and**
negate the other (like ultimate reality, or refute the ultimate

and affirm only the conventional. Appearance and emptiness are indivisible).

53. (To respond to someone who thinks valid cognition and nonvalid cognition are unnecessary:) **If one asks whether someone** (like the Prāsaṅgika school) **can engage in the absolute truth**
merely by seeing the world (by accepting relative reality),
without investigating it according to (whether or not there is) **valid cognition or nonvalid cognition,**
indeed there is nothing to prevent that (engaging in the ultimate) **from happening.**

54. **In seeing how "this"** (a sprout) **arose from "that"** (a seed),
worldly people use inference, which deduces the meaning (such as the unborn)
by relying on direct perception.
Even though they do not designate things with those words ("valid cognition" and "nonvalid cognition") **the meaning** (of valid cognition and nonvalid cognition) **is not forsaken.**

55. (To respond to the non-Buddhist Sāṃkhya school:) **Without both types of** (impure and pure) **conventional valid cognition,**
pure vision would be false (if there were only impure valid cognition and no pure valid cognition),
and for the impure level of seeing something like a conch,
one could not tell (classify) **which is true and which is false—the white conch or the yellow one.**

56. **Without both ways of investigating the absolute truth** (if there were only the expressible absolute),
one would not know (how to abide in) **the unity of the two truths**
and the absolute would be reduced to a fabricated extreme (an existential negation).
In this way, ultimate valid cognition would destroy itself (it could not withstand analysis by the reasoning that investigates the nature of things).

57. Upon investigation, relative truth—the object being
        comprehended—is not established (from the perspective of
        suchness)
     and neither are the mind (which is the six consciousnesses) and self-
        awareness, which do the comprehending.
     They (inseparable appearance and emptiness) are like the moon in
        water.
     Ultimately, the two truths are inseparable;

58. they are a single truth, the final reality of nirvāṇa (free of all
        fabrications),
     because the ultimate is in all phenomena (nothing goes beyond this).
     Consciousness (the mind that knows) and objects of knowledge are
        inseparable
     from the appearance of the kāyas (the wisdom kāya) and wisdoms,
        which are beyond notions of a center or limit.

59. After opening wide the excellent eye of wisdom (that sees through
        reasoning)
     that is profound and vast, as explained above,
     one needs to see (ascertain) the excellent path taken by
     the highly intelligent ones,

60. the descendents of the Sugata (the bodhisattvas).
     So do not let your actions be fruitless (by not tasting this in your
        being)
     by playing around when you could train systematically
     in the vehicles of the sūtras and tantras, so difficult to find (through
        your own merit).

61. Therefore those who exhibit intelligence
     possess the four reasonings as described above,
     and perform their (own) investigation without depending on others
        (like following what others say).
     This is how they become certain about the four reliances (which
        depend on the four reasonings).

62. **Without a mind like this** (which investigates with reasoning based on
    the power of facts),
    it is like the blind leading the blind.
    (Because) **Relying on** (merely worldly) **consensus, literal words**
    (taking the words literally)**, or what is easy to understand** (like
    consensus and literal words)
    goes against the understanding of the four reliances (such as relying
    on the teachings rather than the individual and so on).

    (What goes against the four reliances is: relying on the individual
    rather than the teachings, relying on the words rather than the
    meaning, relying on the provisional meaning rather than the
    definitive meaning, and relying on consciousness that sees mental
    images rather than on wisdom that sees specific phenomena.)

63. **Therefore one should not rely on individuals;**
    one should rely on the Dharma.
    One will be liberated by what is said about the path established
    through authentic reasoning,
    not by those who say it.

64. **If what an individual says is correct** (it is a genuine path established
    through reasoning),
    then it is suitable, no matter what the person is like (good or bad, etc.).
    Even the sugatas have emanated in forms such as butchers
    in order to tame sentient beings (disciples).

65. **However, if what the person teaches**
    contradicts the meaning of the Mahāyāna,
    there will be no benefit, no matter how good the person looks (such
    as his conduct),
    like the form of a buddha emanated by a demon (who has the major
    and minor marks of a buddha and perfect conduct, but his teaching
    contradicts the Mahāyāna. Therefore rely on the teachings).

66. **When intelligent ones hear and contemplate the Dharma,**
    they should rely on the meaning (of the subject matter) **and not on**
    the words (of the subject matter).

If the meaning is understood, there is no contradiction
no matter how it is expressed in words.

67. Things are named because of (a person) wanting to express an
    understandable meaning.
    Once the meaning (of what is to be understood) has been
    understood,
    if the speaker keeps trying to formulate it in words,
    it is like continuing to search for tracks after an elephant has been
    found.

68. If one elaborates further because of attachment to words,
    concepts proliferate endlessly (the words never end).
    Wandering further and further (away) from (realizing) the meaning
    (to be understood),
    immature beings just make themselves tired (and exhausted).

69. For any single phrase, like "Bring me the wood,"
    if wood is differentiated according to its locale, (time,) etc., the
    possibilities are endless.
    Once one has understood the meaning of the phrase (that is, which
    wood is intended),
    then the words (expressed) have fulfilled their purpose.

70. When a man points to the moon with his finger,
    a childish person looks at the finger instead (of looking at the
    moon).
    Foolish ones who adhere to the words (such as "look")
    have difficulty understanding (since they examine only the words),
        even though they think they understand (the meaning of the
        words when they do not examine the meaning).

71. When one engages in the meaning,
    one should know (how to distinguish) the provisional meaning and
        the definitive meaning (of the Buddha's words),
    and (mentally) rely on the definitive
    rather than the provisional.

72. **Since the Omniscient One was all-knowing** (about students and the methods for training them),
he taught the yānas in a sequence (to be gradually traversed to omniscient buddhahood),
like steps ascending a staircase (from the level of the Vaibhāṣikas to the unsurpassable Vajrayāna),
according to students' styles (type), **capacities** (sharp or dull), **and interests** (inclinations).

73. **There are eight categories of** (four) **intentions and** (four) **indirect intentions**
based on the Buddha's purpose regarding the basis (such as the aggregates) **for the intention.**
He spoke this way because it suited his purpose (he had a purpose for what he said),
whereas taking the words literally would impair valid cognition.

74. **Because of his intentions, there are various levels of teachings,**
from the four Buddhist tenets (such as Vaibhāṣika) **up to the sublime Vajrayāna.**
The aspects that are not understood by the lower levels
are clarified by the higher ones.

75. **Having seen which teachings are closer to reasoning** (for as one goes higher and higher, the teachings are based on greater experience or realization) **that accords with scripture** (of the Buddha whose faults are exhausted),
one holds to the definitive meaning (and not the provisional meaning).
(For example) **Like swans who can extract milk from water,**
those of the highest intelligence (are able to) **play in the ocean of the Buddha's speech.**

76. **The profound Vajrayāna teachings**
are concealed (not apparent) **through the six parameters** (whether they follow the literal words or not) **and the four styles of interpretation** (of the words, the meaning, and so on).

They are established through flawless reasoning (such as the four
reasonings that investigate unerringly)
along with the key instructions of the lineage (lamas, because of
being the path of Vajrayāna key instructions).

77. **All phenomena** (all that appears and exists) **are a unity**
    of primordial purity (which is established by divine appearance and
    the mind's timeless awareness) **and great equality** (of saṃsāra and
    nirvāṇa, which is established by Madhyamaka reasoning).
    The two types of accurate valid cognition
    establish (through investigation) **exactly what this means.**

78. **Without contradiction** (of what is taught in the precious tantras), **one**
    penetrates the essence
    of (teachings like illusoriness when illustrated in relation to the body)
    the *Prajñāpāramitā* (where the relative level is illusory), **the**
    creation stage (where the divine form is illusory),
    the completion stage (where the energetic mind is illusory), **and the**
    great completion (such as the spontaneous presence of radiant
    awareness),
    by means of the four styles of interpretation through (in sequence)
    the literal, general, hidden, and ultimate meanings.

    (To illustrate this with the ultimate luminosity, the word meaning
    of luminosity is taught in the Prajñāpāramitā Sūtra. The general
    meaning is like engaging in creation-stage practice as luminosity.
    The hidden meaning is the luminosity of the completion stage
    induced by the four levels of emptiness. The ultimate meaning is in
    accordance with the second part of the completion-stage practice.
    This is the realization of the fundamental, natural state in which all
    phenomena are primordially empty, together with the realization of
    the originally pure timeless awareness of the fourth empowerment.)

79. **Through that, highly intelligent ones** (the heirs of the Buddha)
    become confident (no one could rob this from them) **through**
    certainty (without relying on anyone else) **about the meaning.**
    These heirs of the Buddha hold the inexhaustible (teachings of each
    of the three yānas, the great) **treasure of the Dharma**

and the victory banner (which is victorious over whatever is
not conducive) of the (Buddha's) teachings of scripture and
realization.

80. When practicing (according to one's realization of) the definitive
meaning,
do not rely on consciousness—
(that has the nature of) the perceiving mind and what (objects) it
perceives, which depend on words and concepts.
Rely instead on nondual (without perceiver and perceived) wisdom.

81. That which has reference points (such as being empty, not empty,
both, or neither)
is the mind with a nature of (inner) apprehending the (outer)
apprehended.
Conceiving of things in this way (with reference points) is false
(because it is deluded and cannot withstand analysis).
In reality (free of all fabrications), there is no actual contact (things
are incapable of connecting).

82. (The reason is that) Whether something is conceived of as an entity
or a nonentity (the negation of an entity), or as both (an entity and
an nonentity) or neither,
no matter how it is focused on, there are still reference points (there
is movement of the mind).
The sūtras (such as the *Sūtra of the Manifold Display of Mañjuśrī*) say
that whatever is grasped (as an entity or a nonentity, etc.) through
conceptualization

83. is the domain of demons.
Conceptualization (the habitual way the mind grasps) cannot be
destroyed
by negating (an entity) or affirming (a nonentity, and vice versa,
because one is negating one concept and affirming another concept).
But if (in the true nature) one sees (in such a way that all constructs of
dualistic perception can be there) without removing or adding (or
establishing) anything, there is liberation (from reference points
and conceptual constructs).

84. (In this context, because of being) **Completely free from** (there is no)
perceiver (which focuses) **and perceived** (the objects of focus),
naturally occurring (mind is not blank emptiness), **timeless
awareness is natural luminosity** (its nature is knowingness because
it naturally arises).
Since all fabrications of the four extremes (existence, nonexistence,
etc.) **are** (naturally) **brought to an end,**
timeless awareness is said (by the Buddha) **to be supreme.**

85. **Just like someone blind from birth looking at the form of the sun,**
immature beings (with ordinary, confined perception) **have not
previously seen this** (the true nature).
No matter how they imagine it (it is empty, etc.), **they don't actually
know it** (with a mind of conviction about suchness itself),
so immature beings feel anxious (about being unable to access the
true nature free of all fabrications).

86. **However, by means of authentic scriptures** (of the definitive meaning
taught by the Buddha),
reasoning that refutes all extreme views (all the positions not taught
by the great masters),
and the guru's (who has the lineage instructions) **key instructions,**
(by generating uncontrived devotion for these) **just like a blind man
gaining sight, one will see it** (timeless awareness) **for oneself** (in
the context of being an ordinary person, one reaches the level of
acceptance or the metaphoric wisdom. And in the context of being
on the path of seeing, one has direct perception).

87. **At this time,** (extraordinary certainty arises from seeing this for
oneself) **those with** (confident) **devotion taste the nectar of the
Dharma of the Tathāgata,**
and their eye of increasing joy (which sees the true nature in the
heart)
(This is not the fragile, ordinary eye but the eye of timeless wisdom)
turns toward (and sees the dharmakāya,) **the wisdom body of the
sugatas.**

88. **At this time, all phenomena without exception** (such as saṃsāra
and nirvāṇa, happiness and suffering, good and bad, all these
conventions)
are resolved (through realization) **in the state of equality.**
One gains the inexpressible (by names and words) **confidence**
(which cannot be suppressed by worldly beings, even the gods) **of
certainty**
and (from this point on) **skill in explaining** (all) **the inexhaustible
treasure of the Dharma** (of the three yānas).

89. **By gaining expertise** (through study, contemplation, and meditation)
in the way the two truths (actually) **are,**
one sees (for oneself) **the reality of the two truths in union** (seeing
that which cannot be seen).
When this happens, it is like removing (in stages) **the** (outer) **husk
to reveal the** (subtle) **essence** (of rice, and so on).
One knows how to endeavor in (the unity of the two truths, the
ultimate) **all the skillful means** (for attaining liberation according
to the Buddha's teachings).

(What is realized through those methods is the single basic space of
phenomena. There is nothing not included in this single, ultimate
realization.)

90. **Since the sugatas know about skillful means** (for taming students
sequentially according to their styles, capacities, etc.),
all their methods (of the teachings) **are said to be a genuine path**
(because by endeavoring in them students reach the end, which is
omniscience).
This is why one gives rise to irreversible confidence (even a billion
demons cannot steal one's confidence)
in one's teachers and their teachings.

91. (Because of the essential unity of emptiness and compassion) **By
actualizing supreme, nondwelling** (in saṃsāra or nirvāṇa),
timeless awareness (as it is characterized in the *Prajñāpāramitā
Sūtra* or as naturally occurring timeless wisdom)

one is naturally liberated from the extremes of cyclic existence and
   peace (there is no need to end saṃsāra or remain in nirvāṇa).
Continuous, effortless, great compassion (for sentient beings who
   have not realized this)
boundlessly pervades all directions and times.

92. The supreme, stainless cause
   is possession of the four reliances,
   which comes from contemplating (well) how the Dharma of the
      two truths
   is (unerringly) established by the four types of reasoning.

93. From this comes forth the fruition—profound, timeless awareness,
   and when this fully manifests,
   the eight great treasures of confidence are released
   (as if they had been) from concealment in the basic space of
      (primordial) awareness (which ordinary people do not realize).

94. The treasure of memory
   is not forgetting (at all) the teachings previously studied and
      contemplated.
   (Through holding them in one's memory) The treasure of intelligence
   is discerning (through wisdom) the vast (paths and bhūmis, etc.) and
      profound (emptiness, so difficult to realize) meanings of those
      teachings.

95. The treasure of realization
   is internalizing the entire meaning (which is to be realized) of the
      sūtras and tantras.
   The treasure of retention
   is never forgetting anything one has studied (through having
      attained the four doors of retention).

96. The treasure of confidence is (mentally) satisfying all beings by
      teaching well (in accordance with the meaning).
   The treasure of the Dharma is completely protecting (by fortunate
      ones who adhere to the Dharma and defeat its opponents through
      reasoning)
   the precious treasury of the sacred Dharma.

97. **The treasure of** (relative) **bodhicitta**
    is maintaining the unbroken lineage (by beings the heirs) **of the**
    Three Jewels (through ascertaining the Awakened One, the
    Dharma he teaches, and the Saṅgha that arises from that).
    The treasure of accomplishment is attaining acceptance
    of the true nature, the equality of the unborn (through having
    meditated on the Dharma established through study and
    contemplation).

    (The first four treasures—memory, intelligence, realization, and
    retention—are the causes of confidence, and the four remaining
    ones—the treasure of the Dharma and so on—are the result of
    confidence. These eight are generally labeled as confidence because
    fearless confidence arises from possessing memory and the next
    three, and the treasures after protection of the Dharma occur due to
    having confidence. Since confidence is their primary quality, they
    are called the *eight treasures of confidence*.)

98. (Having attained these) **Those who master the inexhaustible** (each of
    them is limitless) **eight great treasures**
    and never part from them
    (become noble beings) **are praised by the buddhas and their heirs** (as
    "supreme descendents of the buddhas")
    and (quickly) **become** (awareness holders) **the protectors of the three**
    worlds.

99. **The teachings of the Buddha are valid** (because they were presented
    for the benefit of beings)
    since they (in all aspects) **are proven** (to be superior, especially to the
    non-Buddhist tenets) **through valid cognition** (which investigates
    conventional and ultimate reality and is not contradicted by
    reasoning).
    One develops certainty (the highest type of devotion, which is toward
    the teachers and the path they have taught) **through a valid path**
    (of scriptures that investigate the two truths, like those taught of
    glorious Dharmakīrti and Nāgārjuna)

of valid teachings, so one sees the truth, which is the (unsurpassable)
fruition (the pure nectar of the Dharma not known to be this way
by renowned scholars of this world, including the gods, as well as
śrāvakas, pratyekabuddhas, and bodhisattvas).

100. Having completely purified his vision (through the wisdom that
knows the true nature of everything as it is)
and perfected great compassion (that protects others from suffering),
the Sugata (the great being Śākyamuni) demonstrated the path (of
the three yānas to his disciples)
and said, "Taste the deathless nectar I have found.

101. Experience it through the four reasonings
and the four reliances."
Even though he shared (this with this world so that many fortunate
ones have experienced its taste) this nectar (again and again in the
sūtras and tantras),
it is difficult to experience its (the Buddha's teachings) supreme
(sublime) taste

102. because of our current (this contentious time) degenerate era (with
the five degenerations and especially people's mental afflictions and
views)
and the way (people reverse the four reliances and do not give rise to
certainty through reasoning) it goes against the Dharma.
(Clearly) Seeing this, my mind is filled with pure motivation (of
wanting to benefit others)
and the greatest reverence (with devotion through knowing) for the
(very precious) teachings (which rarely appear).

103. Through the (limitless) virtue of expressing (having composed) just a
little (in this short text about a vast subject) of the way (the skillful
methods of the path) to develop (in the mindstreams of fortunate
beings) the stainless (flawless) wisdom,
which comes from contemplating in this way (owing to the special,
final purpose for composing this text as was just explained above)

may all (infinite) **beings** (swiftly, without delay) **attain the state of** (the wisdom being) **Mañjuśrī** (the inseparability of basic space and timeless awareness).

104. **When the lotus of my heart turned** (one-pointedly) **toward Mañjuśrī, the sun of speech,** (the three types of devotion drew forth the sharp rays of the sunlight of his blessings so that) **it blossomed with devotion** (from a hundred flower petals of intelligence)
and this honey pollen of excellent explanations came forth.
May this increase (further and further until saṃsāra ends) **the feast** (of realization in accord with the Buddha's intentions in his words and their commentaries) **of fortunate bees** (who desire to experience the supreme taste of the Buddha's teachings).

In accord with my previous intention to write this, when the learned one Lhaksam Gyaltsen recently urged me to do so, I, Jampal Gyepé, wrote it in a single day, the 29th day of the third lunar month of the Sakyong year. Maṅgalam—may this be auspicious! There are 104 verses. May this be virtuous!

When one sees this excellent explanation of mine,
all one's large and small doubts are self-liberated,
clear intelligence arises and ascertains reality,
and the inexhaustible great treasury of confidence is found.

Appendix B

OUTLINE OF JAMGÖN MIPHAM'S VERSES
BY DEREK KOLLEENY

THE SWORD OF WISDOM THAT ASCERTAINS REALITY

I) Introductory Material 1–2
   A) The validity of the teachings and the teacher 1
   B) The author's promise to compose the text 2

II) Importance and Means of Comprehending the Two Truths 3–4
   A) Importance of the two truths as the foundation of the entire Dharma of the Buddha 3
   B) How to comprehend the two truths through reasoning 4

III) How to Comprehend the Two Truths: The Four Reasonings 5–58
   A) The First Three Reasonings 5–15
      1) General explanation of the first three reasonings 5
      2) Detailed explanation of the first three reasonings 6–14
         (a) Causation
         (b) Functional efficacy
         (c) Nature
      3) Summary of the first three principals 15
   B) The fourth reasoning valid proof 16–58
      1) General explanation 16–17
      2) Detailed explanation 18–47
         (a) Direct perception 18–28
         (b) Inference 29–46
         (c) A summary 47
      3) A response to objections 48–58

Appendix C

OUTLINE OF KHENCHEN PALDEN SHERAB'S COMMENTARY
BY DEREK KOLLEENY

THE RADIANT LIGHT OF THE SUN AND MOON

THE BEGINNING SECTION

The title
The homage
The author's purpose

THE EXPOSITION OF THE SUBJECT MATTER

1) Overview of the Main Topic
   a) The two truths—the topic to be comprehended
      i) Essence
      ii) Definitions
      iii) Characteristics
      iv) Classification
      v) Purpose
   b) The two types of reasoning—what does the comprehending
      i) Brief overview

2) Detailed Explanation of the Four Types of Reasoning
   a) General explanation of the first three reasonings as interdependent appearances
      i) The meaning of interdependence
      ii) The essence of interdependence
      iii) The categories of interdependence

   iv) Outer interdependence
   v) Inner interdependence
  b) The reasonings of causal efficacy and dependency
   i)   What they are
    (1) The meaning of the word "reasoning"
    (2) General definitions of the four reasonings
    (3) Specific definitions of the four reasonings
    (4) How they remove doubts
    (5) The object and gauge of the four reasonings
    (6) Excessive application of the four reasonings
   ii) What their purpose is
  c) The reasoning of the nature
   i)   The relative nature
    (1) Functional things and designations
   ii) The ultimate nature
   iii) Summary of the first three reasonings
  d) The reasoning of a valid proof
   i)   Brief overview
   ii) Detailed explanation

3) Direct Perception
 a) General explanation
 b) Specific explanations
   i)   Sensory direct perception
   ii) Mental direct perception
   iii) Yogic direct perception
    (1) Meaning of the term
    (2) Nature
    (3) Definition
    (4) Categories
   iv) Self-aware direct perception
 c) Summary of direct perception

4) Inference
   i)   Nature
    (1) Inference by the mind
    (2) Inference based on evidence

ii) The three criteria for valid evidence

    (1) The presence of the reason in the subject

    (2) The positive pervasion

    (3) The counter pervasion

iii) Relationship of the same nature

    (1) Causal relationship

iv) Correct signs

    (1) Definition

    (2) Categories

        (a) The sign of being an effect

            (i) Signs of a direct cause

            (ii) Signs of a prior cause

            (iii) Signs of a general cause

            (iv) Signs of a specific cause

            (v) Signs that infer causal properties

        (b) The sign of having the same nature

            (i) Categorized by the reason

                1. Signs that are dependent

                2. Signs that are independent

            (ii) Categorized by the thesis to be proven

                1. Signs that establish the meaning

                2. Signs that establish the term

        (c) The sign of not being perceived

            (i) Definition

            (ii) Categories

                1. Signs that are not suitable to appear

                2. Signs that are suitable to appear

                3. Signs of not perceiving a related object

                    a. That has the same nature

                    b. Because of not perceiving its cause

                    c. Because of not perceiving its pervader

                    d. Because of not perceiving its direct effect

                4. Signs of perceiving a contradictory object

                    a. That is an incompatible opposite

                    b. With a contradictory nature

                        i. Contradicts the nature

4. The relationship of the subject and sign is not established
5. Someone suspects the relationships is impossible
6. Someone suspects there is an underpervasion
7. Someone suspects the relationship takes both sides

(4) Indefinite signs
  (a) Definition
  (b) Categories
    (i) Uncommon indefinite signs
      1. Not different from the term being stated
      2. The subject and the sign are the same
        a. The property to be proven and the sign are the same
        b. The subject, sign, and property proven are the same
        c. The entire thesis and the sign are the same
        d. Not present in the similar or dissimilar class
        e. Does not exist in either of the two classes
        f. Imperceptible which would be in the two classes
        g. The sign is not found although in the similar class
        h. The sign is not found although in the dissimilar class
    (ii) Common indefinite signs
      a. Indefinite in relation to facts
      b. The sign pervades both classes
        i. It pervades similar class and part of dissimilar class
        ii. It pervades dissimilar class and part of similar class
        iii. It partially pervades both classes
      c. Indefinite remainder in relation to someone's mind
        i. The remainder is correct
        ii. The remainder is contradictory

      (b) Inexpressible ultimate

    (5) Summary

  viii) Response to objections

    (1) General objections

      (a) Valid cognition is impossible

      (b) Valid cognition is unestablished

      (c) Valid cognition is unnecessary

    (2) Specific objections

      (a) Objections to investigating conventional reality

      (b) Objections to investigating ultimate reality

      (c) Summary of how these two investigations are concordant

5) The Four Reliances as the Way the Four Reasonings Function

  a) General teachings

  b) Detailed explanation

    i) Rely on the teachings, not on the teacher

    ii) Rely on the meaning, not on the words

    iii) Rely on the definitive meaning, not the provisional meaning

      (1) The four intentions

        (a) Related to equality

        (b) Related to another time

        (c) Related to another meaning

        (d) Related to an individual's mind

      (2) The four indirect intentions

        (a) Related to entry

        (b) Related to characteristics

        (c) Related to antidotes

        (d) Related to change

      (3) The six parameters of the Vajrayāna

        (a) The meaning is either provisional or not provisional

        (b) There is an implicit intention or no implicit intention

        (c) The words should be taken literally or figuratively

      (4) The four styles of interpretation

        (a) The literal meaning

        (b) The general meaning

        (c) The hidden meaning

        (d) The ultimate meaning

THE CONCLUSION

1) The manner in which this text was composed
2) The dedication of virtue
3) The conclusion that makes the text complete
     i)   Mipham's closing verses and colophon
     ii) Khenchen Palden Sherab's closing verses and colophon
     iii) Aspiration prayers for the publication

Notes

1   All these opening verses were adapted from the writings of past masters. Khenchen Palden said that although he has written similar verses of his own, he felt that adapting verses from the great masters would have more blessings. He adapted this verse from one written by Jigmé Lingpa.

2   The two accumulations refer to the two accumulations of merit: conceptual merit and nonconceptual merit. The nonconceptual merit is often referred to as the accumulation of wisdom.

3   Ancient Asian armies had four divisions: elephants, horses, chariots, and foot soldiers.

4   The ten powers of a tathāgata are types of knowledge unique to a buddha: (1) knowing fact from fiction, (2) knowing how actions will ripen, (3) knowing the faculties of sentient beings, (4) knowing their dispositions, (5) knowing the inclinations of sentient beings, (6) knowing where various paths lead, (7) knowing the concentrations, (8) recollecting former lives, (9) having the superknowledge of the divine eye, and (10) knowing the extinctions of defilements.

5   Outwardly, the gods of desire are heavenly beings who live in the desire realm. Inwardly, they symbolize one's dualistic grasping and attachment.

6   Here the metaphor for the Buddha is a lion who can devour other animals, even elephants.

7   The four fearlessness are also qualities that are unique to a buddha: (1) fearlessness in proclaiming the mastery of perfect abandonment, (2) fearlessness in proclaiming the mastery of perfect realization, (3) fearlessness in showing the path to others, and (4) fearlessness in revealing hindrances on the path. The first two refer to the enlightened being and the last two refer to others.

8   Here the metaphor for the tīrthikas, the proponents of eternalism and nihilism, is elephants. The biggest animal symbolizes the greatest ignorance.

9   Continuing with the metaphor for the Buddha as a lion, snow lions live on glacier mountains.

10   The two obscurations are the emotional obscuration and the cognitive obscuration of subtle habitual grasping.

11   The two yogic disciplines refer to meditative equipoise and postmeditation. A realized being knows the wisdom of the true nature in meditation and knows the entire extent of phenomena in postmeditation.

12   This last phrase is Khenchen Palden's request for blessings so that the writing of this book will be auspicious and beneficial.

13   This stanza, like the previous one, was adapted from a verse written by Jigmé Lingpa.

14   This line refers to Padmasambhava as an emanation of the buddhas Amitābha and Amitāyus, the inseparable dharmakāya buddhas of the padma family. Literally, Amitābha means "limitless light" and Amitāyus means "limitless life."

15   This line shows the place from which Padmasambhava emanated.

16   This name means "outshines all that appears and exists," which is also Padmasambhava's activity. It is the name of his most familiar form—shown wearing a lotus hat and brocade robe, his right hand holding a vajra on his right knee and his left hand holding a vase in a skull cup on his lap.

17   This verse was written by Jamgön Mipham Rinpoché to Mañjuśrī. It is the opening verse of Mipham's commentary on Dharmakīrti's *Commentary on Valid Cognition*.

18   This line shows devotion as the basis of the path. The thousand petals indicate that his devotion is in full bloom.

19   Mawé Sengé is one of Mañjuśrī's epithets, which means "lion of speech." Khenchen Palden said this name of Mañjuśrī could also be Mawe Nyima, "sun of speech."

20   This line shows Mañjuśrī's activity.

21   This verse was written by Mipham Rinpoché. Khenchen Palden mentioned that Sarasvatī is also the female deities Tārā and Prajñāpāramitā and the great Tibetan yoginī Yeshé Tsogyal.

22   This verse was written by Shechen Öntrul Gyurmé Thubtop Namgyal of Shechen Monastery. He was a teacher of the first Kongtrul, the first Khyentsé, and Patrul Rinpoché.

23   This refers to the three sections of the Dzokchen teachings: the mind section, space section, and pith instruction section.

24   This is a poetic allusion to the Vedic myth that at one time Śiva swallowed all the water in the rivers because his meditation was disturbed by their noise. The gods, such as Brahmā, and the sages, such as Agastya, beseeched Śiva to release the waters because humans needed it to wash away their sins. Śiva did so from the top of his head, so it seemed as if Agastya had brought forth the Ganges River from underground. This is an allusion to the way the tantras were kept secret in India until the vidyādharas of the three lineages revealed them.

25   Carrying over the metaphor of water, the eight qualities of pure water are its coolness, sweetness, lightness, softness, clearness, and purity. As well, it soothes the stomach and clears and soothes the throat.

26   The Sanskrit term for "genuine masters of awareness" is *ṛṣi vidyādhara*.

27   The original version of this stanza was written by Shechen Öntrul Gyurmé Thubtop Namgyal, and it was later augmented by Khenchen Palden's root teacher, Khenpo Tenzin Drakpa.

28   This verse uses the analogy of Indra, the king of the gods, for Longchenpa. Indra is the chief god in the realm of desire. He resides on the summit of Mt. Sumeru in the Realm of the Thirty-Three. He is also known as Śakra, Ruler of the Devas. Here, the phrase used for the god realm is literally the "three positions," in comparison with

the four positions of humans. Gods have only three main postures—standing, sitting, and moving; they do not lie down and sleep like humans.

29 Indra has thirty-two vassal kings who pay homage to him. Together they comprise the thirty-three gods for whom this realm is named.

30 Indra's elephant is called Sasung in Tibetan, which means "protector of the earth." This powerful royal elephant has thirty-three heads. Indra sits on the central head and the thirty-two vassal kings sit on the surrounding heads.

31 Indra is renowned for having one thousand eyes. The great master Āryadeva once wrote: "Even though Indra has one thousand eyes, he did not realize the true nature. I have only one eye, and I have realized everything."

32 Indra's scepter or weapon is a thousand-pronged vajra. When Indra throws his vajra, it always destroys whatever it hits.

33 Longchenpa possesses the jewels of all knowledge, both Buddhist and non-Buddhist.

34 This verse was written by Kathok Situ Chökyi Gyatso, a student of Mipham Rinpoché. He wrote it after Mipham's death when he was preparing the publication of Mipham's commentary on Candrakīrti's *Entrance to the Middle Way*.

35 Calling Mipham Rinpoché the Lion of Speech is a reference to his being an embodiment of Mañjuśrī.

36 This verse was written by Mipham Rinpoché. It uses the metaphor of the teacher as Indra, holding the scepter of a thousand-pronged vajra.

37 The tertön Pema Drodul Sang-ngak Lingpa was a son of Dudjom Lingpa and lived in the nineteenth century.

38 This is a reference to Nupchen Sangyé Yeshé Rinpoché, one of the twenty-five main students of Padmasambhava, who was particularly connected with the yidam Mañjuśrī Yamantaka.

39 This is one of the names of Dudjom Lingpa, a great tertön of the late nineteenth century.

40 This is another name for Padmasambhava.

41 The eight great treasures of confidence are the treasures of memory, intelligence, realization, retention, confidence, the Dharma, bodhicitta, and accomplishment.

42 The four right discriminations are: right discrimination of the meaning, right discrimination of the Dharma, right discrimination of the explanation of words, and right discrimination of the confidence to teach. For a lengthy discussion of these, see Mipham 2012.

43 Mañjughoṣa, which means "gentle and melodious," is another name for Mañjuśrī.

44 The three levels of the world refers to the planes above the earth where the gods dwell, the earth where the humans dwell, and below the earth where the nāgas dwell.

45 Mipham Rinpoché has many names. Khenchen Palden's main teacher, Khenpo Tenzin Drakpa, wrote a special praise to Mipham Rinpoché that includes twenty of Mipham's names. Mipham Jamyang Namgyal Gyatso means "invincible Mañjughoṣa (gentle and melodious) completely victorious ocean" and Jampal Gyepé Dorjé means "Mañjuśrī (gentle and glorious) joyful vajra."

46   Nupchen Sangyé Yeshé was one of the twenty-five disciples of Guru Padmasam-
      bhava. Both Jamgön Mipham and Khenchen Palden Sherab are considered emana-
      tions of Nupchen Sangyé Yeshé.

47   When consulted on this point, Khenchen Palden quoted Candrakīrti's *Entrance to
      the Middle Way*, saying that "profound" relates to the true nature, or emptiness, and
      "vast" refers to everything else. So the profound and vast meanings encompass both
      the ultimate truth and the relative truth.

48   Titles can show different facets of a text. Some titles show the meaning, or the main
      words, or a metaphor, or the place where the teaching was given, or the name of the
      person who requested it.

49   In Khenchen Palden's commentary below on the third line of the verse, he says these
      three points are the validity of the teachings, the validity of the teacher, and that
      these are established through valid cognition. Before that he interprets this verse as
      a whole in relation to gaining certainty through the three types of investigation (di-
      rect perception for manifest phenomena, inference for hidden phenomena, and valid
      scriptures for very hidden phenomena), and through valid inference based on ful-
      filling the three criteria for valid evidence. This last aspect—valid inference with the
      complete three criteria for valid evidence—is the explanation Jamgön Mipham gives
      in his annotated commentary on this line of verse (see Appendix A).

50   Khenchen Palden said that the Sanskrit word *siddhyanta* should be spelled with a "y,"
      and not *siddhānta*, as is commonly done.

51   Orgyen is another name for Padmasambhava.

52   These four mistaken views are discussed in Padamasambhava's *Garland of Views*.
      Khenchen Palden orally explained these as follows: (1) Materialists are "flat ones"
      (*phyal ba*) whose interests are confined to the surface of life, like having enough food
      and a nice place to live. (2) Hedonists "throw far away" (*rgyangs 'phen*). They think
      there is no past or future karma, and are only interested in present enjoyment. (3) Fun-
      damentalists "depend on limits" (*mur thug*). They are narrow-minded and rigid about
      following rules because they fear punishment by a god. (4) Extremists "stay at the edge"
      (*mu stegs*; Sanskrit: *tīrthika*). Their tenet systems are based on the extreme views of eter-
      nalism and nihilism.

53   These are the two main Buddhist approaches, the Sūtrayāna and the Tantrayāna.
      Both of them transcend worldly views.

54   This analogy refers to all views being concepts. Whether worldly or transcendent,
      they are all conceptual. (KPS)

55   The implication is to accept the one closest to reality and leave the rest.

56   The numbering system for commentary on the verses sometimes has only the verse
      number (e.g., 1.), and sometimes has the verse number followed by the line number
      (e.g., 1:1).

57   The three types of investigation, which are also known as the three types of valid cog-
      nition, are direct perception for manifest phenomena, inference for hidden phenom-
      ena, and valid scriptures for very hidden phenomena.

58   The three criteria for valid evidence are the presence of the reason in the subject of debate, the positive pervasion, and the counter pervasion.

59   The three aspects of a valid inference are inference based on conventional usage, inference based on the power of facts, and inference based on trust.

60   Khenchen Palden emphasized that certainty refers to the first three lines of the verse: that the teachings are unmistaken, that the teacher has eliminated all errors, and that valid cognition brings a doubtless mind.

61   The reasoning of causal efficacy is the first of the four reasonings, which will be explained in detail in chapter 5. Basically it means that causes do indeed produce effects; causes are "efficacious."

62   The formation of correct syllogisms, based on fulfillment of the three criteria of valid evidence, will be fully explained in chapter 10.

63   Ultimate wisdom refers to the omniscience of a buddha. It is beyond the wisdom experienced by bodhisattvas on the bhūmis. (KG)

64   The following two excerpts are from the *Commentary on Valid Cognition*.

65   This is the second verse of the *Entrance to the Middle Way*.

66   This is an epithet of Vajrapāṇi, the chief compiler of the Vajrayāna teachings.

67   Relinquishment refers to clearing away the two obscurations and realization refers to perfecting the two wisdoms.

68   The Buddha's qualities allow him to know what is appropriate for maturing different disciples. (KPS)

69   The Tibetan terms are *khams* (styles), *dbang* (capacities), and *bsam pa* (intentions). *Khams* is *dhātu* in Sanskrit, and in this context is like the Tibetan *rigs*, which means "family, caste, clan, or group." The Mahāyāna teachings mention five families or types of beings: śrāvakas, pratyekabuddhas, bodhisattvas, indeterminate, and cut-off. These are discussed in detail in Gampopa's *Ornament of Precious Liberation*. *Dbang* in this context describes someone's capacity or ability. Five factors are considered in determining someone's capacity: how much devotion, joyful effort, memory, meditative stability, and wisdom they have. *Bsam pa* refers to a person's intentions, wishes, or inclinations. (KPS)

70   This quote comes from the *Prajñāpāramitā Sūtra*. (KPS)

71   Turning the wheel of the Dharma entails more than repeating the Dharma teachings taught to one previously. It means teaching on the basis of personal realization. (KG)

72   This is an example of reasoning by the power of fact. Unless one knows the subject matter, one cannot teach it to others. (KPS)

73   The previous quotations described Buddha's wisdom. The following quotations describe his compassion.

74   Khenpo Gawang suggested leaving the title in Tibetan, as it is simply a name. Khenchen Palden had said that *spar* means "lighting up," like turning on a light, and *khab* means "area," so it is an area that is illuminated with no darkness remaining.

75   For instance, the four Vedas are posited as having no human authorship and as being the divine word. They are said to have come from Brahmā, the four-faced creator of

the world. This lack of human authorship supposedly qualifies the Vedas as scripture. However, Dharmakīrti does not accept this because it cannot be verified through valid cognition. (KPS)

76   In other words, knowing the truth purifies, or removes, one's ignorance.

77   Asaṅga's text, the *Levels according to Yogācāra*, is a very large text with five sections that discuss the levels of the Buddhist path. One of its sections has become renowned on its own as the *Bodhisattvabhūmi*, or *Levels of the Bodhisattva Path*.

78   The first two qualities stated in the first three lines are the six faults, and the last qualities in each line are the three virtues.

79   The Sanskrit word *śāstra*, usually translated as "treatise" or "commentary," has the two functions explained here: *śā* means "transforming" and *tra* means "protecting." Khenchen Palden said that although other philosophical systems say they have *śāstras*, their treatises do not perform the function of transforming and protecting like the Buddhist teachings do. The Tibetan word for *śāstra* is *bstan bcos*, which has two parts: *bstan*, which means "teaching," and *bcos*, which means "transforming."

80   The first two excerpts by Maitreya are from the *Sublime Continuum*.

81   The Sanskrit for "genuine sage" is *ṛṣi*. This is someone whose body, speech, and mind are honest, straightforward, and free of negativity.

82   This excerpt is the first two lines of Dignāga's *Compendium of Valid Cognition*. The entire second chapter of Dharmakīrti's *Commentary on Valid Cognition* covers only these two lines. (KPS)

83   Non-Buddhists are said to have attachment to the self and the world because they do not have a correct understanding of emptiness. Sugatas are very beautiful because they are free of clinging.

84   Those who are still on the path (which means the first four of the five Mahāyāna paths) must return to saṃsāra. In contrast, a sugata is irreversibly freed from saṃsāra.

85   Here, "those beyond training" refers to arhats. Although arhats do not return to saṃsāra, sugatas have completely removed the two obscurations, and this makes their enlightenment more complete than that of arhats.

86   A buddha protects beings from suffering by showing them the cause of suffering and the way out of suffering.

87   This is the opening verse in Vasubandhu's *Treasury of the Abhidharma* (*Abhidharmakośa*).

88   This verse is from a special praise of the Buddha written about one hundred years after Buddha passed away. The author compares the greatness of the Buddha with the ancient Indian gods like Śiva, Viṣṇu, Brahmā, and Indra. He alternates a verse about a particular god's ability with a verse about the Buddha's similar but greater ability because of his wisdom. For example, Śiva had the power to destroy a city of harmful demi-gods with his fiery arrow, but Buddha used the arrow of wisdom to destroy anger itself, which makes the Buddha clearly superior. In these verses the author not only praises the Buddha but he also gives the Buddha's teachings. (KPS)

89   See note 57.

90 See note 58.

91 See note 59.

92 The phases of testing the quality of gold are comparable to the three turnings of the wheel of the Dharma, and can be correlated with the three types of investigation. In the first turning, one burns the gold of manifest phenomena by using direct perception. In the second turning one cuts the gold, going in to the hidden level of emptiness by using inference. In the third turning one rubs the gold and reveals the very hidden buddha nature by relying on valid scripture. So the Buddha's teachings have no internal contradictions, nor are they annulled by direct perception or correct inference. (KPS)

93 This verse was spontaneously composed in a dream by Khenchen Palden Sherab while he was in the hospital in New York City in 1981.

94 The reasoning of dependency uses the evidence of being an effect to show its cause. Since the teachings (the effect) are genuine, the teacher (the cause) is genuine.

95 This homage benefits the author because if an object of homage is genuine and worthy of respect, then the author who pays homage must also be good, and what he writes should be trustworthy and worth reading. (KG)

96 "The topic to be comprehended" or the "object of comprehension" is a translation of *gzhal bya*, that which can arise as an authentic object of valid cognition. Objects of comprehension are the phenomena of saṃsāra and nirvāṇa as they appear and are experienced on the empirical level. This term can be contrasted with *shes bya*, an object of knowledge, that which can arise as an object of the mind. According to this distinction, objects of knowledge include even imaginary objects like a rabbit's horn. Padmakara Translation Committee 2005, 122, 393.

97 The two types of reasoning are the reasoning that investigates conventional reality and the reasoning that investigates ultimate reality.

98 This verse is from Nāgārjuna's most famous Madhyamaka text: *Root Wisdom of the Middle Way*.

99 *Clear Words* is Candrakīrti's commentary on Nāgārjuna's *Root Wisdom of the Middle Way*. Here "aggregates" specifically refer to the five *skandhas* of an individual: form, feeling, perception, mental formations, and consciousness. The form aggregate includes all materiality as well as the physical body.

100 The first two lines of this excerpt are part of the root text of *Clear Words* and the following two lines are part of Candrakīrti's autocommentary on that verse.

101 Things with their own specific characteristics, or specific phenomena, are impermanent, functional things encountered through sense perception. They are located in a given time and place, endowed with specific properties, and produced by causes. They are contrasted with general phenomena, which are general ideas that enable us to identify and classify things. Generalities are nonfunctional things that cannot be pinpointed in space and time. They are static, causally ineffective, conceptually constructed entities.

102 "Something other" refers to words and thoughts. (KG)

103 The sixth sense is the mental sense faculty.

104 Two lion heads joined at the neck, facing opposite directions, is an ancient image for keeping every angle covered. Here valid cognition is watching the relative level, and Madhyamaka philosophy is watching the absolute level, so no mistakes can creep in while comprehending what is true.

105 Equality is another way of saying emptiness, in that all phenomena are equal in being empty of inherent existence.

106 The point here is that all things are interdependent, whether they are dependently arisen owing to causes, like functional things, or are dependently designated by concepts, like space and cessation.

107 The *Formation of Words in Two Volumes* is a commentary on the *Mahāvyutpatti, The Great Volume of Precise Understanding*, which is a standardized dictionary of Sanskrit-Tibetan terminology compiled in the ninth century in Tibet.

108 For a brief description of the perpetuating cause, see chapter 6 and the subdivisions of effective active causes.

109 Among the twelve nidānas (the twelve links of interdependent origination), three are connected with afflictions: ignorance, longing, and grasping. Two are connected with karma: formations and becoming. The remaining seven are connected with suffering: consciousness, name and form, the six senses, contact, feeling, birth, and old age and death.

110 The outer level refers to the world and the inner level refers to sentient beings.

111 As for what "second" refers to, the text said: "The first three reasonings will be explained by means of a general teaching on the interdependence of appearances (this was chapter 4). This will be followed by individual explanations of the reasonings of cause (chapter 5), effect (chapter 6), and nature (chapter 7), and then the three reasonings will be summarized."

112 There are two distinct Tibetan words that sound similar and are written in English as *rigpa*. This *rigpa* is spelled *rigs pa* in Tibetan, and means "reasoning." It is a different word from the Tibetan word *rig pa,* which means "knowledge" or "awareness."

113 Dharmabhadra is the Sanskrit form of Chokyi Zangpo, Rongzom Paṇḍita's given name.

114 *Nyāya* and *yukti* are Sanskrit terms that were translated into Tibetan as *rigs pa.*

115 The attainment of fearlessness is a special quality of a buddha. For instance, the *Sublime Continuum* lists four types of fearlessness that are unique to a fully enlightened being.

116 Production refers to the reasoning of causal efficacy and "what is brought forth" refers to the reasoning of dependency.

117 The Tibetan literally says, "there is heat in a fire crystal." A fire crystal, or sun crystal, is a substance used to start a fire, like Westerners use a magnifying glass. This is expressed in Tibetan as the crystal having the natural quality of fire within it.

118 The lower two Buddhist philosophical schools, the Vaibhāṣikas and Sautrāntikas, are materialists in that they assert that substantial phenomena truly exist. From the higher schools' perspective, this is a mistaken view.

119 In other words, the nature becomes a causally effective thing.

120 The *Discourse on Valid Cognition* is another name for the *Compendium of Valid Cognition* by Dignāga. In this excerpt, the first four lines are the root verse and the ensuing paragraph is Dignāga's autocommentary on these four lines.

121 "Handle" is a translation of the Tibetan word *lung* in the phrase *lung Anuyoga*. When asked about this phrase in their 2009 Shedra teachings, Khenchen Palden Sherab and Khenpo Tsewang Dongyal said that although *lung* is usually translated as "transmission" or "scripture," it also has the less common meaning of "handle." In this phrase *lung* is a metaphor: Anuyoga is like a handle holding Mahāyoga and Atiyoga together. If one understands the meaning of the Anuyoga teachings, then one can effectively hold the Mahāyoga and Atiyoga teachings.

122 Much of this section on the six causes, five effects, and four conditions is identical or a paraphrase of Mipham's writings on these topics in *Gateway to Knowledge*, vol. 3, 252–59.

123 A formless mind refers to the mind of a sentient being in the formless realms.

124 The four types of sustenance are food, sleep, exercise, and meditation.

125 Ancient soldiers would stand their spears on end and lean them together to form a rack. The spears hold each other up, like teepee or tent poles.

126 Noble beings in the formless realms have no physical elements within their respective states and therefore possess no visible vows. However, it is claimed that those born in the formless realms still possess their previous vows, since there is no reason why their undefiled vows from the previous realm would have been abandoned.

127 The realms mentioned here are the desire realm, the form realm, and the formless realm. For the desire realm, which includes humanity, the five omnipresent mental states are intention, feeling, discrimination, attention, and contact. These five factors are always present in every mental factor. (KG)

128 The *Verse Summary of the Gateway to Knowledge* is Jamgön Mipham's verse summary of his own text written for easy memorization of the main points. How the five effects are applied can be seen in Jamgön Mipham's commentary on Maitreya's *Distinguishing Phenomena from Their Intrinsic Nature*, in the section on the functions of nonconceptual wakefulness: "The last of these four forms of complete understanding relates to the functions of nonconceptual wakefulness. One such function is that one distances oneself from the causes of conceptuality since one has conquered their emergence. This is the *result of individual effort*. It also bestows undefiling bliss, which is unexcelled in character, since one realizes all phenomena in an unerring manner and accomplishes perpetual and everlasting bliss. This is the *dominant result*. Wakefulness also divests one of the emotional and cognitive obscurations, as one conquers the subtle developers and their habitual tendencies. This is the *result of separation*. Subsequent to the attainment of nonconceptual wakefulness, wakefulness

unerringly realizes the specific characteristics of phenomena. This wakefulness has unhindered access to all forms of knowledge. This is the *result that resembles its cause.* Finally, purifying buddha fields, completely maturing sentient beings, and establishing and perfecting the qualities of total omniscience in one's own mind stream and granting them to others, when considered a single function, are the *result of maturation.* These five are the distinct functions of nonconceptual wakefulness." Dharmachakra Translation Committee 2013, 55–56.

129   Since the human body is the effect of previous karma, it is a good example of the way an effect could be a support for mundane happiness and suffering.

130   A Vajrayāna example of the four conditions can be found in Jamgön Mipham's commentary on the *Guhyagarbha Tantra,* titled *Luminous Essence:* "As for the four conditions [for empowerment], the causal condition is a devoted and knowledgeable student who is a suitable recipient for the bestowal of empowerment. The ruling condition is a genuine master who is competent when it comes to the path of mantra and is, therefore, capable of conferring an empowerment that blesses the mind of the disciple. The observed object condition consists of substances, mantras, and absorptions of an extraordinary potency. The [similar] immediate condition consists of the preceding empowerments and rituals, since the former empowerments open the gate to those that follow." Mipham 2009, 91.

131   The twelve branches of the Buddha's speech are the sūtra sections, proclamations in song, prophesies, poetic statements, special aphorisms, ethical narratives, illustrative narratives, ancient narratives, former life stories of the bodhisattvas, extensive teachings, miraculous accounts, and decisive explanations. These twelve are discussed as the first of the four right discriminations, the right discrimination of the Dharma, in Mipham 2012, 67–75.

132   An object of knowledge is defined as that which is suitable to be an object of the mind, and includes even imaginary objects like a rabbit's horn.

133   "Emptiness free of extremes is proved by the two basic aspects of logic: refuting and establishing. Madhyamaka has five great reasonings: the first four are connected with refuting misunderstandings and the fifth is connected with establishing correct understanding. In terms of what is refuted, first, causes are analyzed and invalidated through the reasoning called the *diamond fragments.* Second, results are analyzed and invalidated through the reasoning called the *production and cessation of existence and nonexistence.* Third, causes and results are analyzed together and invalidated through the reasoning called the *production and cessation of the four alternatives.* Fourth, the nature itself is analyzed and invalidated through the reasoning called *free of one and many.* And fifth, emptiness is established by analyzing appearances through the reasoning of interdependence." Ringu Tulku 2006, 199–200.

134   Definitions, or defining characteristics, and the thing defined (definiendum) are very important in the study of logic. Nothing qualifies as having a particular definition besides the object being defined, even though some other things may potentially possess those characteristics without having them as their distinguishing and overriding

characteristics. Sermey Khensur Lobsang Tharchin Rinpoché 2005, 26. A definition is perfect when it eliminates the defects of being too narrow, too broad, or impossible to apply. Padmakara Translation Committee 2005, 276.

135 Here the two types of valid cognition are direct perception and inference.

136 Analytical speculation (*yid dpyod*) is also called a *correctly assuming consciousness*. It is a conceptual consciousness that arrives at its conclusion either without reason, in a manner contrary to correct reasoning, or based on correct reasoning but without bringing it to its full conclusion. Most of the information we take in, for example by hearing teachings or by reading, falls into this category. Much is just accepted, and even most of that which we do contemplate and analyze has not been realized with the full force of inference. Because of the weak basis from which it is generated, it is not unfailing and can easily be overturned when presented with an opposite viewpoint. Lati Rinpochay 1980, 23.

137 Inattentive perception (*snang la ma nges pa*) does not ascertain its object because the attention is directed elsewhere or the duration of the consciousness is too brief to be noticed. Chapa would say that although it is a direct perception, it is not a valid direct perception because it is not unfailing and does not newly realize its object.

138 Subsequent cognition is a mind that holds firmly to an object that has been previously realized by valid cognition, which serves as its perpetuating cause. Its abbreviated definition is "realizing what has previously been realized." Chapa would say that this is not a valid cognition because it is not newly realized, and valid cognition entails being a new, unmistaken mind. Sermey Khensur Lobsang Tharchin Rinpoché 2005, 190, 212, 380.

139 There is a difference in the terms "mistaken consciousness" (*khrul shes*) and "wrong consciousness" (*log shes*). Mistaken consciousness includes all conceptual consciousnesses, even correct inference. This is because the object that appears to a conceptual consciousness is a mental image and not the object itself. However, in relation to the mental image, a correct inference is a reliable form of knowledge; it is valid cognition. In contrast, wrong consciousness is mistaken with respect to the object being got at, the object it comprehends. Wrong consciousness can be either nonconceptual, like seeing a white snow mountain as blue, or conceptual, like conceiving of a truly existent self. Lati Rinpochay 1980, 21, 25.

140 There are two types of doubt: doubt tending toward the fact and doubt tending away from the fact. Sometimes a third type is added: doubt that tends equally toward and away from the fact.

141 For example, the word "vase" refers to a particular, functional object. The general attributes of a vase, like being produced, being impermanent, and so on, are unstated but implicit in that term.

142 As for which of these fits which description, in terms of having an effect, specific phenomena are capable of performing functions and general phenomena are incapable of performing functions. In terms of their identity, general phenomena have similar things in common and specific phenomena do not; they are unique objects. In terms

of applying terminology to these objects, specific, functional objects are stated directly and general, nonfunctional objects are indirectly implied. In terms of the subjective consciousness involved, general appearing objects are known through concepts and specific appearing objects are known without concepts. In terms of the way these two types of objects appear, specific objects are manifest phenomena and general objects are hidden phenomena.

143 See note 58.

144 In Tibet, it is customary to see the shape of a rabbit in the full moon, whereas in the West it is customary to see the face of a man in the moon.

145 See note 57. In other words, we can make inferences by trusting scriptures written by highly realized beings on the basis of their direct perception.

146 According to the Sūtrayāna, there are three categories of superior beings: śrāvaka arhats, pratyekabuddhas, and bodhisattvas.

147 "And so forth" refers to other ways of describing the ultimate nature, such as suchness, clarity, and awareness-emptiness.

148 This is Dharmakīrti's *Nyāyabindu*, a relatively short text that is a distillation of his seven treatises on logic.

149 The traditional examples of distorted consciousness are: because of an eye disease, two moons are seen at the same time; because of rapid movement, one sees a twirling firebrand as a circle; because of being on a moving boat, the trees on the shore seem to be moving; and because of the disturbance of the gaseous and the bilious elements in the body, objects look fiery.

150 This is the Sautrāntika view, not the Madhyamaka view.

151 For both direct perception and inference, the cognition itself is the result, for the nature of cognition is comprehension of an object. Direct perception and inference are called *means of cognition* because they appear to involve an activity. Tachikawa 1971, 128.

152 "In explaining the identity of *pramāṇa* [valid cognition] with its effect, Dignāga (in the *Compendium of Valid Cognition* i:11) says that pramāṇa, its object, and the effect are not three different entities. They can all be represented by a single cognition. The object would be the cognized aspect, *pramāṇa* would be the cognizing aspect, and the cognition itself would constitute the effect." Gangopadhyaya 1971, 130, translator's note 34.

153 Vinītadeva was an Indian Buddhist scholar who lived around 700 CE. Tāranātha said that Vinītadeva was an ācārya of Nālandā monastery. He wrote twelve commentaries, mostly on the works of Dharmakīrti, which are in the *Tengyur*, the Buddhist canon of commentarial literature. His commentary on Dharmakīrti's *Essence of Reasoning* has been translated into English by Mrinalkanti Gangopadhyaya in *Vinītadeva's Nyāyabindu-Ṭīkā*.

154 "Dissimilar type" means things that are contradictory, incompatible, or opposite.

155 Dharmottara (c. 740–800) wrote several important commentaries on the works of Dharmakīrti, including a commentary on the *Essence of Reasoning*, which is translated into English in Stcherbatsky 2008, vol. 2.

156 Direct perception contacts its object directly and unmistakenly, but conceptualization must get at its object through the medium of a mental image. The mental image appears as if it was the actual object, but it is not. In this respect a conceptual consciousness is mistaken about the object appearing to it. Lati Rinpochay 1980, 21.

157 Dignāga is distinguishing the Buddhist definition of direct perception as nonconceptual from the non-Buddhist definition of direct perception as conceptual.

158 The "early valid cognition view" is based on Chapa's interpretation, which says that direct perception is not necessarily valid cognition, because valid cognition entails newly realizing the object. This is contrasted with the "later valid cognition view," which is Sakya Paṇḍita's interpretation that direct perception is always valid cognition, and there is no need to specify that the object is newly realized. The Nyingma lineage holds the position of Sakya Paṇḍita.

159 In other words, specific phenomena are perceived in the present instant only, and in being specific they are not mixed up with any other objects. Validly cognizing them is similar to taking a photo with a camera: it happens instantly and the objects are not mixed up.

160 Jamyang is the Tibetan for Mañjughoṣa, another of Mañjuśrī's names.

161 The dependent nature (*gzhan dbang*) is one of the three natures explained in Cittamātra and Yogācāra philosophy. In general the dependent nature refers to consciousness, which is colored by various habitual tendencies, which can be pure or impure.

162 For sensory direct perception, the objects other than themselves are form, sound, smell, taste, and touch, and for mental direct perception the object other than itself is a mental phenomenon.

163 Yogic direct perception, while perceiving the ultimate nature of the mind, also perceives appearances.

164 An example of different names with the same nature is: being a functional thing, being a product, and being impermanent.

165 They have the same nature in that they are pervaded by self-knowing awareness.

166 The Nyāya is a non-Buddhist, Indian philosophical school that emphasizes logic and epistemology, and asserts that direct perception is not valid cognition.

167 The Vaiśeṣika is a non-Buddhist school of atomists; the Vaibhāṣika is a Buddhist school of atomists. They say that sensory and mental direct perception are enough; there is no need for self-aware direct perception.

168 The Cārvāka is a non-Buddhist school that holds the view of nihilism.

169 As noted in the root verse 20, "and so forth" refers to other ways of describing the ultimate nature, such as suchness, clarity, and awareness-emptiness.

170 Generally speaking, when a Tibetan philosophical text refers to the *Treatise* (*bstan bcos*) it is referring to Nāgārjuna's *Root Wisdom of the Middle Way*.

171 "Their" refers to śrāvaka arhats, pratyekabuddhas, and bodhisattvas.

172 The four permutations are the "four corners," or *mu bzhi*. For example, if there are two things, A and B, then (1) there are things that are A and not B, (2) things that are B and not A, (3) things that are both A and B, and (4) things that are neither A nor B.

173 This is because self-aware direct perception and yogic direct perception are not dependent on the senses.

174 Although mistaken sensory perception is dependent on the senses, it is not direct perception because it is mistaken.

175 Two instances of consciousness cannot occur simultaneously, and for two instances of consciousness that occur sequentially, no contact can be proven between them. How could the second instance know and verify the first?

176 Conceptualization is self-awareness because it is inference, which must be based on direct perception, which is based on self-awareness.

177 This refers to the threefold reification of agent, action, and object.

178 Inference is indeed mistaken, but only in one sense: that which appears to it is not the object's true nature. What appears is a mental construct, but that construct can be correct and a true reflection of the phenomenon, and can enable one to experience the phenomenon's true nature. Rogers 2009, 23.

179 Concerning direct perception, the *Essence of Reasoning* was quoted in chapter 9 as stating: "A directly perceiving consciousness itself is established as the effect of valid cognition." Inference is similar; the fact that a correct inference occurs is its own effect.

180 A class is defined as a set or category of things having a property or feature in common and differentiated from other things by kind or quality.

181 The dissimilar class in a proof is that which does not exist in accord with the way the property to be proven is stated in the proof. There are three types of dissimilar class: (1) the thing does not exist, like a rabbit horn; (2) The object is an overextension, it is too large to be in a similar class; for example, an object of knowledge is in a dissimilar class to impermanence since objects of knowledge include permanent phenomena as well as impermanent phenomena; and (3) it is a contradictory phenomenon, like a permanent phenomenon in relation to an impermanent phenomenon. Sermey Khensur Lobsang Tharchin Rinpoché 2005, 290, 306.

182 The "locus" is another word for the subject of the argument, the basis for the argument. This is the particular person, place, or thing in which the existence or nonexistence of the sign is to be inferred. Prasad 2002, 48.

183 In *Essence of Reasoning* Dharmakīrti defines a product as a positive entity that depends on the functioning of something else for the production of its nature. Gangopadhyaya 1971, 164.

184 The word "pervasion" is sometimes translated as the "entailment" or the "invariable concomitance" of the relationship. "Pervasion" is used here because it is the literal

meaning of the Tibetan word *khyab*, and because it expresses the fact that the sign is pervaded or covered by the property to be proven.

185 For example, if fire is absent, it is impossible for smoke to be present. If the opposite of fire is present, such as a lake, it is impossible for smoke to be present.

186 The similar class consists of things compatible with the property to be proven in that proof. For example, for impermanence, the similar class would include things like cups, humans, and rain. The dissimilar class for impermanent things is nonimpermanent things, like uncompounded space and nirvāṇa. The similar and dissimilar classes are called *one-pointed features*, which means that similarity or dissimilarity need to apply in one respect only—in having or not having the predicated property mentioned in that argument. For example, consider the syllogism: "On that smoky hill there is fire because there is smoke." To be in the similar class to the hill on which there is smoke, there needs to be similarity in only one respect: that it has fire. No other similarity is required. A hearth is in the similar class to the hill in this respect. To be the dissimilar class, a thing must be dissimilar only in not having fire as the property to be proven, so a pond would be in the dissimilar class. See Prasad 2002, 42.

187 One way to understand the three criteria is by using formulas. Syllogisms are usually stated in this way: A (the subject) is or has B (the property to be proven) because of C (the sign/reason). A sample syllogism is: The subject, a lemon (A), is a fruit (B) because it is a citrus (C). The presence of the reason in the subject is seeing whether C is a quality of A. (Is a citrus present in a lemon? Yes.) If so, next, the positive pervasion is seeing whether the presence of C entails the presence of B. (Does being a citrus entail being a fruit? Yes.) The counter pervasion is seeing whether the negation of B entails the negation of C. (Does negating fruit negate citrus? Yes.) If these three criteria are fulfilled, then there is a valid proof.

188 For the presence of the reason in the subject to be contextually faultless, there must be an appropriate person who has some doubt about the thesis and consequently is investigating the matter. For example, no one doubts that sound is the object of hearing (its definition), or that sound is the object of smelling. So there is no presence of the reason in the subject when one of these logical signs is used. However, someone could have perceived that sound is something produced but doubt that sound is impermanent; this person would be an appropriate respondent.

189 One can use something as an example if one has already ascertained that it fits the thesis. In the syllogism "Sound is impermanent because it is produced, like a pot," the pot is the basis, or example, which has been previously ascertained to be impermanent.

190 A correct similar example is something that has already been ascertained to fit the pervasion and the thesis. In the syllogism, "Sound is impermanent because it is produced, like a pot," the pervasion is that if something is produced, it is necessarily impermanent. A pot fits this pervasion since it is produced, and it also fits the thesis by being impermanent.

191 A correct dissimilar example is something that has already been ascertained to fit the counter pervasion, which means it is the opposite of the pervasion. For this syllogism, a correct dissimilar example would be something that is not produced, like space.

192 What makes an inference valid for Dharmakīrti is that it deals with genuine qualities that causally interact, and their relationship can be either of the same nature or of causal dependency. Knowledge of either of these two natural relations is sufficient to guarantee our knowledge of universal concomitance. Such natural relations would make the logical sign concomitant with the property to be inferred. Matilal 1998, 122, 127.

193 *Ascertaining Valid Cognition* is the second of the seven treatises on logic by Dharmakīrti. It is a verse and prose abridgment of Dharmakīrti's *Commentary on Valid Cognition*. More than half the verses are borrowed from the principal work. The *Essence of Reasoning* is a further abridgement of the same subject. The latter two texts have three chapters: one on sense perceptions, one on inference, and one on syllogisms.

194 As discussed in chapter 6 on the six causes, the substantial cause and its cooperating conditions are a subdivision of the producing cause, which is the first type of active cause. The substantial cause is like the seed that gives rise to a sprout, or the way a previous moment of consciousness gives rise to a later moment of consciousness. The cooperating conditions are externally like water, fertilizer, warmth, etc., for a seed, and internally like the observed object condition and the sense faculty for a consciousness.

195 An example of dependently designated causes is a mother and child. Designations can be said to "cause" each other because there is no mother unless there is a child, and no child unless there is a mother.

196 The Buddhist view is that a thing is delineated by conceptually isolating it by excluding everything it is not. A mental image serves the purpose of excluding everything other than the represented object, so that it describes the image of a table as an appearance as opposed to describing it as everything that is not the table. See Klein 1998, 206.

197 For example, in the syllogism "Sound is impermanent because it is produced," everything that is not impermanent is excluded, but in terms of having a relationship, "being produced" is not discarded because it has the same nature as "impermanent."

198 For example, in the syllogism "On the smoky hill there is fire because there is smoke," everything that is not fire excluded, but in terms of having a relationship, smoke is not discarded because it arose from fire. They have a causal relationship.

199 For example, when hot and cold come together, they cannot continue with the same strength they had alone. Since they are opposites, they are "harmed" by each other. Both of them diminish in strength.

200 There are two kinds of formal arguments: the syllogism, which is a statement asserted by the proponent, and the consequence, which is a response to the opponent's assertion that shows its unwanted consequences. The typical syntactic structure of a

syllogism is that the subject is or has the property to be proven because of the logical sign.

201 Here the word "pervasions" explicitly indicates the positive pervasion and implicitly indicates the counter pervasion. Sermey Khensur Lobsang Tharchin Rinpoché 2005, 266.

202 The definition of a "basic existent" is anything that is established by valid cognition. Wilson 1992, 44.

203 The perpetuating aggregates are all the aggregates (*skandhas*) that are produced by karma and mental afflictions. The perpetuating aggregates arise sometimes and sometimes not, because of having their own unique causes. When those causes are absent, the perpetuating aggregates do not arise. Sermey Khensur Lobsang Tharchin Rinpoché 2005, 350.

204 "A sense consciousness appearing as blue" means that the visual consciousness is focusing on the blue color of some object. Being a sense consciousness, it is a functional thing that needs an observed object as a condition for its arising.

205 An argument that states the meaning is used to communicate with someone who is familiar with a term, like "impermanence," but does not know what it means. Impermanent phenomena are always produced, so this reason helps explain the meaning of "impermanence."

206 An argument that states the term is used to communicate with someone who is not familiar with a term. The sign and the property to be proven are related as the definition and term being defined. So the term "impermanent" is illustrated by the sign "momentary," which is its definition.

207 The object to be negated refers to the property to be proven in the logical argument, which will be refuted or negated if it is not perceived. In the following example, the object to be negated is a ghost.

208 It is unreasonable to hold that whatever one does not perceive definitely does not exist. This statement is directed in part to nihilists, who assert that liberation, omniscience, and the relationship of cause and effect do not exist because they do not perceive them. The sign of not perceiving what does not appear is set forth mainly to refute such views. Rogers 2009, 203.

209 Objects beyond someone's perceptual capacity are called "supersensory objects." These are things that ordinary people cannot perceive, like ghosts and enlightened qualities in others. Supersensory objects are always designated in relation to an individual mind. These objects may be perceptible to others who have higher perceptions such as clairvoyance.

210 "Objects beyond someone's perceptual capacity owing to their place or time" refers to specific environments and occurrences that are very far away in space and time. Objects that are supersensory by their nature are things that are too subtle for ordinary people to perceive. Rogers 2009, 198–99.

211   An example of an object that is suitable to appear is a cup or a book or any object within one's perceptual abilities. If that object does not appear, its presence is negated.

212   The point is not whether the person does or does not have a valid cognition; the point is that a person for whom the object is unsuitable to appear cannot be certain whether the object is there or not.

213   Not being able to perceive hidden qualities is not a sufficient basis for judging that they are not there. There may be others who are capable of perceiving them and definitely know whether they are present or not.

214   An object unsuitable to appear because of being beyond one's perceptual ability cannot be definitely established as present or not. However, an object suitable to appear because it is within one's perceptual ability but that does not appear can be definitely established as not present.

215   "Related objects" refers to partners in a relationship, such as smoke and fire, a definition and what is defined, a generality and its specifics, and so on. Sermey Khensur Lobsang Tharchin Rinpoché 2005, 402.

216   For the "existential negation," see note 281 and chapter 12 on affirmations and negations.

217   A nonexistent is something that is not perceived by valid cognition. Conversely, an existent is defined as something that is perceived by valid cognition.

218   Here trees are the "pervader," a general category that covers, or pervades, all specific instances of trees, like aśoka trees, which are "what is pervaded" or the "object of pervasion." In saying "This is a tree because it is an aśoka," if trees are eliminated, then an aśoka is eliminated, but if an aśoka is eliminated, trees are not eliminated. So it is correct to say "This is a tree because it is an aśoka," but false to say "This is an aśoka because it is a tree."

219   Direct causes and direct effects are distinguished from cause and effect in general. A direct cause immediately precedes its direct effect; there should be no gap between them. The direct cause of a sprout is the seed that is just about to ripen and emit the sprout.

220   The classic example of incompatible opposites is hot and cold, which is used in the syllogisms that follow.

221   In these twelve syllogisms, the subject is much the same, the sign is much the same, and the property to be proven is not perceived because instead there is the perception of a contradictory sign. The distinction is that the sign opposes either the nature, the cause, the effect, or the pervasion of the property to be proven.

222   Here the presence of a contradictory effect proves that there could not have been a direct cause.

223   Here the effect is contradicted because without any direct cause there will be no effect.

224   The object pervaded is always part of the larger category of the pervader. Snow is an object pervaded by cold, which is the larger category, so fire contradicts the pervader, cold.

225 The perception of the sign smoke, which is the effect of fire, contradicts the property to be proven, which sequentially is cold's nature, cause, effect, or cold as a pervader.

226 Smoke is the effect caused by fire, whose nature is heat, which is the opposite of the nature of cold.

227 In these syllogisms, the pervader is fire and the pervaded object is a sandalwood fire.

228 In this example, the sign "being produced" is pervaded by impermanence. Since impermanence and permanence are mutually exclusive, perceiving the sign of being produced contradicts permanence as the pervader.

229 In this example, there is no pervasion, or concomitance, between something naturally disintegrating and it needing something else to cause it to disintegrate.

230 Here the purpose of the sign refers to what is being refuted, such as a cause, effect, nature, pervaded object, and so on.

231 A fallacious sign is one that does not possess all three aspects of a correct sign, as follows: unestablished signs lack the first aspect of a correct sign—the presence of the reason in the subject, indefinite signs cannot be found in the similar or dissimilar class, and contradictory signs lack both the positive pervasion and the counterpervasion. Tachikawa 1971, 119.

232 The phrase "impossible to have doubts" means the statement is so obviously false or true that it is impossible to seriously question it.

233 No one doubts whether sound is an object of hearing, because that is the definition of sound. Nor does anyone doubt whether sound is apprehended by the eyes. If either of these logical signs is used, it is said to be unestablished. For the presence of the reason in the subject to be contextually faultless, there must be an appropriate person who has some doubt about the thesis and consequently is investigating the matter. But with these reasons, there is no doubt about the presence of the reason in the subject, so the reason is considered false and unestablished.

234 A definition is said to be incorrect if it has any one of three defects: (1) it is an underpervasion or too narrow, (2) it is an overpervasion or too broad, or (3) it is impossible. In other words, a definition excludes characteristics that are either: (1) not possessed by the totality of the thing being defined, (2) belong to other things as well, or (3) are impossible. Padmakara Translation Committee 2005, 283. Here the sign is false because it is too narrow to encompass the totality of the subject. Although some sounds do come from a previous moment of mind since they are produced by human effort (like singing), other sounds do not come from a previous moment of mind and therefore are not produced by effort (like thunder).

235 Here the pervasion and nonpervasion refer to the subject and the reason. There is a pervasion when part of the reason pervades the subject and there is a nonpervasion when part of the reason does not pervade the subject.

236 To review, being both nonconceptual and unmistaken is the definition of valid direct perception.

237 Indefinite signs are the second category of false signs, and will be covered next. They are often overpervasions, which is what usually makes them indefinite.

238 In syllogisms, an overpervasion is a reason that is too broad, that is, it includes characteristics that belong to other things as well as the thing in question. An example of an overpervasion is: "Sound is impermanent because it is an object of knowledge." The reason "objects of knowledge" is too broad since objects of knowledge include permanent as well as impermanent phenomena, and permanent phenomena are the dissimilar class for impermanent phenomena.

239 This sign is unestablished because it has aspects of both a pervasion and a nonpervasion.

240 The six categories of false, unestablished signs in relation to facts are the first three categories and the three subcategories of the fourth; the fourth is not an illustrated category in itself. To name these six categories, it is a false, unestablished sign in relation to facts: (1) because the subject does not exist; (2) because the sign does not exist; (3) because both the subject and the sign do not exist, and (4) even though the subject and the sign do exist, there is no relationship between them because it is impossible to have doubts about the sign; (5) even though the subject and the sign do exist, there is no relationship between them because there is an underpervasion; and (6) even though the subject and the sign do exist, there is no relationship between them because the sign has aspects of both a pervasion and a nonpervasion.

241 It is helpful to remember that unestablished signs are signs that cannot be shown to be present in the subject of debate.

242 The respondent in the debate does not have the ability to know if someone is an arhat, so from the perspective of the respondent's mind, this reason cannot be established.

243 This argument is connected with the eternity of the Vedas. The Sāṃkhyas insisted that words/sounds are always present, in unmanifest but potentially creative form, and that they become manifest under some circumstances. They are not produced by anything. Tachikawa 1971, 131. Please note that the Tibetan word *sgra* (Skt. *śabda*) is translated in several ways, including "words" and "sound." Some scholars, like Musashi Tachikawa, point out that in the context of arguments about the eternity of the Vedas, the correct meaning is "words," that the words of the Vedas are eternal. Here, *sgra* is translated as "sound" because every other located translation uses "sound" in this classic syllogism. See Tachikawa 1971, 131 n.7.

244 This classic Buddhist reason is unestablished, and therefore false, for the Sāṃkhyas, who do not accept that sound is produced. When the respondent in debate does not accept the presence of the reason in the subject (for example, that sound is produced), then the way the debate proceeds is to find another subject, like a vase, which the subject accepts as being produced through causes and conditions. Then the proponent shows that the same reason applies to this subject, sound.

245 In contrast to the previous example concerning "words" and "sounds," in this example the Tibetan text says *tshig*, "words," rather than *sgra*, which is both "sound" and "words."

246 This is an underpervasion because the reason is too narrow for the respondent who believes that some words are produced by beings and other words (like those of the Vedas) are not produced by beings.

247 Here taking both sides at the same time is like saying that a functional thing is both permanent and impermanent. It cannot be both at the same time.

248 A term generality can refer either to the mere internal reverberation of the sound of a term, like to a young child, or to an image that appears in the mind of a person who has never seen the actual thing represented by that image, like the city of Timbuktu. Klein 1998, 119.

249 The six categories of false, unestablished signs in relation to someone's mind are the first three categories and the three subcategories of the fourth; the fourth is not an illustrated category in itself. To name these six categories. It is a false, unestablished sign in relation to someone's mind because: (1) the subject does not exist; (2) the sign does not exist; (3) both the subject and the sign do not exist, and (4) even though the subject and the sign do exist, there is no relationship between them because someone suspects that the relationship is impossible; (5) even though the subject and the sign do exist, there is no relationship between them because someone suspects there is an underpervasion; and (6) even though the subject and the sign do exist, there is no relationship between them because someone suspects that both the relationship is impossible and there is an underpervasion.

250 In the syllogism "Sound is impermanent because it is an object of hearing," it is not possible to ascertain an object of hearing without ascertaining sound, since the defining characteristic, or definition, of sound is that it is an object of hearing. One would have to realize "whatever is an object of hearing is necessarily impermanent" in relation to a similar example before realizing it in relation to sound, but this is not possible since nothing but sound is an object of hearing. In other words, there is no similar class of impermanent phenomena that are objects of hearing. Also, an object of hearing is not found in the dissimilar class, which is permanent phenomena, so the sign does not exist in either class. Rogers 2009, 339.

251 This example makes it especially clear that what makes a sign a false indefinite sign is the ascertainment of the respondent, since the syllogism is correct if the respondent is a Buddhist but not if the respondent is a Vedantist.

252 From the perspective of the Vedas, sound is permanent and simply manifests and disappears under certain circumstances. It is not produced and never perishes, as the Buddhists assert.

253 The sign is found in the similar class: there are many things like sound that are produced, and all of them are impermanent.

254 The sign (being produced) is found in the dissimilar class (impermanent phenomena are the opposite of permanent phenomena), where it shouldn't be found. That in itself would make this syllogism false.

255   Common indefinite signs are indefinite signs that are ascertained to be present in the subject as well as in one or both of the similar and dissimilar classes of the property to be proven.

256   This type of sign is said to "have a remainder" because there is something left to be done in order for the sign to be a correct sign.

257   When a sign "pervades" the similar or dissimilar class, it means that the sign is necessarily present in that class. It cannot be in both classes at the same time.

258   An object of comprehension is defined as that which can arise as the object of valid cognition. Objects of comprehension are the phenomena of saṃsāra and nirvāṇa as they appear and are experienced on the empirical level. These can include impermanent phenomena (the similar class) as well as permanent phenomena, like emptiness (the dissimilar class). As the logical sign, "an object of comprehension," pervades both classes, it is a false sign.

259   The sign (impermanent) pervades the similar class, "arises through effort," since whatever arises through effort is necessarily impermanent.

260   This sign is found partly inside and partly outside the dissimilar class, "does not arise through effort." Some things that do not arise through effort are not impermanent (like uncompounded space), and others are not necessarily not impermanent (like lightning). "Not necessarily not" is the formally correct way of negating a negative, which makes a positive. So "not necessarily not (impermanent)" is a convoluted way of saying "it is (impermanent)."

261   The sign "impermanent" pervades the dissimilar class, "arises through effort." Anything that arises through effort is necessarily impermanent. One way in which this reason is false is that a correct sign pervades the dissimilar class.

262   The sign is found partly inside and partly outside the similar class, "does not arise through effort," since some phenomena that do not arise through effort are not impermanent (like uncompounded space) and some phenomena are not necessarily not impermanent (like lightning).

263   According to the non-Buddhist Vaiśeṣika school, substance is ninefold: earth, water, fire, air, space, time, direction, soul, and mind. The first four substances (the four elements) are in the form of an atom or an aggregate of atoms. Tachikawa 1971, 137.

264   Remember this is oriented to the Vaiśeṣikas, for whom atoms are considered permanent.

265   See note 256.

266   A "correct remainder" refers to ascertaining the presence of the reason in the similar class, so it is potentially almost correct and all that remains is to perceive the sign's relationship to the dissimilar class. However, sometimes, as in our example, it is impossible to ascertain the sign's correlation with the dissimilar class and so it is not a correct sign but an indefinite one.

267   Something is a negative phenomenon because it complies with the definition of a negative word that states: "A word is made negative by applying a negative grammatical

particle to it." In English negations are often formed with a prefix like non-, in-, im-, or un-; for example, nonexistent, indestructible, impermanent, uncompounded.

268 This example is connected with the non-Buddhist Sāṃkhya school, which asserts that things arise from themselves. For example, a pot made of clay: Even at the time of the cause, which is the unshaped clay, there is the potential of it becoming a pot. There is no visible pot, but when the clay is shaped it becomes a pot. The pot does not produce pots, but the clay produces pots, and the pot is clay.

269 This is the complete opposite of a correct sign that is not perceived, because that kind of sign refutes the property to be proven, which is an object to be negated. Here the syllogism affirms the property to be proven as an object to be established.

270 By nature, permanent phenomena are never produced. Whatever is produced is always impermanent.

271 Permanent phenomena never arise through effort. Whatever arises through effort is necessarily impermanent. Also, some sounds do not arise through effort, so the reason is not valid in that sense as well.

272 This syllogism may be connected with the Vaiśeṣika assertion that existence itself is the cause of the notion "it is existent." See Tachikawa 1971, 138 n.47.

273 The three ways of presenting the object being comprehended are from the perspective of pure appearance, the emptiness of appearance, and inseparable appearance-emptiness. In Thrangu Rinpoché's commentary on the *Union of Mahāmudrā and Dzogchen*, he says: "All of this is summarized in a clear way by Jetsun Milarepa in one of his songs, in which he says: 'Appearance, emptiness and their inseparability, these three things summarize the view.' Now appearance here means not only external appearance but the whole aspect of appearance or lucidity. So it includes the cognitive lucidity that is the mind's defining characteristic as a mind, which is at the same time utterly empty. And not only is the mind's cognitive lucidity empty, but cognitive lucidity and its emptiness are also not two different things. Knowing this summarizes the view." Extracted from the unpublished transcript of his teaching in Vancouver, 2008.

274 The object being comprehended is the main subject of this text—the two truths.

275 This is a quotation from the *Prajñāpāramitā Sūtra*.

276 These are called an appearing affirmation, an excluding affirmation, an existential negation, and a predicate negation.

277 There is a well-known story related to this verse in Jamgön Mipham's early life when he was studying Dharmakīrti's *Commentary on Valid Cognition*. Sakya Paṇḍita appeared to him in a dream, saying, "What don't you understand about valid cognition? It has two parts: affirmation and negation." Sakya Paṇḍita then tore in half a copy of the *Commentary on Valid Cognition* and told Mipham to put it back together. When Mipham did this, the book became a sword, and when Mipham waved the sword, he instantly cut through all phenomena. Mipham later told his teacher Sölpön Pema that from then on he had no trouble understanding logic. Petit 2002, 28.

278 Functional things are connected with appearing objects and appearing affirmations. Nonfunctional things are connected with nonappearing objects and excluding affirmations.

279 An example of an appearing affirmation is "There is a blue vase."

280 An example of an excluding affirmation is "This vase is not a red vase."

281 The Tibetan word for an existential negation is *med dgag*. This term is also translated as a "nonimplicative negation" or "nonaffirming negation" because when something's existence is negated nothing further is implicated. For example, "There is no horse."

282 The Tibetan word for a predicate negation is *ma yin dgag*. This term is also translated as "implicative negation" or "affirming negation" because when one aspect is negated there is the implication of something else. For example, "This is not a horse."

283 The two ways of presenting inference in relation to how it is used are through proofs and refutations.

284 "Unobscured" is another way of saying "manifest phenomena," and "obscured" is another way of saying "hidden phenomena."

285 In Dharmakīrti's texts on valid cognition, he divides the discussion on inference into "inference for oneself" and "inference for others." One must gain certainty through inference for oneself before showing inference to others.

286 Dignāga says that the counter pervasion is based on the logical sign not being known to occur in any other loci in which the property to be proven is absent. "Not being known to occur in any other loci" is another way of saying "the dissimilar class." Here the dissimilar class is impermanent things that are not unproduced (i.e., that are produced). Space is not an impermanent thing and it is not produced, so it is not found in the dissimilar class, and the counter pervasion is correct. Here sound acts as a correct dissimilar example because it does not possess the qualities of either the sign or the predicate. Unlike space, sound is not unproduced and it is not permanent. Matilal 1998, 121.

287 This false proof statement is related to a non-Buddhist philosophy, possibly the Sāṃkhya school, that believes that happiness is found in objects and is not in the mind. For them, the mind is always existent and never changes.

288 The reason (whichever is suitable) does not seem to make sense, but saying "sound is permanent" is enough to make this syllogism a false statement in relation to facts.

289 Consequences are stated on the basis of positions being attacked, not on positions being held. In showing the consequences, the reason may be acceptable in the context of opponent's position, but the thesis statement—that the subject is or has the predicate—presents an unwanted consequence for the opponent. Wilson 1992, 351.

290 The three main sections of inferential valid cognition are its nature, its classifications, and a response to objections. The entire discussion of inference up to this point has been on the nature of inference.

291 The "lords of the three families" refers to the bodhisattvas Vajrapāni, Avalokiteśvara, and Mañjuśrī. They are embodied in these three masters of the Early Translation

tradition in Tibet: Śāntarakṣita is an emanation of Vajrapāni, Padmasambhava is an emanation of Avalokiteśvara, and Trisong Detsen is an emanation of Mañjuśrī.

292   The author of the commentary, Khenchen Palden Sherab, wrote this verse.

293   To clarify which school holds which characteristics Svātantrika accepts conventional, specific phenomena and Prāsaṅgika does not. Svātantrika presents logical reasoning and Prāsaṅgika does not. Svātantrika applies the qualifier "ultimately" to the object of refutation and Prāsaṅgika does not. Svātantrika accepts a commonly agreed-on subject for debate and Prāsaṅgika does not.

294   Khenchen Palden Sherab, wrote this verse.

295   Emptiness arises out of appearance because without some appearance there would be nothing to be empty. Conversely, appearances arise out of emptiness, like the form kāyas radiating from the dharmakāya, so appearance and emptiness are always inseparable.

296   "And so forth" means that negation of the other three extreme views (nonexistence, both existence and nonexistence, and neither existence and nonexistence) is included as well.

297   The Saha world is the trichiliocosm where the present Buddha Shakyamuni has manifested. It is called the "world of no fear" because sentient beings here are not afraid of desire, they are not frightened by anger, and they have no fear of ignorance.

298   The Nyingma lineage has been criticized for upholding the view of Hashang, a Chinese master defeated in debate by the Indian master Kamalaśīla in ninth-century Tibet. This famous debate was pivotal in Tibetan Buddhism adopting the gradual approach of Indian Buddhism over the instantaneous approach of Chinese Buddhism. Hashang's view was that one attains enlightenment instantaneously by generating a blank, nonconceptual state of mind. His approach was determined to be wrong by all the Tibetan schools, including the Nyingma.

299   The approximate absolute truth is another way of saying the expressible absolute truth.

300   In his commentary to Maitreya's *Distinguishing the Middle from the Extremes,* Jamgön Mipham adds this reason to adhere to the intended meaning rather than the literal words: "Factors such as not knowing the profound intended meaning of the scriptures and taking their words literally hinders wakefulness from arising, as well as its result, perfect enjoyment. Perfect enjoyment refers to one's own enjoyment of the Great Vehicle's teachings and also bringing all other sentient beings to full maturation by teaching them correctly." Maitreya 2006, 62.

301   Here *khams* is similar to *rigs*, meaning "type," "family," or "class." It refers to types of students in relation to their training on the paths of the śrāvakas, pratyekabuddhas, or bodhisattvas.

302   The six parameters apply to how we understand a Vajrayāna text as a whole, and the four styles of interpretation relate to the ways of interpreting each word and line of the text.

303   Buddha Vipaśyin in Sanskrit, or Namparzik in Tibetan, was the first buddha of this
      eon. The intention behind this statement will be given in the upcoming commentary
      from Kawa Paltsek on the four intentions.

304   The three natures are a teaching upheld by the Cittamātra and Yogācāra schools. The
      three natures are the imaginary nature (dualistic, conceptual imputations), the de-
      pendent nature (awareness that exists as dualistic experience), and the thoroughly
      established nature (suchness, the essential emptiness of duality). See Dharmachakra
      Translation Committee 2006, 71. The Tibetan term for the "three natures" is *mtshan
      nyid gsum*. *Mtshan nyid* is more commonly translated as "characteristics," as in the
      indirect intention related to characteristics.

305   Here the intention related to another meaning seems more like an intention related to
      another aim, such as attaining realization. The Tibetan word *don*, commonly translated
      as "meaning," can also mean "aim" or "goal," so an alternate meaning is being used for a
      term.

306   The Sanskrit word *sāra*, or the Tibetan word *snying po*, which means "essence"
      and "distraction," would have two negatives: "essenceless" and "nondistraction."
      Here what is usually understood as "essenceless" is meant by the Buddha to be
      "nondistraction."

307   The Tibetan word *nyon mongs* is the translation of the Sanskrit word *kleśa*, or men-
      tal afflictions. *Nyon mongs* can also mean "difficulty," or "being tired in body and
      mind." Here Buddha used *nyon mongs* to mean "difficulty" rather than "affliction."
      He uses the less common meanings of words to show that his teachings are not easy
      to understand.

308   The Tibetan word *phyin ci log* usually means "mistaken," but it can also mean "the
      opposite or the reverse." This is another example of Buddha using a less common
      meaning of a word to complicate matters.

309   The notions of "purity," "bliss," "permanence," and "the self" are the reverse of the
      Buddha's realization that the characteristics of saṃsāra are impurity, suffering, imper-
      manence, and nonself.

310   Khenpo Gawang said this quote has the same general meaning as the previous one
      from Ngok Loden Sherab: For the "intentions," do not rely on the words but on what
      is meant by the speaker. For the "indirect intentions," one should rely on the mean-
      ing behind the words. Khenpo Gawang repeatedly emphasized that the function of
      the "intentions" and "indirect intentions" is to counteract claims that the Buddha's
      teachings are simplistic. These statements are deliberately difficult to understand.

311   Mentioning the aggregates refers back to the previous example of "indirect intention
      in relation to entry," where Buddha told the śrāvakas that the aggregates exist so that
      they would gradually enter the Mahāyāna. The Buddha meant that the aggregates
      exist only relatively, not absolutely.

312   Khenpo Gawang pointed out that the *Guhyagarbha Tantra*, for example, includes a
      significant amount of special reasoning. (KG)

313 "The fortress of the view (*lta ba'i rdzong*) is the recognition of awareness, the ravine of meditation (*sgom pa'i 'phrang*) is the visualization manifesting as undistracted awareness display, and the life-force of the action (*spyod pa'i srog*) is the application of ritualistic procedures." *Rangjung Yeshé Dictionary*, http://nitartha.pythonanywhere.com /search, search for entry *rdzong 'phrang srog gsum*.

314 The "lady" is Yeshé Tsogyal.

315 The four styles of interpretation provide the framework for Khenchen Palden Sherab's commentary on the "Praise to the Twenty-One Tārās" titled *The Smile of the Sun and Moon: A Commentary on the Praise to the Twenty-One Taras*.

316 The four kinds of reasonings that investigate flawlessly are the reasonings of causal efficacy, dependency, the nature, and valid proofs, which were explained earlier.

317 The reasonings of the four realizations is, according to the Mahāyoga tantra, a way of establishing that the phenomena of saṃsāra and nirvāṇa, the spontaneous display of the ordinary mind and of primordial wisdom, manifest within the indivisibility of the two truths. Padmakara Translation Committee 2005, 395, n.151.

318 An example of a common word with a higher meaning is "emptiness."

319 For an excellent explanation of these four realizations, see Mipham 2009, 61.

320 Khenpo Gawang commented that this is the most important verse in the *Guhyagarbha Tantra*, and that its meaning is very subtle and complex. Ngöndzok Gyalpo is a wrathful emanation of Samantabhadra, the primordial dharmakāya buddha.

321 In their commentary on the Guhyagarbha Tantra, Khenchen Palden Sherab and Khenpo Tsewang Dongyal explain: "Here the *Guhyagarbha Tantra* uses the example of the *ah* syllable. *Ah* has no particular source. It comes from the unborn state. *Ah* is the source of all the other syllables, and thus all letters and sound systems emerge from it." Sherab and Dongyal 2012, 163.

322 The Khenpo brothers' commentary says: "Power and blessings naturally come upon stabilizing the recognition that the unborn nature and its unceasing display are inseparable." Ibid., 164.

323 The Khenpo brothers' commentary says: "This reasoning builds upon the previous one, further explaining that the blessings and power we have been discussing are actually inseparable from one's own self-born awareness." Ibid., 165

324 To correlate the *Guhyagarbha* quote with Khenchen Palden's commentary, the world is composed of the five elements (earth, water, fire, wind, and space), beings are composed of the five aggregates (form, feeling, perception, formations, and consciousness), and the mindstream is the consciousnesses. A well-known verse on these three purities is the final testament of Terdak Lingpa, the founder of Mindroling Monastery, which begins: "Deity, mantra, and dharmakāya are the nature of appearance, sound, and awareness / The pervasive kāya and wisdom display of the buddhas."

325 In their true nature the five elements are the five female buddhas, the five aggregates (*skandhas*) are the five male buddhas, and the eight consciousnesses are the five wisdoms.

326 The seven riches of the absolute are enlightened body, speech, mind, qualities, activities, space, and wisdom.

327 In terms of the "two equalities that are superior to two equalities," the third and fourth of these syllogisms are superior to the first two because in addition to emptiness they include timeless awareness and the kāyas and wisdoms as the true nature.

328 The magical net is one of the names of the *Guhyagarbha Tantra*, and is an analogy for inseparable awareness-emptiness.

329 Here the pāramitās refer to the Sūtrayāna teachings.

330 Earth and water are in union as the nirmāṇakāya, fire and wind are in union as the saṃbhogakāya, and space and mind are in union as the dharmakāya.

331 The completion stage has two aspects: the completion stage with characteristics, which refers to the subtle body practices, and the completion stage without characteristics, which refers to Dzokchen meditation.

332 See note 131.

333 Several contemporary translators translate *spops pa* as "eloquent confidence" rather than "confidence." When asked about this, Khenchen Palden Sherab was emphatic that *spops pa* is not a quality of speech but a quality of mind.

334 The first Jamgön Kongtrul explains the four doors of retention thus: (1) the retention of the Dharma is the mind ascertaining the Dharma without fear of emptiness; (2) the retention of mantra is the ability to apply awareness mantras in order to pacify or harm, (3) the retention of words is not forgetting terms, symbols, and meanings, and (4) the retention of the meaning is not forgetting the specific characteristics of phenomena. Duff 2006, entry *gzungs kyi sgo bzhi*.

335 Jampal Gyepé is one of Mipham's names, which means Joyful Mañjuśrī.

336 The Sakyong year is the nineteenth year of the sixty-year cycle, which would date this colophon as having been written in 1885.

337 See Appendix A for Mipham's annotated verses.

338 During Mipham's lifetime the Fire Horse year was in 1906.

339 The "twofold excellence" refers to being learned and disciplined.

340 The four precepts of pure conduct refer to the basic vows of not killing, not stealing, not lying, and not engaging in sexual misconduct.

341 The three ancestral Dharma kings of Tibet were Songtsen Gampo, Trisong Detsen, and Ralpachen.

342 According to the Nyingma lineage, the three main founders of Buddhism in Tibet were the Abbot Śāntarakṣita, the Master Padmasambhava, and the Dharma King Trisong Detsen.

343 The Lion of Speech is an epithet of Mañjuśrī. Jamgön Mipham is considered an emanation of Mañjuśrī.

344 Verses 7–10 use the compositional device of the eight auspicious symbols.

345 The nine transmission lineages of the Nyingma lineage are: (1) the mind lineage of the victorious ones, (2) the symbolic lineage of the vidyādharas, (3) the hearing lineage of individuals, (4) the entrustment lineage of the ḍākinīs, (5) the word lineage

of yellow parchment, (6) the lineage of aspiration and empowerment, (7) the lineage of the blessings of compassion, (8) the lineage of prophesied transmission, and (9) the lineage of liberation through the taste of samaya substances.

346 The magical net is a metaphor for the unity of purity and equality. It is also one of the names of the *Guhyagarbha Tantra*.

347 Presumably this is a reference to Khenpo Tenzin Drakpa, Khenchen Palden's main teacher at Riwoché Monastery in Tibet.

348 Ajita is the Sanskrit form of the Tibetan name Mipham.

349 This is a reference to Śākyamuni Buddha.

350 This was the Western year 1986.

351 The five states of being are the same as the six realms, with the gods and demigods counted together as one.

352 All the words in bold print are the root verses. All the words in parentheses are Mipham's own annotations to the verses.

Glossary
of Sanskrit and Tibetan Terms

Anuyoga. According to the Nyingma system of nine yānas, Anuyoga is the eighth yāna, and the second of the three inner tantras: Mahāyoga, Anuyoga, and Atiyoga. The practice of Anuyoga is the completion-stage practice with characteristics.

Atiyoga. According to the Nyingma system of nine yānas, Atiyoga is the ninth yāna, and the third of the three inner tantras: Mahāyoga, Anuyoga, and Atiyoga. The practice of Atiyoga is the completion-stage practice without characteristics.

Bhagavān. An epithet of the Buddha, sometimes translated as the Blessed One. The Tibetan form, pronounced *chom den de* (*bcom ldan 'das*), is glossed as the one who has conquered (*bcom*) the four demons, possesses (*ldan*) all good qualities, and is beyond (*'das*) saṃsāra and nirvāṇa.

bhūmis. The ten levels of the bodhisattva path.

bodhisattva. An advanced Mahāyāna practitioner who is committed to attaining full enlightenment in order to help all beings attain enlightenment as well.

buddha. An awakened or enlightened being. Buddhas have awakened from all ignorance and their enlightened qualities are fully developed.

ḍākinīs. The Tibetan *khandro* (*mkha' 'gro*) literally means "one who goes in space," which refers to someone who has realized emptiness. Ḍākinīs are female tantric practitioners or deities with either mundane or transcendent spiritual accomplishments, and they fulfill the activities of serving and protecting the Buddhist teachings and practitioners.

Dharma. This Sanskrit word has many meanings, foremost among them are "the teachings of the Buddha," "phenomena," and "reality."

dharmadhātu. The basic space of phenomena, which refers to suchness, or emptiness, which pervades and encompasses all things.

dharmakāya. The buddha body of reality, which is the all-pervasive emptiness of awareness, inseparable from the mind's clarity.

kāya. This literally means 'body' but can also signify dimension, field or basis. This term designates the different manifestations or dimensions of a buddha.

mahāsattva. A great bodhisattva.

Mahāyoga. According to the Nyingma system of nine yānas, Mahāyoga is the seventh yāna, and the first of the three inner tantras: Mahāyoga, Anuyoga, and Atiyoga. The practice of Mahāyoga is the creation-stage practice.

maṇḍala. Literally "center and surroundings." A maṇḍala most commonly refers to a tantric deity and its supporting retinue and environment.

nirmāṇakāya. The "buddha body of emanation" is the union of the empty (dharmakāya) and luminous (sambhogakāya) aspects of awareness, which manifests as an unceasing display of wisdom and compassion. A nirmāṇakāya (Tibetan *'sprul sku*, pronounced *tulku*) can also refer to a physical emanation of an enlightened being.

nirvāṇa. The "state beyond sorrow" is the state of being that transcends *samsaric* existence with its mental afflictions and dualistic conceptions, and therefore it is beyond all suffering.

padma. Lotus.

pāramitā. "Having reached the far shore" refers to the Mahāyāna practice of virtue in a way that transcends the threefold reification of subject, object, and action.

ṛṣi. A "genuine sage" is someone whose body, speech, and mind are honest, straightforward, and free of negativity.

samaya. Sacred words, which refers to the Vajrayāna commitments practitioners make in relation to their view, meditation, and conduct.

sambhogakāya. The "buddha body of complete enjoyment" refers to the energetic, compassionate, and luminous aspect of awareness.

samsāra. Cyclic existence, which is characterized by mental afflictions, karmic cause and effect, ignorance, and suffering.

siddha. "One with spiritual attainments" due to great accomplishment in Vajrayāna meditation.

siddhi. Spiritual attainment, which could manifest as mundane accomplishments or the supreme accomplishment of enlightenment.

skandha. The aggregates that make up the forms of all phenomena and the body and mind of human beings. There are five aggregates: form, feeling, perception, mental formations, and consciousness.

śrāvaka. A "hearer," a follower of the Buddhist foundation teachings who focuses on becoming individually liberated from the suffering of saṃsāra and is not aspiring or working for the complete enlightenment of all beings.

sugata. A "blissfully gone one" is a fully enlightened being. Often the term refers to Buddha Śākyamuni.

tarka. Generally meaning "logic" or "reasoning," sometimes used to refer to non-Buddhist philosophy.

tathāgata. A "thus-gone one" is a fully enlightened being. The term often refers to Buddha Śākyamuni.

terma. Treasure texts and objects hidden by enlightened beings, most famously Padmasambhava, to be found at the right time in the future in order to benefit beings.

tīrthika. A non-Buddhist logician.

vajra. Vajra means "indestructible" and refers to the buddha nature, or intrinsic awareness, which is never altered or destroyed by conditions.

vidyādhara. An "awareness-holder" is someone who has attained high realization in the Vajrayāna.

vyākaraṇa. Refers in Sanskrit to grammar, or more generally to the study of language.

yāna. A "vehicle" that can take a practitioner through a particular level of the spiritual journey. Each yāna has its own special view, meditation, conduct, and result.

yidam. A personal or chosen deity in Vajrayāna practice, particularly as the object of meditation in creation-stage practice.

Bibliography

Berzin, Alexander. "Explaining Vajra Expressions: 6 Alternatives and 4 Modes." https:// studybuddhism.com/en/advanced-studies/vajrayana/tantra-advanced/explaining-vajra-expressions-6-alternatives-4-modes.

Dharmachakra Translation Committee, trans. 2013. *Distinguishing Phenomena from Their Intrinsic Nature: Maitreya's Dharmadharmatāvibhāga with Commentaries by Khenpo Shenga and Ju Mipham.* Boston: Snow Lion Publications.

———. 2006. *Middle beyond Extremes: Maitreya's Madhyāntavibhāga with Commentaries by Khenpo Shenga and Ju Mipham.* Ithaca, NY: Snow Lion Publications.

Dongyal, Khenpo Tsewang. 2013. *Homage to the Nine Stupas of the Tathagata: Reliquaries of the Khenchen Palden Sherab Rinpoché (1938–2010).* Sidney Center, NY: Padma Samye Ling.

Dreyfus, Georges. 1997. *Recognizing Reality: Dharmakīrti's Philosophy and Its Tibetan Interpretations.* Albany: State University of New York Press.

Duff, Tony. 2006. *The Illuminator: Tibetan-English Encyclopaedic Dictionary.* Online edition. http://www.pktc.org/pktc/tibddiction.htm. Kathmandu, Nepal: Padma Karpo Translation Committee.

Dunne, John D. 2004. *Foundations of Dharmakīrti's Philosophy.* Somerville, MA: Wisdom Publications.

Gangopadhyaya, Mrinalkanti. 1971. *Vinītadeva's Nyāyabindu-Ṭīkā.* Calcutta: R. D. Press.

Klein, Anne Carolyn. 1998. *Knowledge and Liberation.* Ithaca, NY: Snow Lion Publications.

Lati Rinpochay. 1980. *Mind in Tibetan Buddhism.* Translated by Elizabeth Napper. Ithaca, NY: Snow Lion Publications.

Maitreya. 2013. *Distinguishing Phenomena from Their Intrinsic Nature: Maitreya's Dharmadharmatāvibhāga with Commentaries by Khenpo Shenga and Ju Mipham.* Translated by Dharmachakra Translation Committee. Boston: Snow Lion Publications.

———. 2006. *Middle beyond Extremes: Maitreya's Madhyāntavibhāga with Commentaries by Khenpo Shenga and Ju Mipham.* Translated by Dharmachakra Translation Committee. Ithaca, NY: Snow Lion Publications.

Matilal, Bimal Krishna. 1998. *Character of Logic in India.* Albany: State University of New York Press.

Mipham, Jamgön. 2002. *Gateway to Knowledge.* vol. 3. Hong Kong: Rangjung Yeshé Publications.

————. 2012. *Gateway to Knowledge*. vol. 4. Hong Kong: Rangjung Yeshé Publications.

————. 2009. *Luminous Essence*. Ithaca, NY: Snow Lion Publications.

Padmakara Translation Committee, trans. 2005. *The Adornment of the Middle Way: Shantarakshita's Madhyamakalankara with Commentary by Jamgön Ju Mipham*. Boston: Shambhala Publications.

Petit, John W. 2002. *Mipham's Beacon of Certainty: Illuminating the View of Dzogchen, the Great Perfection*. Boston: Wisdom Publications.

Prasad, Rajendra. 2002. *Dharmakirti's Theory of Inference: Revaluation and Reconstruction*. Oxford: Oxford University Press.

Rangjung Yeshé Dictionary. *The Nitartha International Online Tibetan-English Dictionary*. http://nitartha.pythonanywhere.com/index.

Ringu Tulku. 2006. *The Ri-me Philosophy of Jamgön Kongtrul the Great*. Boston: Shambhala Publications.

Rogers, Katherine Manchester. 2009. *Tibetan Logic*. Ithaca, NY: Snow Lion Publications.

Sermey Khensur Lobsang Tharchin Rinpoché. 2005. *Pointing the Way to Reasoning*. Howell, NJ: Mahayana Sutra and Tantra Press.

Sherab, Khenchen Palden. 2004. *The Smile of the Sun and Moon: A Commentary on the Praise to the Twenty-One Taras*. Boca Raton, FL: Sky Dancer Press.

Sherab, Khenchen Palden, and Khenpo Tsewang Dongyal. 2012. *Ceaseless Echoes of the Great Silence*. Sidney Center, NY: Dharma Samudra Publications.

————. 2007. *Opening the Door of the Madhyamaka School*. Sidney Center, NY: Dharma Samudra Publications.

————. 2007. *Opening the Door of the Rangtong and Shentong Views*. Sidney Center, NY: Dharma Samudra Publications.

————. 2011. *The Splendid Presence of the Great Guhyagarbha*. Sidney Center, NY: Dharma Samudra Publications.

————. 2007. *Tara's Enlightened Activity*. Sidney Center, NY: Dharma Samudra Publications.

Stcherbatsky, Theodore. 2008. *Buddhist Logic*. 2 vols. Delhi: Motilal Banarsidas.

Tachikawa, Musashi. 1971. "A Sixth-Century Manual of Indian Logic: A Translation of the *Nyāyapraveśa*." *Journal of Indian Philosophy* 1: 111–45.

Wilson, Joe Bransford. 1992. *Translating Buddhism from Tibetan*. Ithaca, NY: Snow Lion Publications.

Sources Cited in the Commentary

English and Sanskrit titles used in the text, along with the Wylie transliteration of the Tibetan and, if known, the author.

Abridged Prajñāpāramitā Sūtra. Prajñāpāramitāratnaguṇasañcayagāthā. 'Phags pa shes rab kyi pha rol tu phyin pa sdud pa tshigs su bcad pa.

Adornment of the Middle Way. Madhyamakālaṃkāra. Dbu ma rgyan. Śāntarakṣita.

All-Creating Monarch. Kulayarājatantra. Kun byed rgyal po'i rgyud.

Ascertaining Valid Cognition. Pramāṇaviniścaya. Tshad ma rnam nges. Dharmakīrti.

Clear Words. Prasannapadā. Tshig gsal. Candrakīrti.

Commentary on Valid Cognition. Pramāṇavarttika. Tshad ma rnam 'grel. Dharmakīrti.

Compendium of the Abhidharma. Abhidharmasamuccaya. Mngon pa kun btus. Asaṅga.

Compendium of Authentic Teachings on Valid Cognition. Bka' yang dag pa'i tshad ma'i mdo btus pa. Trisong Deutsen.

Compendium of the Mahāyāna Teachings. Mahāyānasaṃgraha. Theg pa chen po bsdus pa. Asaṅga.

Compendium of Valid Cognition. Pramāṇasamuccaya. Tshad ma kun btus. Tshad ma'i mdo. Dignāga.

Dictionary of Dharma Terminology. Chos kyi rnam grangs brjed byang chen mo. Kawa Paltsek.

Distinguishing the Middle and the Extremes. Madhyāntavibhāga. Dbus dang mtha' rnam par 'byed pa. Maitreya/Asaṅga.

Eight Herukas Fortress, Ravine, and Life Force. Bka' brgyad rdzong 'phrangs.

Entering the Way of the Mahāyāna. Theg chen tshul 'jug. Rongzompa Chokyi Zangpo.

Entrance to the Middle Way. Madhyamakāvatāra. Dbu ma la 'jug pa. Candrakīrti.

Essence of Interdependence. Pratītyasamutpādahṛdayakārika. Rten 'brel snying po. Nāgārjuna.

Essence of Reasoning. Nyāyabindu. Rigs pa'i thig pa. Dharmakīrti. (This text is included in the translation of Vinītadeva's *Nyāyabindu-Ṭīkā* by Gangopadhyaya.)

Explanation of the Levels of the View. Lta ba'i rim pa bshad pa. Kawa Paltsek.

Explanation of Reasoning. Vyākhyāyukti. Rnam bshad rigs pa. Vasubandhu.

Extensive Commentary on the Sūtra of the Definitive Explanation of the Intent. Dgongs 'grel chen mo. Chokro Lui Gyaltsen.

Formation of Words in Two Volumes. Sgra sbyor bam po gnyis pa.

Garland of Views. Upadeśadarśanamālā. Man ngag lta phreng. Padmasambhava.

Gateway to Knowledge. Mkhas 'jug. Jamgön Mipham.

Great Commentary on the Kālacakra Tantra. Dus 'khor 'grel chen. Puṇḍarīka. See *Stainless Light.*

Great Scripture of the Embodiment of the Realization of All Buddhas. Sangs rgyas thams cad kyi dgongs pa 'dus pa'i mdo.

Guhyagarbha Tantra. Rgyud gsang ba snying po.

Guru Rinpoché's Response to the Questions of the Lady. Jo mos gu ru rin po che la zhus len. Padmasambhava.

Heart Sūtra. Prajñāpāramitāhṛdaya. Shes rab snying po.

Heruka Galpo Tantra. He ru ka gal po'i rgyud.

King of Meditative Stabilization Sūtra. Samādhirāja. Ting nge 'dzin gyi rgyal po'i mdo.

Lamp of the Eye of Meditation. Bsam gtan mig sgron. Nupchen Sangyé Yeshé.

Lamp of Proven Reasoning. Rigs pa grub pa'i sgron me. Candragomin.

Levels according to Yogācāra. Yogācārabhūmi. Rnal 'byor spyod pa'i sa sde. Asaṅga.

Light of the Middle Way. Madhyamakāloka. Dbu ma snang ba. Kamalaśīla.

Litany of the Names of Mañjuśrī. Mañjuśrīnāmasaṅgīti. 'Jam dpal gyi mtshan yang dag par brjod pa.

Mahāparinirvāṇa Sūtra. Mya ngan las 'das pa chen po'i mdo.

Mantra of the Second Verse. Tshig su bcad pa gnyis pa'i gzungs.

Māyājāla Guhyagarbha Tantra. Sgyu 'phrul drva ba chen po gsang ba'i snying po.

One Hundred Fifty Praises. Śatapañcāśatka. Bstod pa brgya lnga bcu pa. Aśvaghoṣa.

Ornament of Clear Realization. Abhisamayālaṃkāra. Mngon rtogs rgyan. Maitreya/ Asaṅga.

Ornament of the Commentary on Valid Cognition. Rnam 'grel rgyan. Sherjung Bepa.

Ornament of the Mahāyāna Sūtras. Mahāyānasūtrālaṃkāra. Mdo sde rgyan. Maitreya/ Asaṅga.

Ornament of the Middle Way. Madhyamakālaṃkāra. Dbu ma rgyan. Śāntarakṣita.

Overview of the Great Scripture of the Embodiment of the Realization of All Buddhas. Sangs rgyas thams cad kyi dgongs pa 'dus pa spyi mdo.

Parkhap. Spar khab. Lalitavajra.

Praise of the Inconceivable Middle Way. Acintyastava. Dbu ma bsam gyis mi khyab par bstod pa. Nāgārjuna.

Praise to the Unsurpassable One. Niruttarastava. Bla na med par bstod pa. Nāgārjuna.

Prajñāpāramitā Sūtra. Shes rab kyi pha rol tu phyin pa'i mdo.

Precious Illuminator. Rin po che snang byed.

Precious Key for Assessing the Provisional and the Definitive. Drang nges 'jal byed rin chen lde mig. Longchen Rabjam.

Radiant Light of the Sun and Moon. Nyi zla 'bar ba'i sgron me. Padmasambhava.

Root Guhyagarbha Tantra. Rtsa rgyud gsang snying.

Root Mañjuśrī Tantra. Mañjuśrīmūla tantra. 'Jam dpal rtsa rgyud.

Root Wisdom of the Middle Way. Prajñāmūlamadhyamakakārikā. Dbu ma rtsa ba'i shes rab. Nāgārjuna.

Salu Sprout Sūtra. Śālistamba Sūtra. Sa lu ljang pa'i mdo.

Scripture That Embodies the Realization of All the Buddhas. Sangs rgyas thams cad kyi dgongs pa 'dus pa spyi mdo.

Secret Essence of the Magical Net. Māyājālaguhyagarbha tantra. Sgyu 'phrul dra ba chen po gsang ba'i snying po.

Self-Arising Awareness Tantra. Svotthavidyā tantra. Rig pa rang shar rgyud.

Stainless Light. Vimalaprabha. Dri med 'od. Puṇḍarīka. See *Great Commentary on the Kālacakra Tantra.*

Sublime Continuum. Uttaratantra śāstra. Rgyud bla ma. Maitreya/Asaṅga.

Supplement to the Guhyagarbha Tantra. Sgyu 'phrul le lag.

Sūtra Connected with Questions on What Happens after Death. Āyuspattiyathākāraparipṛcchā sūtra. Tshe 'pho ji ltar zhus pa'i mdo.

Sūtra of the Definitive Explanation of the Intent. Saṃdhinirmocana Sūtra. Dgongs pa nges par 'grel ba'i mdo.

Sūtra of the Descent to Laṅkā. Laṅkāvatāra sūtra. Lang kar gshegs pa'i mdo.

Sūtra of the Manifold Display of Mañjuśrī. Mañjuśrīvikrīḍita sūtra. 'Jam dpal rnam par rol pa'i mdo.

Sūtra of the Meeting of the Father and Child. Pitāputrasāmagama sūtra. Yab sras mjal ba'i mdo.

Sūtra of the Teaching of Inexhaustible Intelligence. Akṣayamatinirdeśa sūtra. Blo gros mi zad pa bstan pa'i mdo.

Sūtra of the Vast Display. Lalitavistara sūtra. Mdo rga cher rol pa.

Sūtra on Repaying Kindness. Drin lan gsab pa'i mdo.

Sword of Wisdom That Ascertains Reality. Don rnam par nges pa shes rab ral gri. Jamgön Mipham.

Tantra of Deliverance. Abhyudayatantra. Mngon par 'byung ba'i rgyud.

Tantra of the Enlightenment of Vairocana. Vairocanabhisaṃbodhitantra. Rnam snang mngon byang rgyud.

Thirty-Five Hundred Stanzas. Stong phrag phyed dang bzhi pa. Dharmakīrti.

Treasury of the Abhidharma. Abhidharmakośa. mngon pa mdzod. Vasubandhu.

Two Truths. Bden gnyis.

Udānavarga: A Collection of Verses from the Buddhist Canon. Ched du brjod pa'i tshoms. Buddha Śākyamuni.

Vajra Mirror Tantra. Vajradarpaṇa Tantra. Rgyud rdo rje me long.

Verse Summary of the Gateway to Knowledge. Mkas 'jug gi sdom byang. Jamgön Mipham.

Way of the Bodhisattva. Bodhicharyāvatāra. Byang chub sems dpa' spyod pa la 'jug pa. Shantideva.

Index

U

About the Author

KHENCHEN PALDEN SHERAB RINPOCHÉ (1938–2010) was born in eastern Tibet. He received his early education at Gochen Monastery and his higher education as a khenpo at Riwoche Monastery. He and his family escaped from Tibet in 1960. In 1965 Khenchen Rinpoché was asked by H. H. Dudjom Rinpoché to represent the Nyingma lineage as a founding member of the Central University for Tibetan Studies in Sarnath, India, where Khenchen taught Buddhist philosophy for seventeen years. In the early 1980s Khenchen Rinpoché moved to New York to work closely with Dudjom Rinpoché, and in 1988 he and his brother Khenpo Tsewang Dongyal Rinpoché founded the Padmasambhava Buddhist Center, which has monasteries and Dharma centers in the United States, India, and Russia. Khenchen Rinpoché is the author of over thirty books in Tibetan and English.

What to Read Next
from Wisdom Publications

Mipham's Beacon of Certainty
Illuminating the View of Dzogchen, the Great Perfection
John W. Pettit and His Holiness Penor Rinpoche

"A riveting and wonderful work, which gives the reader a real education in some of the most compelling issues of Buddhism, especially their impact on Dzogchen." —Anne Klein, Rice University

Journey to Certainty
The Quintessence of the Dzogchen View:
An Exploration of Mipham's Beacon of Certainty
Anyen Rinpoche and Allison Choying Zangmo

"Remarkably accessible, this book is essential reading for anyone attempting to understand or practice Dzogchen today."
—John Makransky, author of *Awakening Through Love*

About Wisdom Publications

Wisdom Publications is the leading publisher of classic and contemporary Buddhist books and practical works on mindfulness. To learn more about us or to explore our other books, please visit our website at wisdompubs.org or contact us at the address below.

Wisdom Publications
199 Elm Street
Somerville, MA 02144 USA

We are a 501(c)(3) organization, and donations in support of our mission are tax deductible.

Wisdom Publications is affiliated with the Foundation for the Preservation of the Mahayana Tradition (FPMT).